中国国际减贫中心
IPRCC **International Poverty Reduction Center in China**

The Sharing
Dev

U0686574

Edited by International Poverty Reduction Center in China

2024 Annual Report on

International Rural Revitalization

CHINA AGRICULTURE PRESS

BEIJING

图书在版编目（CIP）数据

国际乡村振兴年度报告.2024：英文 / 中国国际减贫中心编著. -- 北京：中国农业出版社，2024.10.（国际乡村发展经验分享系列）. -- ISBN 978-7-109-32540-1

Ⅰ.F313

中国国家版本馆CIP数据核字第2024642PT6号

中国农业出版社出版

地址：北京市朝阳区麦子店街18号楼

邮编：100125

责任编辑：郑　君

版式设计：杨　婧　责任校对：张雯婷

印刷：中农印务有限公司

版次：2024年10月第1版

印次：2024年10月北京第1次印刷

发行：新华书店北京发行所

开本：700mm×1000mm　1/16

印张：22.25

字数：365千字

定价：88.00元

2024 Annual Report on International Rural Revitalization

Research Group

Group Leaders: Gao Boyang, Li Xin

Group Members: Jiang Ling, Dai Juncheng, Wang Yourong, Wen Fenghua, Ou Bianling, Geng Ximei, Xu Liping, He Shengnian, Liu Huanhuan, Yao Yuan, Meng Yue, Jiang Yiyao, Han Xiangting, Liu Beitong, Jiang Yating, Zhao Zhihao, Meng Hanyu, Suo Cheng, Chen Qi, Pi Fuling

◎ Preface

The eradication of poverty has always been a wish to be fulfilled. The history of humankind is the history of relentless struggle against poverty. As the world's largest developing country with a population of 1.4 billion, China had long been plagued by poverty because of its weak foundations and uneven development. Ending poverty, improving people's well-being and realizing common prosperity are the essential requirements of socialism and important missions of the Communist Party of China (CPC). In order to fulfill this solemn political commitment, over the past century, the CPC has united and led the Chinese people to wage a long and arduous struggle against poverty with unwavering faith and will. Since the launch of reform and opening up, China has carried out well-conceived and well-organized initiatives for development-driven poverty alleviation on a massive scale, and devoted its focus to releasing and developing productive forces and to ensuring and improving public wellbeing, securing great and unprecedented achievements in the process. Since the 18th National Congress of the CPC in 2012, the CPC Central Committee with Comrade Xi Jinping at its core has prioritized poverty elimination in its governance. President Xi Jinping has assumed leadership, made plans and directed the battle in person in order to implement the basic policy of a targeted strategy in poverty alleviation and mobilize the whole Party, the entire nation and all sectors of society, thus scoring the largest battle against poverty and benefiting the largest number of people in human history.

The complete victory in the battle against poverty is inseparable from the organic combination of a capable government and an effective market. Over the eight years since the 18th CPC National Congress, the CPC Central

Committee, with Comrade Xi Jinping at its core, has centrally and uniformly led the fight against poverty, leveraged the political advantages of the country's socialist system with Chinese characteristics which can bring together the resources necessary to accomplish great tasks, and placed poverty reduction in a prominent position in national governance, providing strong political and organizational guarantees for the fight against poverty. The active participation of market and social forces has been widely mobilized, with the implementation of actions such as the "Ten Thousand Enterprises Helping Ten Thousand Villages" campaign, to encourage private enterprises, social organizations and individual citizens to participate in the fight against poverty, and facilitate the agglomeration of factors such as capital, talent and technology in poverty-stricken areas. By the end of 2020, all of the 98.99 million rural residents, 832 counties, and 128,000 villages that fell below the current poverty line had been lifted out of poverty. Regional poverty had been eliminated on the whole, and the arduous task of eradicating absolute poverty had been completed. China has built the largest education, social security, and healthcare system in the world, and achieved rapid development in step with large-scale poverty reduction, and economic transformation in step with the elimination of extreme poverty.

China has always been an active advocate, strong promoter and important contributor to the international cause of poverty reduction. According to the World Bank's international poverty line, since the launch of reform and opening up in 1978, the number of people lifted out of poverty in China has amounted for more than 70 percent of the global total and 80 percent of that in East Asia and the Pacific over the same period. China is home to nearly one fifth of the world's population. Its complete eradication of extreme poverty–the first target of the United Nations 2030 Agenda for Sustainable Development–10 years ahead of schedule, is a milestone in the history of the Chinese nation and the history of humankind, making an important contribution to the cause of global poverty alleviation.

On the basis of the national conditions and the understanding of the patterns underlying poverty alleviation, China has pioneered a Chinese path to poverty alleviation, given shape to Chinese theory on fighting poverty, and created a "China example" of poverty reduction. Adherence to the people-centered development philosophy, and unswervingly following the path of common prosperity are the fundamental driving force behind China's cause of poverty reduction. Highlighting poverty alleviation in the governance of China, all Party members, from top leaders to the grassroots officials work together towards the same goal. China has strengthened top-level design and strategic planning, mobilized forces from all quarters to participate in poverty alleviation, improved the institutional system for poverty eradication and maintained the consistency and stability of policies. China is committed to eradicating poverty through development, and its experience with poverty alleviation has proven that development is the most effective way to eradicate poverty and the most reliable path towards a more prosperous life. Pressing ahead with poverty alleviation based on reality, China has constantly adjusted and reformed its strategies and policies as circumstances and local conditions change. The strategy of targeted poverty alleviation has been the magic weapon for winning the battle against poverty, while the development-driven approach has emerged as the distinctive feature of China's path to poverty reduction. Letting the poor residents play the principal role in eliminating poverty, China has committed to mobilizing the enthusiasm, initiative, and creativity of impoverished people and inspiring them with the motivation to fight poverty, so that they can benefit from success in the undertaking of poverty alleviation and at the same time contribute to development in China.

Following the decisive victory in the fight against poverty, the Chinese government has set out a five-year transition period for counties lifted out of poverty to consolidate and expand these achievements, and comprehensively promote rural revitalization. In accordance with the deployment of the 20th CPC National Congress, on the new journey of comprehensively promoting the rejuvenation of the Chinese nation on all fronts through a Chinese path to modernization, China is advancing rural revitalization across the board, building a beautiful and harmonious countryside that is desirable to live and work in, and moving towards the higher goal of realizing the all-round human development and common prosperity for all. China's exploration and practice of consolidating and expanding the achievements in poverty alleviation and rural revitalization will continue to provide new Chinese experience and wisdom for human poverty reduction and rural development, and contribute to the promotion of building a community with a shared future for mankind free of poverty.

In the face of new trends and features in the international situation, General Secretary Xi Jinping has put forward the Belt and Road Initiative, the Global Development Initiative and other common global actions, with poverty reduction as a key area of cooperation, and has endeavored to promote the building of a community with a shared future for mankind free of poverty and with common development. It has become a global consensus to strengthen the sharing of international experience in poverty reduction and rural development and to contribute to the global poverty reduction and development process.

To this end, since 2019, the International Poverty Reduction Center in China (IPRCC) and the Bill & Melinda Gates Foundation have jointly implemented international cooperation projects. With persistence in carefully planning the project topics from a policy-based and future-oriented perspective, we are committed to leading the frontier hot spots and research trends of poverty reduction and rural development at home and abroad. We have always insisted on bringing China's poverty reduction and rural development experience into line with international standards, explaining China's poverty reduction and rural revitalization path through the international discourse system, and promoting the international dissemination of China's poverty reduction and rural development experience. So far, more than 30 research projects have been implemented, and a number of research results in various forms and with wide influence have been formed, some of which have been released in relevant international exchange activities.

In order to implement the Global Development Initiatives and further promote global exchanges and cooperation on poverty reduction and rural development, IPRCC has carefully sorted out the research results and launched four series of books, including *The Sharing Series on Global Poverty Reduction and Development Experience*, *The Sharing Series on China's Poverty Reduction and Development Experience, The Sharing Series on International Rural Development Experience,* and *The Sharing Series on China's Rural Revitalization Experience.*

The Sharing Series on Global Poverty Reduction and Development Experience aims to track the progress of global poverty reduction, analyze the trends of global poverty reduction and development, summarize and share the experiences of countries in poverty reduction, and provide knowledge products for promoting the United Nations 2030 Agenda for Sustainable Development and participating in global poverty governance. This series mainly includes global poverty reduction knowledge products, such as the *Annual Report on International Poverty Reduction* and *Theory and Frontier Issues in International Poverty Reduction*, as well as regional poverty reduction knowledge products covering Africa, ASEAN, South Asia, Latin America and the Caribbean.

The Sharing Series on China's Poverty Reduction and Development Experience aims to tell the story of China's poverty reduction, share China's poverty reduction experience with the international community, and provide practical experience for the majority of developing countries to achieve poverty reduction and development. This series focuses on China's experience and practices in targeted poverty alleviation, poverty eradication as well as consolidation and expansion of poverty eradication achievements, and forms knowledge products for sharing China's poverty reduction experience based on international perspectives.

The Sharing Series on International Rural Development Experience focuses on the history, policies and practices of international rural development, compares the experiences and practices of rural development between China and other countries, and provides knowledge products for exchange and mutual understanding for the cause of global rural development. This series mainly includes the *Annual Report on International Rural Revitalization, Comparative Analysis Report on International Experience in Rural Governance, Urban-Rural Integrated Development and Rural Revitalization in Counties*, and other research results.

The Sharing Series on China's Rural Revitalization Experience focuses on telling the story of China's rural revitalization, summarizing the experiences, practices and typical cases of rural revitalization in time, and providing references for domestic and foreign policy makers and researchers. This series mainly focuses on rural development, rural planning, common prosperity and other topics, summarizes relevant policies, experiences and practices, and develops and compiles typical cases based on international perspectives.

Finally, I would like to extend my heartfelt appreciation to all the relevant project teams, publishers and editors who have worked diligently for the publication of the series, as well as the government agencies, universities and research institutes, social organizations and friends from all walks of life who have shown their concern and support for IPRCC. All these series have been generously funded by the Bill & Melinda Gates Foundation and have received careful guidance and assistance by the China Office of the Gates Foundation, for which we would like to express our heartfelt thanks.

Global poverty reduction and rural development are dynamic and ever-changing. The book is far from exhaustive, and we look forward to receiving comments from the readers of the books.

Liu Junwen

Director General of the International Poverty Reduction Center in China

January, 2024

◎ Introduction

For centuries, rural areas have played an indispensable role in fostering human civilization by providing the means of production, driving social progress, fostering economic development, and safeguarding the ecological environment. They have been pivotal in advancing global sustainable development. Currently, rural areas are home to over 40% of the world's population, shouldering the vital responsibility of supplying food, agricultural products, and other essential resources for over 7 billion people. Endowed with rich ecological resources including abundant water, extensive land, and forests, rural areas are critical for global carbon cycling, climate regulation, and natural disaster mitigation. Moreover, these regions serve as custodians of traditional culture, contributing to human cultural diversity and social cohesion, thus holding immeasurable value.

Rural areas are a key driver of global sustainable development and a cornerstone of global poverty alleviation efforts. The United Nations' 2030 Agenda for Sustainable Development places "end poverty in all its forms everywhere" as its primary objective. The international community is actively committed to reducing poverty and achieving goals related to poverty eradication, social equity, and sustainable development. It is well recognized that poverty is predominantly concentrated in rural areas. Since 2010, the global population living in absolute poverty has decreased by nearly 40%, while those in multidimensional poverty have declined by almost half, with rural areas contributing more than two-thirds of this progress due to economic development and improved infrastructure. Nevertheless, it is crucial to note that globally, 667 million people still endure extreme poverty, with the vast majority residing in rural areas. Consequently, poverty reduction remains a major challenge shared by all nations worldwide, underscoring the critical role of rural development in advancing the global poverty reduction agenda.

Actively promoting rural development and realizing rural revitalization is an important initiative to promote the achievement of global sustainable development goals. At present, poverty alleviation among the rural poor is highly dependent on employment opportunities in agriculture and related fields; by upgrading agricultural production, infrastructure development and social security in rural areas, the incidence of poverty can be effectively reduced and the livelihoods of residents improved. Secondly, rural revitalization focuses on talent training and improving the quality of education, so as to raise the skill level and employability of farmers and provide them with more opportunities to escape poverty. Third, rural revitalization attaches importance to cultural heritage and ecological protection, providing a better living environment and social welfare for rural areas and further improving the quality of life of rural residents. In addition, rural development can help to realize broader sustainable development goals, including zero hunger, gender equality and clean water.

Promoting rural revitalization and development is an important part of the development strategies of many countries. In 2020, China's poverty eradication campaign has achieved a comprehensive victory, and through improving infrastructure, providing education and medical services, and developing the rural economy, the rural poor population has been fully lifted out of poverty, 832 poverty-stricken counties have been removed from their hats, and 128,000 poverty-stricken villages have all been lifted out of poverty. This has historically solved the arduous task of eradicating absolute poverty, and has also provided a Chinese model and Chinese program for global poverty reduction. On this basis, China has further promoted the implementation of the strategy of rural revitalization. The 14th Five-Year Plan for Promoting Modernization of Agriculture and Rural Areas, which was released in 2022, explicitly identifies "effectively linking the consolidation and expansion of the results of poverty eradication with rural revitalization, strengthening the endogenous development capacity of poverty-stricken areas, and enabling the people who have been lifted out of poverty to lead a better life and gradually embark on the road to common prosperity" as one of the key tasks. The rural revitalization strategy aims to achieve balanced development in urban and rural areas, promote economic growth in the countryside and improve the quality of life of rural residents. This strategy clearly sets out to comprehensively promote the realization of the five major revitalizations of rural industries, human resources, culture, ecology and organizations. First, promote the revitalization of rural industries. Deeply push forward the reform of agricultural supply structure, promote the transformation of agriculture from total expansion to quality improvement, and accelerate the cultivation and development of rural industries and local industries. The second is to promote the revitalization of rural talents. Accelerate the cultivation of local talents, encourage talents to return to their hometowns, cadres to return to their hometowns, and enterprises to go to their hometowns, so as to provide stronger talent support for the revitalization of the countryside. The third is to promote the revitalization of rural culture. Promote the formation of civilized countryside, good family style, simple folk style. The fourth is to promote rural ecological revitalization. Deepen the improvement of rural habitat, promote the green development of agriculture and rural areas, strengthen the prevention and control of soil pollution on agricultural land, promote the transformation of the value of high-quality ecological products, and enhance the concept of ecological civilization. Fifth, promote the revitalization of rural organizations. Further enhance the capacity of rural grassroots organizations, gather the power of the masses to create good governance in the countryside, and promote the common construction and sharing. Overall, for countries around the world, promoting rural industrial development, talent training, cultural heritage, ecological protection and organization building, and promoting economic prosperity, social progress and ecological health in rural areas are important ways to effectively promote rural revitalization and development.

The world is currently experiencing changes that have not been seen in a century, and affected by multiple factors, such as the COVID-19, the global rural areas are also facing a series of challenges, such as outflow of population, insufficient infrastructure, climate change and the digital divide, and the road to revitalization of rural development is faced with a number of challenges and opportunities. Looking ahead, the world should work together to build a sustainable countryside, promote urban-rural integration and diversified synergies, and build a "green, inclusive, affluent, resilient and well-governed" countryside, so as to comprehensively promote the development of the global countryside.

To sum up, this annual report will comprehensively analyze the policy initiatives, experiences and practical cases in the five aspects of rural industry, talents, culture, ecology and organization in the world and major regions, and sort out China's rural revitalization strategies and positive practices, so as to provide theoretical foundations and scientific support for the understanding of the long-term trend and future development direction of global rural revitalization and the achievement of the SDGs, with a view to contributing to the promotion of rural revitalization and the joint realization of the goal of poverty reduction.

The report is divided into seven chapters, each focusing on a core area of rural revitalization, aiming to comprehensively reveal the diverse connotations and implementation paths of rural revitalization.

Chapter 1, "International Rural Industrial Development," analyzes the current status, trends, and challenges of rural industries worldwide, exploring how to promote rural industrial revitalization through technological innovation, industrial upgrading, and other means.

Chapter 2, "International Rural Talent Development," focuses on issues such as talent shortages and outflow in rural areas, discussing how to attract and cultivate rural talents through education, training, policy guidance, and other measures to provide strong support for rural revitalization.

Chapter 3, "International Rural Cultural Revitalization," explores the unique value of rural culture, discussing how to protect and inherit rural culture while promoting its integration with urban culture to enhance the soft power of rural culture.

Chapter 4, "International Rural Ecological Governance," addresses rural ecological environmental issues, exploring how to improve the rural ecological environment and achieve sustainable rural development through measures such as ecological restoration and environmental protection.

Chapter 5, "International Rural Organizational Development," analyzes the role and status of rural organizations in rural revitalization, discussing how to strengthen rural organizational construction to enhance rural governance capacity and level.

Chapter 6, "China's Rural Revitalization and Practices," focuses on the implementation, achievements, and experiences of China's rural revitalization strategy, providing reference and inspiration for other countries around the world.

Chapter 7, "Global Outlook on Rural Revitalization," integrates the content of the previous chapters, prospects the future development trends of global rural revitalization, and puts forward targeted policy recommendations and development ideas.

◎ Summary

The countryside is the key to promoting the sustainable development of human society, carrying more than 40 per cent of the global population and assuming the important responsibility of providing food, agricultural products and other survival capital for more than 7 billion people around the world. Rural industries are the foundation of the national economy, and the rural economy is an important part of the modernized economic system. Rural revitalization is also an important initiative to promote global sustainable development. In order to share rural development experiences, join hands to promote global rural revitalization, and help achieve the Sustainable Development Goals, the International Poverty Reduction Center in China (IPRCC) compiled the *2024 Annual Report on International Rural Revitalization*, sorting out policies, experiences, practices and practical cases of the world and major regions in the five aspects of rural industry, talents, culture, ecology and organization, summarizing the successful experience of the current rural revitalization strategy, and providing reference for the development of other countries and regions in the world.

The report concludes:

(1) Rural industrial development models are diverse, but economic development still faces many challenges. Global agricultural production and output have steadily increased, agricultural productivity has improved, forestry, animal husbandry, and fisheries have grown and transitioned towards green development, and rural industrial development models have become more diversified. The integration of agricultural and non-agricultural industries has

made significant contributions to promoting rural industrial development and prosperity. However, there are significant regional and national disparities in agricultural production, total agricultural output, and agricultural productivity. The sustainable development of agriculture and rural non-agricultural industries lacks driving force. The potential for rural industrial development and innovation in models is constrained by various factors such as climate change, land resources, agricultural technology, agricultural policies, and international trade. Under the background of globalization and free trade, the disparity in food self-sufficiency rates among countries has further widened. The economic impact of the COVID-19 pandemic has exacerbated food insecurity, leading to an unprecedented global food crisis.

(2) The internal driving force for rural talent development is insufficient, and problems such as depopulation and aging are prominent. Due to rapid urban development, rural areas face development constraints in terms of economy, society, and ecology. A large number of rural laborers migrate to cities for work, resulting in depopulation, aging, and feminization of rural areas. Within the context of rapid urban development, there are issues such as insufficient internal driving force for rural development, low agricultural production levels, and low levels of education in rural areas. Due to differences in the natural conditions of rural economies, societies, ecologies, etc., different countries have implemented different models of talent development policies and practices for rural talent development to meet their specific needs.

(3) Rural cultural revitalization is an important aspect and strong support for rural revitalization. The protection and utilization of agricultural cultural heritage can stimulate the vitality of local culture. The construction of rural public cultural facilities in China has laid a solid cultural foundation for the development of grassroots rural society. By relying on key village construction, various regions have achieved creative transformation and innovative development of high-quality rural cultural resources, driving the integration of rural industries and becoming exemplary demonstrations for upgrading rural tourism. Many places have intensified efforts to build unique rural public

cultural spaces, continuously improving the spiritual outlook of farmers, and enhancing the cohesion and attractiveness of villages. Rural festivals and celebrations are effective carriers for showcasing agricultural civilization and folk culture, as well as catalysts for the development of rural tourism and the prosperity of rural economies. To deepen the construction of rural civility, it is necessary to fully mobilize the enthusiasm and initiative of farmers, form a conscious ideology, establish norms through institutions, and create an atmosphere of civilized conduct that nurtures the happiness of rural residents.

(4) Rural ecological governance is complex and urgent, facing issues such as climate change and biodiversity loss. Rural ecological governance has attracted increasing attention globally due to its involvement in numerous issues, including climate change, biodiversity loss, and pollution, making rural ecological governance exceptionally complex. Global rural ecological governance is complex and urgent, requiring the joint efforts of governments, businesses, and the public worldwide. Global rural ecological governance policies are gradually shifting from partial environmental management to comprehensive ecosystem management, encompassing not only agricultural environments but also the entire rural environment, including forests, wetlands, and water bodies. The governance approach is moving from single-government management to multi-stakeholder participation involving government, market, society, and technology. Global rural ecological governance policies should focus more on technological innovation and green development, promote rural industrial upgrading and transformation, and achieve coordinated unity between rural ecological environment and economic development.

(5) Rural organizations are vital forces in achieving rural revitalization. The development of rural organizations relies on government policy guidance. Governments provide financial support, improve laws and regulations, and integrate various social resources to assist the development of rural organizations. With the support and guidance of the government, rural organizations have made significant progress. However, due to differences in development stages, political systems, historical experiences, and traditional

customs among countries or regions, the specific forms of rural organizations vary. The development of rural organizations should improve organizational policies, enhance organizational coordination, mobilize market forces, fully leverage the collective strength of various social organizations, and strengthen international cooperation in agriculture.

(6) China's rural revitalization has significant value for global rural development. By analyzing the effects of China's rural revitalization efforts, this paper explains how China's rural areas embody values for global rural development, reviews China's rural revitalization policies, and illustrates how to effectively link consolidating and expanding poverty alleviation achievements with rural revitalization. Secondly, the paper summarizes the experiences of China's rural revitalization efforts, highlighting that developing high-quality rural industries, expanding employment opportunities, developing and growing new rural collective economies, and enhancing poverty alleviation capabilities through skills training are all important measures to enhance endogenous driving forces in poverty-stricken areas and their residents.

(7) Currently, global rural development faces numerous difficulties and challenges. Population loss is a serious challenge for rural revitalization, and improving infrastructure construction is an urgent task for current rural revitalization efforts. The scarcity of educational and medical resources presents a difficult problem for rural revitalization, while the single industrial structure constrains the development of rural revitalization. Environmental protection and ecological issues are crucial for the sustainable development of rural revitalization. Looking towards the future of global rural areas, we have proposed development goals in five aspects: rural industry, talent, culture, ecology, and organization, and provided corresponding strategies and suggestions.

◎ Contents

Preface   V

Introduction   XI

Summary   XVI

Chapter I   International Rural Industry Development   1

  I. Current situation and mode of rural industry development   2

  II. The policies for the development of rural industries   23

  III. Experience and enlightenment of rural industry development   46

Chapter II   International Rural Talents Development   50

  I. Current situation and model of rural talent development   51

  II. Policies and measures for the development of rural talents   66

  III. The experience and enlightenment of rural talent development   126

Chapter III   International Rural Cultural Revitalization   145

  I. Current status of rural cultural revitalization   146

  II. Typical modes of rural cultural revitalization   156

  III. Experiences and insights in rural cultural revitalization   168

Chapter IV   International Rural Ecological Governance   174

  I. Current status of rural ecology   175

  II. Rural ecological governance policy   195

III. Typical cases of rural ecological governance 221

IV. Experience and enlightenment of rural ecological governance 236

Chapter V Development of International Rural Organizations 257

I. The development status and policy measures of international rural
organizations 258

II. Practical cases of the development of international rural
organizations 270

III. Experience and inspiration from the construction of international
rural organizations 294

Chapter VI Rural Revitalization and Practice in China 298

I. Analysis of the effect of China's promotion of rural revitalization 299

II. Typical practices for continuing to promote rural revitalization 311

Chapter VII Looking to the Future of Rural Development 315

I. Current difficulties and challenges 315

II. Towards a global future for rural development 320

III. Suggestions and recommendations 326

◎ Chapter I International Rural Industry Development

Abstract

Since the beginning of 21st century, the global total output and value of agricultural products have been growing steadily. The agricultural productivity has been continuously improving. Forestry, animal husbandry and fishery have been growing and transforming to green development. The development model of rural industries has been diversified, and agriculture and non-agricultural industries have been developing together. Rural non-agricultural industries have made significant contributions to the development and the prosperity of rural economy.

However, the international rural industry development is facing many challenges. There are significant regional and national differences in total agricultural output, total agricultural value and agricultural productivity, and it is lack of sufficient motivation of the sustainable development of agriculture and rural non-agricultural industries; the development potential and model innovation of rural industries are restricted by many factors such as climate change, land resources, agricultural technology, agricultural policies and international trade; under the background of globalization and free trade, the national differences in food self-sufficiency rate have further widened; the economic impacts of the COVID-19 have led to the worsening of food insecurity and the world is facing an unprecedented global food crisis.

I. Current situation and mode of rural industry development

1. The status of rural industry development

According to the data released by Food and Agriculture Organization of the United Nations (FAO), the global total crop output (including grains, oil crops, sugar crops, vegetables and fruits) and the total agricultural output value are growing continuously. The total output of crops, which was 4,995 million tons in 2001, increased to 7,517 million tons in 2021, by an increase of 2,522 million tons and with an average annual growth rate of 2.08%. In 2001, the global total agricultural output value was US$ 1,279 billion, and that was US$ 4,447 billion in 2020, by an increase of US$ 3,168 billion and with an average annual growth rate of 6.79%. There are significant regional differences in total agricultural output and total agricultural value.

Global agricultural productivity showed a steady growth trend with significant regional differences. Global per capita agricultural output value and per capita agricultural production index[1] increased steadily. Per capita agricultural production index rose from 84.61 in 2001 to 103.16 in 2021. There are great differences in agricultural productivity among continents in the world, with the highest level in Europe and Oceania and the lowest level in Asia and Africa, and the gap between continents is widening. Take per capita agricultural output value as an example, Africa's per capita agricultural output value was only US$ 700 per person in 2001 and increased to US$ 1,300 per person by 2019; Asia's per capita agricultural output value increased from US$ 700 per capita in 2001 to US$ 4,300 million per person in 2019; in 2001, the per capita GDP of agriculture in Europe and Oceania was US$ 8,100 and US$ 7,800, respectively. By 2019, the per capita GDP of agriculture in Europe and Oceania were as high as US$ 27,300 and US$ 21,200.

Forestry, animal husbandry and fishery have made increasingly outstanding

---

1　Per capita agricultural production index = agricultural production index/population index.

contributions to the development of rural industries. The global total forest cover decreased, and the output of forest products and the export of forest products increased. According to the Food and Agriculture data database of the FAO, the global forest area decreased by 2.38% (99 million hectares) in total from 2000 to 2020, the area of other forest lands decreased by 9.133 million hectares, and the area of artificial forests increased steadily. The global output of forestry products showed an overall growth trend with significant regional differences. Among the world's forestry products, round logs produced the largest volume (3,967 million cubic meters in 2021), while wood fuel (1,948 million cubic meters in 2021) and industrial round logs (2,019 million cubic meters in 2021) remained at the same level. The global total export of forest products showed an increasing trend in the fluctuation from 2001 to 2021. The total export of forest products in 2001 was US$ 130,816 million, which had reached US$ 283,713 million by 2021.

The output value of animal husbandry has steadily increased and is one of the fastest-growing sectors in developing countries. In 2020, the output value of three major animal husbandry products, namely livestock, meat and milk, reached US$ 2.32 trillion, increased by US$ 0.71 trillion from US$ 1.61 trillion in 2001, with an average annual growth rate of 1.93%. Developing countries contributed most of the growth in global livestock production. The advantages of being latecomers have brought great opportunities for small-scale livestock industry practitioners in developing countries, but there are also many challenges, including food safety problems in livestock industry, environmental pollution problems and greenhouse gas emissions. The proportion of land occupied by animal husbandry is relatively high, but through the circulation of ecological system, it can realize coordinated development with planting industry, establish a sustainable food system and promote the development of circular agriculture.

Global fishery production has been steadily increasing, and fishery industry is undergoing a blue transition. In 2021, total fishery output reached 218 million metric tons, of which Asia was the major production area, driving up global production. With the rapid increase in the consumption demand of fishery products and the development of aquaculture technology, more and more aquatic products come from artificial aquaculture instead of direct fishing. Artificial cultivation can not only make fishermen react more quickly to changes in consumers' preferences, but also realize the sustainable development of fishery. Thanks to the improvement of aquaculture technology, inland fisheries have developed rapidly.

2. The main model of rural industrial development

(1) Utilizing regional advantages, and developing the local characteristic products

The mode of developing the local characteristic products refers to the cultivation of products with unique quality and cultural value that meet the market demand through scientific planting, breeding, processing and other technical means for a region with unique climate condition, land resource, special environment and other characteristics. It is not limited to agricultural products, but also includes handicrafts and cultural products with special characteristics.

Characteristic product development model has the following characteristics in product development, product production, product operation and sales. First, the products have differentiated competitiveness in terms of raw materials, production process and historical background, and the local areas often have certain industrial bases. Second, the production of products is characterized by industrial agglomeration and modernization. Generally speaking, the advantaged industries in the villages are also the leading industries in the locality, which will gather various resource elements and gradually expand the upstream and downstream industrial chains. Third, in terms of product operation and sales, featured industries often focus on building product production standards and brand image, binding geographical indications with featured products to create long-term product reputation.

The implementation path of the mode of developing the local

characteristic products: First, identify and screen the categories and varieties of local featured products. This step requires attention to the product's locality and competitiveness. The so-called " locality" refers to the degree of adaptation of products to local social and economic conditions, and the so-called "competitiveness" refers to the differentiated advantages of products facing the same category of products. Locality and competitiveness are important conditions to ensure the long-term healthy development of characteristic industries. From the perspective of regional environment, the selection of featured products needs to consider the local resources endowment, business environment, industrial base, ecological carrying capacity, etc. From the perspective of product industry, the selection of featured products needs to consider factors such as product characteristics, industry coverage, market capacity, etc.

Second, standardize the production process and improve the processing technology. The development mode of characteristic products is not simply to introduce some agricultural products or make some handicrafts, but also to improve the quality of products and build heterogeneous competitiveness around the high-quality characteristics or cultural heritage of products. The focus of global economic development has been on cities for a long time, and the level of modernization in rural areas of most developing countries is relatively low[2]. The development model of featured products needs to rely on the power of agricultural science and technology and modern industry to improve the output and quality of the products, strengthen the processing and packaging process of the products, and increase the added value of the products.

Third, improve product reputation and build brand image. Brand and product differentiation complement each other. Brand helps consumers distinguish products. High-quality products can leave a deep brand impression on consumers. When the featured products have sufficient competitiveness

---

2   UNEP. Global resources outlook 2019 [R]. Nairobi: United Nations Environment Programme, 2019.

and customer base, their brand image is easier to gain popularity. For the rural industry, we should pay attention to the geographical and cultural connotation behind the products, strengthen the brand planning and design, and formulate a complete brand strategic plan for the characteristic industry.

Fourth, strengthen marketing and promote the product reproduction process. The sales link of products is the "breathtaking leap" in commodity circulation, especially for the newly cultivated characteristic rural products. First of all, it is necessary to expand all kinds of marketing channels, such as participating in agricultural exhibitions and trade fairs, holding rural tourism activities, digital marketing and so on, so as to expand product popularity and sales channels. Second, develop from point to surface, combine point with surface. Today, with the development of basic logistics, the marketing activities of rural characteristic products need not be confined to the surrounding areas, but can also expand the marketing network through online marketing and other means.

Japan's "One Village One Product" movement is a representative case of the mode of developing the local characteristic products. After World War II, Japan focused on the construction of large cities, with production factors concentrated on cities. By the 1970s, Japan's rural development had almost stagnated, and its basic industry, agriculture, was also facing the problem of abandoned arable land[3]. In 1961, the village head of Oita prefecture selected two kinds of crops with high input-output ratio, plum and chestnut, and called on the town to replace the main plants from rice and wheat with plum and chestnut and equipped with tourist facilities. After accumulating the original capital by planting cash crops, Oita improved its agricultural production technology through overseas studies, gradually improved its production and living conditions, and further promoted the construction of Lentinus

---

3 Chang Wei, Wang Wei, Kan Qingyun. The enlightenment of Japan's "One Village One Product" movement on rural revitalization in China: Based on the perspective of government function transformation [J]. Reform and Strategy, 2020, 36 (5):111-118.DOI:10.16331/j.cnki.issn1002-736x.2020.05.012. (in Chinese)

edodes industry.In 1979, based on the successful practice, the governor of Oita prefecture launched the "One Village One Product" movement. The movement has achieved remarkable results. From 1980 to 1999, the number of characteristic products in Oita prefecture increased from 143 to 319, of which the sales volume of 19 products exceeded 1 billion yen. By 2018, Oita has cultivated more than 330 kinds of special products, such as plum honey, shiitake mushrooms, wheat soju, Fenghou beef, Yukiko Sushi and so on.

During the same period, the grapefruit industry in Umaji Village of Japan started in the 1980s aiming to replace the forestry industry that was banned by the environmental protection policy. The pomelo produced here is not outstanding in appearance, but is rich in nutrition, and the product quality is continuously improved through agricultural techniques such as organic recycling planting method. As a result, Umaji Village has opened up all the major links of production, processing and sales, giving full play to the product features of the category of grapefruit, and has developed various products such as grapefruit juice, grapefruit jam and grapefruit skin care products, forming a diversified product matrix that combines agricultural products, industrial products and tourism. Today, Umaji Village sells more than 10 million pomelo products a year, with an income of 200 million RMB, and the number of the village is less than 400.

Through the "One Village One Product" movement, Japan's rural areas have successfully combined featured agricultural products with local culture, tourism and other resources, thus realizing the upgrading of agricultural industry and the prosperity of rural economy. The success of Oita County has attracted the world's attention, and relevant successful experiences have practical cases in Asian, African and Latin American countries. Under the "One Village One Product", both the introduction of new products and the re-development of existing products need to fully mobilize people's subjective initiative and innovation, and to upgrade production, product packaging, business models and other aspects.

The enlightenments of the mode of developing the local characteristic

products: First, mobilize the enthusiasm of various market players and actively develop featured industries. The characteristic product development model requires the development of local high-quality industries. Breakthroughs from zero to one require the active participation of various business entities, including large farmers, returning entrepreneurs, leading enterprises, agricultural associations, etc. The yuzu industry in Umaji Village and the plum and chestnut industry in Oita Prefecture's Oyama Town were both initiated by local village chiefs and agricultural associations, while Yukiko Sushi was jointly developed by sushi makers and shiitake mushroom growers. It can be seen that various market operating entities have different advantages and resources, and exploring a diverse entity operating model is conducive to resource integration and normal industry operation.

Second, track the market demand and identify the products with local advantages in the villages. The development model of special products often requires the introduction of new industries that "I have what others don't have, I have the best when others have it, and I have more professional products when others have excellent products." Whether the introduced industry meets market demand will need to be verified after the product is launched. From the production stage to the sales stage, various uncertain factors will affect market fluctuations. Agricultural products have low entry barriers and long production cycles. If you fail to grasp the relationship between market supply and demand and choose to develop industries with oversupply or insufficient demand, it is easy to have short-term oversupply and large fluctuations in product prices, which will ultimately affect the income of business entities and the sustainable development of rural areas.

Third, explore the connotation of products, and create products but also create industries. The product connotation can not only support the marketing link, but also scientifically guide the extension direction of the industrial chain. Umaji Village has fully explored the fresh and natural native gene of pomelo, which is a product category, so as to be able to continuously innovate and carry out primary processing and finishing of agricultural products. The connotation of products may not only be based on the characteristics of the products themselves, but also from the local history and culture, rural geographical environment, local conditions and cultural characteristics and other aspects.

(2) Specializing the production, and extending the agricultural industry chain

The model of extending agricultural industry chain refers to the combination of product sales, brand building, research and development innovation and other links with the agricultural industry, to carry out professional division of labor and large-scale production, and to establish a new agricultural industry chain.

This model has the following three characteristics in product positioning, production and sales. First, there is a prominent industry-led chain in the agricultural industry chain. The development of the industrial chain does not mean putting average effort on each industry. Instead, the industry chain is extended by relying on the leading industry with scale effect and agglomeration effect to promote the diversification, specialization, and modernization of the agricultural industry. Second, the standardized production system runs through the whole chain. The industrial chain means the continued circulation of semi-finished and finished goods. The standardized production system not only improves the efficiency of docking between upstream and downstream and the quality of the whole process of products, but also enhances industrial scale effect and synergy through standardizing production standards, unifying procurement of materials and co-constructing of infrastructure, and finally enhances industrial scale effect and synergy. Third, take the brand management as a concept to integrate the whole upstream and downstream products. In terms of sales, brand management can empower upstream and downstream products at the same time; in terms of increasing the enthusiasm of participants, brand management can unite small farmers, leading enterprises, collective economic organizations and other actors in the countryside.

The key steps to implement the model of extending agricultural

industry chain include: First, promote specialized production in all links of the industry chain. Through the introduction of high-tech equipment and advanced agricultural technology, the efficiency and quality of agricultural production will be improved and large-scale production and modern production will be realized. The connotation of specialized production is divided into three levels: leading industry, additional industry and the whole industrial chain. For the leading industry, it is necessary to increase the input and conversion rate of scientific research, improve the productivity and product quality of the leading industry, and build the competitiveness of the leading industry. For the additional industries, we should do a good job in professional positioning, serve the upstream industries well, and take the production link as the core, expand the categories of the upstream industries it serves, and strengthen the scale effect.

Second, collaborate and integrate all links in the industrial chain. Strengthen the collaboration and cooperation among all links of the agricultural industry chain, including scientific research, planting/cultivation, processing, transportation, sales and other links, to realize the whole closed-loop of crops from production to sales. There is a smile curve in the value-added structure of the agricultural industry chain, that is, the value-added is more reflected at both ends of the industry chain, such as design and sales, while the value-added in the middle of the production chain is the lowest. We should emphasize the positive interaction between the major production links, take the leading industry to drive the development of additional industries, and vigorously develop the agricultural product processing industry. Promote the progress of leading industries with the development of additional industries, such as expanding the functions of leading products and expanding the market of leading products.

Third, innovate the agricultural industry chain. In order to promote the innovation of agricultural industry chain, we should pay attention to innovation and diversification, combine with modern market demand, develop agricultural products with unique characteristics and high added value, and improve the market competitiveness of products. Scientific research investment and cultural connotation are the two core driving forces to promote the innovation of the industrial chain. Scientific research investment mainly acts on the production side, while cultural connotation mainly acts on the sales side. For the reprocessing industry, innovation should be strengthened, the development direction of the industrial chain network should be explored through scientific and technological innovation, and small farmers with insufficient accumulation of original capital should be encouraged to participate. For back-end processing industry and marketing industry, we should fully tap the connotation of local culture and products.

The Netherlands "Chain Strategic Action Plan" has achieved remarkable results and is a typical representative of the model of extending agricultural industry chain. As a high-latitude coastal country, the Netherlands is not endowed with high agricultural development and is one of the representatives of "low-lying countries" in Europe. The Netherlands has insufficient light and low temperature. The country is facing the threat of seawater flooding and the area of agricultural land is relatively limited. Under the premise of limited agricultural volume, the best way to increase agricultural output value is to increase agricultural productivity and land productivity. At the end of the 20th century, the Netherlands began to promote the "Chain Strategic Action Plan", starting from each link of the agricultural industry, improving the cohesion between each link, and creating a relatively perfect industrial cluster and industrial system. Holland's flower industry and animal husbandry are world-famous. The Netherlands is not only the world's largest flower producer, but also the world's second largest dairy producer.

The model of the Kingdom of the Netherlands includes three key points, namely, high investment in research and experimental development, integration of production, supply and marketing, and cultural empowerment. The remarkable feature of Netherlands agricultural model is its high input and high output paradigm. This model has achieved high efficiency through capital-intensive advanced technology, and all these benefits are supported by advanced agricultural science and technology. The highly scientific and technological input has laid a solid scientific and technological foundation for Netherlands agriculture, which has achieved remarkable economic benefits under the limited land resources. The Netherlands has adopted a series of advanced agricultural science and technology, such as greenhouse agriculture, to skillfully solve the problem of limited arable land resources. By using sophisticated computer technology to control the greenhouse environment, the Netherlands has achieved high yields while saving arable land resources. Greenhouse fish culture also makes effective use of water resources. In addition, Netherlands agriculture has made high-level investment in means of production and agricultural equipment, such as milking equipment and industrial mushroom production equipment. In the production of grain, Netherlands agriculture pays attention to the selection of good varieties and adopts modern cultivation techniques to achieve high yield. This kind of technology investment has also created significant economic benefits for Netherlands agriculture under the limited land resources.

In addition, the Netherlands government is relying on the "Chain Strategic Action Plan" to gradually strengthen the collaboration and integration of the agricultural industry chain. It integrates the planting, harvesting and preservation of crops with the processing, transportation, storage and sales of agricultural products, and realizes the organic combination of production, supply and sales. This mode of integration of production, sales and supply makes the best use of resources and forms an integration of benefit sharing and risk sharing.

Finally, Netherlands agriculture also pays attention to cultural empowerment and skillfully integrates cultural elements into creative agriculture. For example, in the flower industry chain, Holland successfully integrated the tulip culture, making it a part of the industry chain, and achieved remarkable success. This cultural empowerment can add color to agricultural products and enhance market competitiveness.

The enlightenments of the model of extending agricultural industry

chain: First, pay attention to the importance of science and technology and cultural investment. In every link of the industrial chain, the investment in science and technology and culture has been proved to be effective in increasing the added value of products, generating significant economic benefits and enhancing market competitiveness. We will step up research and development of key processing technologies for agricultural products, cultivate new varieties of excellent agricultural, forestry, animal husbandry and fishery, and promote the upgrading of crops and livestock and poultry varieties. At the same time, the establishment of scientific and technological innovation and training promotion system, improves the comprehensive quality of grassroots rural cadres and farmers, promotes mature technological achievements, cultivates brand-name products with strong competitiveness, thus laying a solid foundation for the sustainable development of the industrial chain.

Secondly, strengthen the guiding role of the government in the development of the industrial chain. The government plays an irreplaceable role in promoting the development of the industrial chain. First, through the establishment of relevant research institutions and the provision of information services, sufficient information and management experience are provided for the development of the creative industry, thus providing intellectual support for the sustainable development of the industrial chain. Second, the government should set up a corresponding management system to promote the integrated management of the industrial chain and provide the farmers with the guarantee of the organization system, so as to ensure the orderly operation of the industrial chain.

Finally, pay attention to the cultivation of leading enterprises and the development of talents. In the initial stage of the rural industrial chain, it is especially critical to focus on cultivating leading enterprises. It is suggested to set up a consultancy group to support the development of leading enterprises and formulate development strategies for enterprises in line with the actual situation, so as to speed up the establishment and improvement of modern enterprise system. At the same time, it is necessary to introduce urgently needed talents, cultivate a high-quality workforce, and accelerate the formation of a group of backbone forces with market expansion capabilities to safeguard the healthy operation of the enterprise.

(3) Expanding the multi-function of agriculture, and promoting the diversification of rural economy

The model of expanding multi-function agriculture refers to the development of agricultural ecology, culture, society and other functions on the basis of traditional agricultural production, to realize the diversified development and sustainable development of the rural economy.

This model has the following three characteristics. First, it emphasizes the comprehensive function of agriculture. The model of expanding multi-function agriculture highlights the multiple functions of agriculture, not only limited to food production, but also integrating ecological, cultural and social functions. Through the development of agricultural tourism, leisure agriculture and other strategies, effectively expands the diversified development of rural economy, and thus significantly enhances the economic income of farmers. **Second, it realizes ecological protection and sustainable development.** The multi-function expansion model of agriculture focuses on maintaining the stability of the ecological system and advocates rational use of resources and environmental protection measures to realize the sustainable development of the rural economy. For example, the practice of organic agriculture in Japan has significantly protected the local ecological balance and has also attracted tourists who are highly concerned about environmental issues. **Third, itpromotes community and cultural heritage.** The multifunctional expansion model of agriculture has actively promoted the prosperity and stability of rural communities. Through the protection and inheritance of traditional agricultural skills and local culture, the cohesion of the community is strengthened and the farmers have a stronger sense of belonging. Take Italy's Tuscany region as an example, through the protection of traditional agricultural methods, the long-standing agricultural tradition has been continued, and a sustainable and stable economic source has been provided for the community.

The key paths to the success of the model of expanding multi-function agriculture: The first is to deeply develop rural resources. Developing the natural landscape, human history and agricultural resources in rural areas to create a unique tourism destination and attracting tourists to the natural landscape in rural areas is one of its unique resource advantages. Scientific planning, integration and ecological restoration are needed to create an attractive and characteristic tourism destination. Such as a reasonably designed scenic route, a set of viewing facilities and a continuous trail network, can significantly enhance the natural experience of tourists. Secondly, we need to dig deeply into the human history. Rural areas contain rich historical and cultural connotations, including ancient villages, traditional buildings and precious historical sites. Through professional archaeological research and cultural interpretation, combined with cultural relics protection, tourists can have a deep understanding of the local historical accumulation. The last is to use agricultural resources in a diversified way. Traditional agriculture is not only a mode of production but also a part of a multifunctional system. Agricultural resources are endowed with multi-level values and experiences by means of excavating characteristic agricultural products and developing agricultural experience activities.

The second is to intensify infrastructure construction and build infrastructure and tourism facilities that cater to the needs of rural tourism. Firstly, transportation and communication infrastructure need to be optimized. The transportation and communication conditions in rural areas are crucial factors that determine tourists' willingness to visit and reside there. We should enhance the transportation network and improve traffic convenience. At the same time, we need to improve communication facilities to ensure smooth information flow for tourists in rural areas. Secondly, for guesthouses and rural hotels, intelligent planning is a crucial prerequisite for building a high-quality rural tourism industry. The success of rural tourism hinges on providing a high-quality accommodation environment. Attention should be paid to the intelligent and unique planning of infrastructure, including smart home systems and distinctive decorations, to offer tourists a comfortable and convenient accommodation experience. Finally, it is essential to diversify the development of leisure agriculture facilities. As a significant component of rural tourism, leisure agriculture must fully consider the diverse needs of tourists. Facilities encompassing agricultural experiences, leisure and entertainment, and health and wellness should be established to provide tourists with a comprehensive and enriching experience.

The third is to strengthen cultural heritage and enhance tourists' experiences. Firstly, traditional festivals and cultural activities need to be systematically designed. These activities serve as significant carriers of rural cultural heritage. Through meticulous planning and design, we aim to endow these festivals with profound cultural meanings and encourage active participation, thus attracting more tourists. Secondly, vibrant exhibition windows for folk culture should be established. Folk performances, demonstrations of traditional skills, and other events are the cultural highlights of rural tourism. They must present the authentic folk cultural characteristics in engaging formats, allowing tourists to immerse themselves in the experience. Lastly, interactive experiences in handicraft production should be provided. As an integral part of cultural heritage, these activities should be presented in an interactive manner, enabling tourists to participate actively in the production process and enrich their cultural experiences.

A typical successful case of the model of expanding multi-function agriculture is the flower town of Grasse, France. Located on France's Côte d'Azur, Grasse is renowned for its rich perfume history and unique fragrance industry. The town has cleverly leveraged the cultivation of flowers and spices to foster the production of innovative industrial perfumes and drive the booming tourism industry. Over the years, Grasse has undergone numerous industrial transformations, evolving from leatherworking to flower cultivation, and ultimately to perfume manufacturing. This evolution has culminated in an economic model anchored by green agriculture, emerging industries, and modern services. These transformations have not only successfully upgraded the industrial structure but also significantly enhanced the quality of life for local residents. A comprehensive set of functional amenities serves as a crucial prerequisite for its diversified development. Grasse boasts a picturesque natural environment and a complete range of supporting facilities encompassing medical care, community services, cultural activities, and entertainment, providing utmost convenience to both locals and tourists. In summary, with its unique geographical setting and rich industrial heritage, Grasse has successfully implemented the multifunctional expansion model of agriculture through multiple industrial transformations, emerging as one of the exemplary models of global agricultural development.

The enlightenments of the model of expanding multi-function agriculture: First, adaptation to local conditions, one village, one policy. In the rural revitalization centered on tourism, the development strategy adapted to local conditions is of fundamental significance. The core of this is to accurately position the products according to the actual conditions of each region and avoid blindly applying the general model. For example, China's *Strategic Plan for Rural Revitalization (2018—2022)* classifies villages into four categories: agglomeration and promotion, suburban integration, feature protection and relocation and merging. It formulates corresponding policies according to local conditions, avoiding blind development in advance, helping to achieve accurate allocation of resources and ensuring the sustainability of the revitalization process.

Second, increase residents' participation and realize cultural revitalization. The revitalization process can be greatly promoted by strengthening training and promotion and motivating residents to participate. The government's manpower training work can effectively improve the residents' participation in the rural revitalization and realize the organic combination of government guidance and villagers' autonomy.

Third, fully invest, and avoid excessive emphasis on hardware construction. Carry out long-term and overall development planning research to prevent the negative benefits from rural tourism development from exceeding the positive benefits. Scientific resource allocation and reasonable layout design will effectively reduce the risks of blind development, including financial risks, repeated construction risks, market risks, etc.

Fourth, pay attention to scientific and technological innovation and digital development. The application of science and technology is a great help to the revitalization of the countryside. Through the application of scientific and technological achievements, not only can the upgrading of hardware facilities be promoted, but also the sustainable economic development can be realized through the feedback of scientific and technological achievements. Through the deep integration of science and technology and rural revitalization, the rural areas assume urban functions. It provides a brand-new development path for rural revitalization.

(4) Integrating the primary, secondary and tertiary industries, and promoting rural modernization

The model of integration of primary, secondary and tertiary industries refers to the introduction of industrial, service industries and modern information technology into the countryside on the basis of traditional agricultural production, to achieve the organic integration of "primary, secondary and tertiary" industries, and to promote the diversified development and modernization of the rural economy.

The most remarkable feature of the model of integration of primary, secondary and tertiary industries is that it promotes the diversification and modernization of the rural economy, which is mainly reflected in the following two aspects: First, it emphasizes the integration of industries. The integration development model of primary, secondary and tertiary industries highlights the organic integration between industries, and not only focuses on the linear connection of industrial chains. It is unique in that it emphasizes the mutual cooperation and symbiotic relationship between different industries, breaks down the barriers between various industries, promotes the circulation and sharing of resources, information and value, helps to improve the comprehensive utilization efficiency of rural resources, and thus enhances the overall competitiveness of the rural economy. Second, it emphasizes the dominant position of agriculture in the industrial chain. Agriculture is regarded as the leading force in the industrial chain, and farmers are no longer simple producers of agricultural products in this model, but have become a key link in the entire industrial chain by participating in the deep integration of multiple industries. They can directly participate in the processing, packaging, sales and other links of agricultural products, and can also participate in the industrial chain by providing services, carrying out tourism and other ways to achieve all-round participation and benefits.

The implementation path of the model of integration of primary, secondary and tertiary industries includes: Firstly, focusing on the cultivation and development of advantageous agriculture. Through in-depth exploration of local resource endowments and climatic conditions, the cultivation of crops or livestock and poultry breeding industry suitable for local characteristics will be emphasized. This will not only help to increase the output, but also ensure the quality of agricultural products. At the same time, the introduction of advanced agricultural technology, such as precision agriculture and green planting technology, will improve the efficiency of agricultural production and provide a solid foundation for the production and marketing of agricultural products.

Secondly, the agricultural products produced are processed into semi-finished products or finished products, laying the foundation for subsequent processing and utilization. At the same time, we must pay attention to technological innovation and adopt modern production technology and equipment to ensure the quality of agricultural products and food safety. Through this step, not only the added value of agricultural products is increased, but also the market space is expanded, laying a solid foundation for subsequent industrial development.

Then, through deep processing, agricultural products are processed into derivatives with higher added value. For example, fruit is processed into sauce, or characteristic agricultural products are used to make medicines and cosmetics. This process not only increases the value of agricultural products, but also provides a new development direction for rural industries and makes a substantial contribution to the diversification of rural economy.

Finally, combine industry and service industry with agriculture to realize industrial integration and service expansion. The development of food processing industry and the provision of services such as rural tourism, farm entertainment and experience of agricultural products have provided strong support for the modernization and transformation of the rural economy. This step not only provides more employment opportunities for local farmers, but also provides new impetus for the countryside to attract tourists and foreign investment, thus promoting the diversified development of the rural economy.

Typical cases of the model of integration of primary, secondary and tertiary industries include the "wine plus" industrial system in the Napa Valley of the United States and the "six industrialization" in Japan. The typical case of Napa Valley has provided vivid practice for the integration model of primary, secondary and tertiary industries. The four key points of resource integration, industrial integration, brand effect and national participation blend with each other, and jointly weave a picture scroll of regional sustainable development. Napa Valley, located in northern California, 95 kilometers away from San Francisco, is a world-famous wine-producing region with a history of 180 years. Its development has experienced extensive stage, brand building stage and industrial integration stage. The key points of its development include the following four points. First, resource integration. Napa Valley has fully integrated rich natural landscape, agricultural landscape and wine cultural resources, constructed a global tourism space based on wine industry, and realized the efficient use of resources and diversified development of the industry. Second, industrial integration. In the stage of industrial integration, Napa Valley combines tourism development with urban development, controls the development scale and direction of each small town through joint management of the government and the community, forms a compound development model with wine industry as the core, and promotes the extension of the industrial chain. Third, the brand effect. Taking advantage of the brand effect of the world's top wine producing areas, Napa Valley has successfully built a wine cultural resort in the United States, attracting wine lovers around the world and promoting the international development of the wine industry. Fourthly, the participation of the whole people. The Napa Valley government and the community committee participate in the political system of the city. Through the formulation of the sustainable development plan, the environmental protection and community construction are emphasized, realizing the participation of the whole society and jointly promoting the sustainable development of the region.

In order to promote the rural revitalization, Japan proposed the "six industrialization" model. The core of the "six industrialization" model is to organically integrate different industries, including traditional agriculture (primary industry), processing and manufacturing of agricultural products (secondary industry), service industry (tertiary industry), information technology and high-tech industry (fourth industry), environmental protection and ecological industry (fifth industry) and cultural, sports and leisure industry (sixth industry). Specifically, agricultural products focus on the enhancement of added value. Through the processing and manufacturing of the secondary industry, agricultural products can be added value, thus improving their market competitiveness. This includes food processing and intensive processing of agricultural products, making it easier for agricultural products to enter domestic and foreign markets. The tertiary industry plays an important role in the "six industrialization", including agricultural consultation, rural tourism, sales of agricultural products and other services. These services not only meet the needs of local residents and tourists, but also create more employment opportunities in rural areas. The development of the fourth industry, especially the application of information technology and high and new technology, has improved the level of intelligence in agriculture. The adoption of smart agriculture, agricultural information technology and other technologies makes agricultural production more efficient and accurate, which helps to improve the yield and quality. The fifth industry pays attention to environmental protection and the development of ecological industry, and encourages sustainable development methods such as organic agriculture and ecological agriculture to ensure the ecological balance in rural areas. The development of the sixth industry emphasizes the cultivation of local culture, sports and leisure industry. This way of multi-industry integration and development enriches the economic activities in rural areas, improves the comprehensive utilization efficiency of resources, solves the problem of uneven development in rural areas, and realizes the transformation of rural modernization.

The enlightenments of the model of integration of primary, secondary and tertiary industries: First, optimize the top-level design and guide the industry integration and development. Optimizing the top-level design is the foundation of rural revitalization. Good top-level planning and policy guidance can provide strong support for industrial integration and development. Through policy guidance and overall planning, we will promote the integration and development of the primary, secondary and tertiary industries. This kind of precise guidance enables all industries to be organically combined to form an industry model with unique local characteristics, thus avoiding blind development and industrial conflicts.

Second, strengthen platform construction and promote integration and development. The construction of integration platform is an important way to realize the integration and development of primary, secondary and tertiary industries. By building diversified integration platforms, opportunities are provided for interaction between different industries. The multi-format integration platform and the multi-subject integration platform allow the government, enterprises, academia and other parties to participate in the industrial development, forming a benign interactive situation. These platforms also provide a role of demonstration and guidance and a useful reference for industrial integration in other regions.

Third, strengthen the scientific and technological empowerment to improve the quality of agriculture. Science and technology is the power source to promote the development of the industry and an important means to enhance the added value of the industry. Through research and development of advanced planting technology and ecological protection technology, the quality and yield of agricultural products have been improved. This not only makes agricultural production more efficient, but also provides reliable raw material guarantee for the development of other industries.

Fourth, pay attention to the basic agricultural industries and create special brands. When developing small towns with agricultural characteristics, we must dig deep into the basic industries and form an industrial chain with local characteristics and competitive advantages. For example, based on grape planting, it has developed into a world-class wine culture town, indicating that the agricultural industry is the source of development. This successful experience suggests that when developing small towns with agricultural characteristics, we should cultivate basic industries and form a sustainable industrial chain based on local resources and advantages.

Fifth, cultural excavation and brand export. The combination of agricultural industry and local culture is one of the important means to create a brand with rural characteristics. Through in-depth excavation of local culture, the formation of a brand of agricultural products with unique cultural connotations can make the industry more competitive in the market. In addition, building a model room is also an effective way to cultivate the industrial brand and provide a development model for other regions.

II. The policies for the development of rural industries

1. Protecting arable land and improving land use efficiency

(1) Strengthening the protection and quality construction of arable land to ensure food security

With the development of urbanization and industrialization, the area of urban construction land continues to expand, while the area of arable land gradually decreases. Arable land, as the important carrier of food and the most basic means of agricultural production, is related to national food security and the stable development of society. It also holds significant importance for the protection of the ecological environment and serves as the foundation and guarantee for promoting the development of rural industries. Both developed countries and developing countries have adopted various policies of the protection of arable land.

As the country with the largest arable land area, the United States adopts a centralized and vertical arable land management method, emphasizing the social function and benefits of land. Through tax reductions and agricultural subsidies, it protects the agricultural use of land and encourages farmers to improve the soil. By employing measures such as preferential taxation, deferred taxation, and restrictive agreements, landowners are required to maintain the agricultural use of the land for 10 years as a condition for lower taxes, thereby preventing changes in land use. Cash subsidies are used to directly increase farmers' income, encouraging fallowing, crop rotation, or increased investment in arable land to improve its quality.

The UK coordinates urban and rural development to protect arable land through planning. By granting development rights to control land use, with land ownership belonging to private individuals and the development rights belonging to the state, the increased value benefits from land development investments are returned partially to the society. Such policies effectively alleviate arable land loss, improve land quality through land improvement subsidies and loans, and promote the development of small farms into larger, more scaled operations through the transfer of land by farmers, facilitating intensive and scaled agricultural development.

Japan focuses on ensuring high-quality arable land rather than the total land area in its policy orientation, establishing a comprehensive legal system of land and agriculture laws that are interwoven and mutually supportive, with detailed provisions and strong operability.This system forms a relatively systematic institutional design, comprehensive support, scientific structure, and strict enforcement in the process of arable land protection and utilization.

India implements arable land protection through the promotion of agricultural cooperative mechanisms. The development of agricultural cooperatives in India promotes farmers' enthusiasm to integrate arable land resources, significantly weakening the exploitation of farmers' assets by agricultural usurers. Through these cooperatives, the use of large-scale agricultural machinery and other new agricultural technologies is promoted, enhancing agricultural production efficiency, expanding the scale of agricultural production, reducing cultivation costs, increasing farmers' income, reducing the proportion of India's impoverished population, and ultimately promoting the progress of modern agriculture in India.

Brazil implements a policy to promote conservation tillage technology, which has had remarkable effects in the protection of arable land. In the early 1970s, after a Brazilian farmer actively studied conservation tillage technology in the United States, this technology was widely promoted in Brazil. Brazil specifically established professional institutions and grassroots organizations for conservation tillage, allocated funds to these institutions through public finances, and set up experimental sites across the country dedicated to the development of conservation tillage technology. For farmers who adopt conservation tillage technology, the government provides preferential policies such as reducing insurance and providing subsidies. With the promotion of conservation tillage technology policy, the area under conservation tillage in Brazil increased from 1.28 million hectares to 12.95 million hectares, accounting for 58.9% of the total arable land area. This led to improved land productivity and food quality, reduced production costs, and brought significant benefits to the Brazilian government and people.

The enlightenments of farmland protection policies are as follows: Firstly, it is essential to establish comprehensive farmland protection laws. Secondly, strict enforcement of land use planning should be carried out to prohibit any activities that change the use of cultivated land. Thirdly, the establishment of tax reductions or subsidies should be implemented to prevent farmers from altering the use of land and encourage them to improve the quality of the land. Finally, the establishment of land development rights or special funds for agricultural land protection is necessary to maintain the overall balance of cultivated land.

(2) Establishing agricultural industrial parks to improve the utilization efficiency of rural land and attract investment in rural industries

Establishing agricultural industrial parks, rationalizing and integrating rural land, and improving the efficiency of land use to attract more investors and businesses to enter the rural industrial sector are important means to promote the revitalization of rural industries. Countries such as Germany, the Netherlands, the United States, Singapore, and Japan started the modernization of agriculture relatively early. With the development of agricultural modernization, these countries have gradually established modern agricultural industrial parks. Currently, a large number of modern agricultural industrial parks have been built in these countries, integrating functions such as agricultural technology promotion, technical demonstration, ecotourism, and agricultural education, achieving a positive interaction between agricultural modernization and the development of agricultural industrial parks.

Different countries have different characteristics in the construction of agricultural industrial parks. The construction of agricultural industrial parks in the United States mainly emphasizes technological and large-scale operations. Its agricultural industrial parks adopt the main operating model of family farms, integrating agricultural production, processing, circulation, and financial services. They also carry out industry division and production segmentation in different regions, thus avoiding homogeneous competition and effectively dividing the functions of rural land, thereby improving agricultural production efficiency.

In Japan, agricultural industrial parks integrate leisure tourism to realize the multi-functionality of agriculture and increase the value of land use. In recent years, Japan has attached great importance to the construction of experiential agricultural parks and has incorporated it into an important agricultural policy for the development of multifunctional agricultural land. By combining the operational concepts and management methods of public parks, agricultural production and processing, agricultural internships, and leisure tourism are integrated. Moreover, Japan has used advanced agricultural technology to create a large number of distinctive and attractive sightseeing agricultural parks in addition to professional agricultural parks for vegetables, fruit trees, and flowers.

The construction of agricultural parks in Germany is committed to the industrialization and scale of the main agricultural products planting and processing. To promote the industrialized development of the parks, Germany first adjusts its agricultural industry structure and agricultural trade policies according to market orientation. It then further promotes the specialization, automation, and standardization of the production system, forming a distinctive ecological industrial development chain. Based on the production chain, a strong agricultural product marketing system is built as the basic driving force for agricultural development. Finally, a standardized agricultural technology system is constructed to promote the use of organic fertilizers, thereby increasing the added value of agricultural products and establishing highly industrialized agricultural industrial parks.

Singapore has rich experience in establishing multifunctional agricultural industrial parks and has developed its own characteristic path. Under the government's policy of vigorously developing agricultural industrial parks, Singapore currently has six agricultural industrial parks covering an area of 1,465 hectares. These parks feature ecological corridors, vegetable gardens, flower gardens, crocodile farms, marine aquaculture, and display advanced technologies for intensive agricultural production at home and abroad. They integrate agricultural production, sales, and sightseeing, exporting high-value products and services, generating substantial tourist income, with an average annual export value exceeding 60 million US dollars and attracting nearly 6 million visitors.

The experience of establishing agricultural industrial parks provides the following insights: Firstly, adopting modern high-tech agricultural technology, using big data, and the Internet of Things to improve the quality of agricultural products, promoting cooperation between agricultural parks, universities, and research institutions, and driving agricultural technology innovation. Secondly, fully utilizing local resources to promote the planting and export of local specialty crops, avoiding homogeneous competition, and maximizing economic benefits. Thirdly, organizing and standardizing the operation of agricultural industrial parks to achieve high production efficiency. Fourthly, actively promoting the comprehensive development of agricultural industrial parks, integrating production, leisure, agricultural technology promotion, and fully tapping into the multifunctionality of agriculture to enhance the added value of agricultural crops and their processed products. Fifthly, actively carrying out cooperation between agricultural industrial parks to form industrial clusters.

(3) Implementing land protection and compensation policies to encourage farmers to engage in land conservation and ecological environment restoration work

Many countries and regions have implemented land conservation and ecological compensation policies. The green payment policy in the United States is a typical policy for protecting and compensating land. Its main content involves individuals who benefit from land protection paying those who provide protection services. The key practices of this policy include: providing subsidies for the use and restoration of forestland, offering subsidies and services to farmers who operate ranches and farms in environmentally friendly ways, and controlling land development through purchasing land development rights. The Conservation Reserve Program (CRP) in the United States is one of the largest land conservation programs in U.S. history, and it has shown significant implementation effects. The program aims to remove erodible soils from cultivation in order to protect and improve soil quality, thereby enhancing crop quality. Under the program, farmers voluntarily sign 10-15 year contracts with the government to assist in land protection efforts, withdrawing environmentally sensitive land from agricultural production while receiving annual subsidies from the government. Since its implementation in 1985, the government has allocated 200 million dollars annually from the national treasury for land compensation, effectively controlling soil erosion and improving water quality.

The green direct payment within the European Union's Common Agricultural Policy is the most direct form of compensation and incentive for land ecological protection. It is used to support farmers who adopt cultivation methods that contribute to achieving environmental and climate goals. Farmers who comply with three environmentally beneficial mandatory practices receive green direct payments. Failure to adhere to the regulations governing green direct payments results in corresponding funding deductions, and governments may impose administrative penalties on top of funding reductions.

Germany's land conservation and compensation policy mainly consists of two forms of ecological subsidies and fallow subsidies. The ecological subsidies are primarily targeted at enterprises or farmers engaged in organic agriculture, requiring them to refrain from using any chemicals or fertilizers in the agricultural production process. Farmers meeting the requirements of organic agriculture production receive certain subsidies to offset the additional costs incurred by implementing environmental protection measures. Additionally, free training and assistance with expanding crop sales channels are provided to these farmers.

The experience of land conservation and compensation policies provides several insights: Firstly, these efforts rely on comprehensive legal frameworks. With the support of relevant laws and regulations, the compensation subjects, recipients, and methods of land conservation and compensation policies become clearer, and the compensation procedures and standards are more defined, ensuring the legitimacy and rationality of compensation measures and to some extent strengthening the land conservation awareness of the recipients. Secondly, the subjects and standards of land conservation and compensation policies are diversified. In many countries' compensation policies, the compensation subjects are not solely the government; governments of countries such as Germany and

Canada actively widen financing channels and involve social organizations and private businesses to jointly carry out compensation work for farmers. Different standards are set based on various land characteristics and production conditions. Furthermore, specialized land conservation and compensation banks are established to prevent issues like low efficiency and lack of focus in government compensation, ensuring that the compensation funds are used for their intended purpose. Lastly, land conservation and compensation mechanisms are dynamic, continually adjusted and improved in response to changes in socio-economic conditions and environmental protection requirements.

2. Providing financial support for the development of rural industries

(1) Providing financial services for agricultural products, agricultural technology, and equipment, to stabilize agricultural production

Increasing financial support for grain and important agricultural product production, strengthening financing services for high-standard farmland and water conservancy infrastructure construction, and providing financial services for the diversification of food supply systems. Strengthening financial support for agricultural science and technology equipment and green development, developing key core technologies in agriculture and promoting financial services, increasing financing support for the research and development of modern facility agriculture and advanced agricultural machinery. There are mainly two approaches: The first is to provide financial service support for agricultural products' prices, support the circulation and sales of agricultural products, and stabilize farmers' income in coordination with government agricultural policies; The second is to support investments in water conservancy, soil improvement, rural infrastructure construction, agricultural structure adjustment and other agricultural projects through providing lower interest rates and longer terms loans.

The United States' policy-based agricultural credit is composed of mutual cooperative agricultural credit institutions and government agricultural credit institutions, providing a variety of credit services to meet the diversified needs of rural areas. Various financial institutions in the United States comprehensively provide financial services to the rural economy, and there is clear division of labor among these institutions. Agricultural credit companies provide low or interest-free loans to farmers using unripe agricultural products as collateral, Federal Land Banks mainly provide long-term real estate loans, Intermediate Credit Banks mainly support agricultural production and operation, and Cooperative Banks mainly provide loans to agricultural cooperatives. To support agricultural product exports, the U.S. government often uses export credits.

Rural financial policy of the Republic of Korea is mainly implemented by agricultural cooperatives. In the early stage of "Saemaul Undong" (New Village Movement), a policy of simultaneous support for finance and fiscal was adopted. On the basis of government subsidies, agricultural cooperatives generally provide long-term, low-interest loans of up to 30 years to help farmers build houses, level land, and realize agricultural mechanization, to assist farmers in better conducting agricultural activities. In addition, its policy-based agricultural financial institutions also provide guarantees to agricultural producers, making up for the insufficient guarantee power of agricultural producers and expanding the financing scale of agricultural producers.

Thailand's agricultural financial policy combines the above two models, which is of specially typical significance. The Bank for Agriculture and Agricultural Cooperatives (BAAC) established by the Thai government provides more than 100 specialized financial services to farmers, covering multiple agricultural production areas, and provides financial services to 45 million farmers, successfully solving Thailand's rural financial problems. Regarding agricultural products, BAAC provides financial support for the circulation of agricultural products. In 1989, agricultural marketing cooperatives (AMCs) were established in various provinces of Thailand to provide farmers with production materials, transportation, and other services. At the same time, BAAC established joint guarantee groups, combined with AMC loans, greatly promoting the circulation speed of agricultural products. In addition, BAAC also established three national agricultural product trading markets, accelerating the circulation of agricultural products. In terms of rural construction, BAAC undertakes certain policy-based financial services, providing loan services for agricultural infrastructure construction and agricultural circulation facilities. As of 2013, BAAC has provided a total of 523 billion baht in policy-based financial services, benefiting 7.8 million farmers and playing a huge role in promoting Thailand's agricultural production.

Enlightenments from agricultural financial policies: Firstly, the government should combine monetary, fiscal, and financial policies to create a favorable macro environment for agricultural financial services, while providing certain subsidies and funds to support the development of rural finance for commercial financial institutions. Secondly, building a sound rural financial organizational system, which should not rely solely on single commercial bank credit but should also be comprehensive through the improvement of the financial organizational system. Thirdly, enriching rural financial service products and innovating in credit varieties, settlement methods, and financing methods to expand the coverage of agricultural financial services and meet the different needs of farmers.

(2) Providing financial support for rural small enterprises and farmer entrepreneurship, to promote the development of rural industries

Rural industrial revitalization cannot be achieved without effective entrepreneurial financial support. Innovation and entrepreneurship activities are important sources for promoting sustainable economic growth in rural areas. Many countries have established financial support policies for rural entrepreneurship.

The United States government adopts a "small government, big society" approach in supporting rural small business startups through financing management. It establishes a guided commercial institution with the government at its core and the market as its foundation, which indirectly regulates loans or investments from commercial entities and private capital to rural entrepreneurial enterprises. This increases the market financing channels for rural entrepreneurs. In addition, the United States has long implemented policies such as low-interest or subsidized loans, government credit guarantees, and "non-recourse loans" for family farmers. These policies offer diverse loan forms, significant preferential rates, and longer repayment periods. The guarantee system in the United States has national, regional, and community characteristics, meeting the financing guarantee needs of entrepreneurs at different levels. In the United States, there is a specialized type of rural entrepreneurship investment fund called the Community Development Venture Capital (CDVC) and Rural Business Investment Companies (RBICS). CDVC is specifically targeted at entrepreneurship investment funds for rural community development, while RBICS is an entrepreneurial investment program aimed at small and medium-sized businesses and new markets in rural America. The Small Business Administration (SBA) can help specific entrepreneurs obtain financing in a more targeted manner, including the "Rural Lender Advantage Program (RLA)" for rural development, making the U.S. entrepreneurship financing system more robust. In recent years, the U.S. government has doubled its investment in SBA for rural small businesses, promoting the interaction between private equity, venture capital, and rural startups, and better assisting rural startups in obtaining entrepreneurial investment.

Japan's *Act on Promotion of Agriculture, Industry and Commerce Cooperatives* clearly stipulates that recognized agricultural, industry and commerce cooperative plans or support plans can enjoy low-interest financing and insurance benefits. The Netherlands provides financial products and services for farmers, agricultural producers, and small and micro enterprises in all aspects of the industrial chain, including loan products, project financing, financing leasing, trade and commodity financing, acquisitions and mergers.

The enlightenments from the experience of financial support for rural small enterprises and farmers' entrepreneurship: Firstly, the orderly development of rural entrepreneurial finance requires institutional norms and policy support. Under the management of the government, relevant laws and regulations should be enacted for rural entrepreneurial finance to ensure the standardized implementation of the rural financial policies. Secondly, fiscal taxation should be combined with financial credit and other policies. For example, tax incentives or a certain proportion of credit financing support should be provided for the entrepreneurial income of rural small and micro enterprises. The equity financing and enterprise value-added services should also be provided for rural innovation and entrepreneurship. Thirdly, it is important to encourage the active participation of private capital and establish risk funds, compensation funds, and guarantee funds to enhance the risk-bearing capacity of rural financial institutions in supporting of farmers' entrepreneurship.

(3) Promoting the establishment of agricultural insurance system, to ensure the production efficiency of farmers

Agricultural insurance primarily aims to provide compensation insurance for agricultural producers who suffer economic losses due to natural disasters, accidents, epidemics, diseases, and other insured events in the process of engaging in crop farming, forestry, animal husbandry, and fishery production. The insurance covers crop cultivation, forest construction, livestock and poultry farming, aquaculture, fishing, and subsidiary activities related to agricultural production in rural areas. The main purpose of establishing an agricultural insurance system is to provide protection for the agricultural production process, minimize the losses caused by various risks to agricultural production, and safeguard the income of farmers.

The U.S. government has been committed to building a comprehensive and mature rural insurance system, with a high degree of marketization for rural agricultural insurance. Although the government does not directly intervene in the insurance business in the agricultural production process, it transfers specific insurance business to relevant market institutions such as private insurance companies and commercial insurance agencies. However, the U.S. government focuses primarily on top-level design of macro policies, supervision and management of insurance companies, and forecasting and analysis of market conditions.

Japan adopts a mutual insurance cooperative model for private insurance, and the organizational form of agricultural insurance adopts a "three-tier" villager mutual aid system, characterized by strong policy orientation and mutual assistance in operating organizations. Farmers join agricultural insurance mutual companies for mutual relief and assistance. These insurance mutual companies do not aim for profit. Under the guidance and supervision of higher-level governments, they handle insurance enrollment, collect premiums from insured farmers, assess the extent of disaster losses, and pay compensation to farmers by directly serving farmers. They also carry out disaster prevention work, such as pesticide spraying and setting up veterinary clinics.

Western European countries adopt a government subsidy model. In this model, agricultural insurance is not operated by the government but mainly by private insurance companies and insurance cooperatives. There is no unified agricultural insurance system at the national level, and farmers are not obliged to participate in insurance, as it is voluntary. To reduce the burden on farmers participating in agricultural insurance, the government provides subsidies and tax exemptions for participating farmers.

France, as a country with relatively developed agriculture, started early in agricultural insurance and has accumulated a wealth of successful experiences. In 1986, France established the Agricultural Mutual Insurance Group, a joint-stock company primarily controlled by the government with social participation. The group includes four insurance companies: agricultural mutual insurance company, non-agricultural property insurance company, farmer life insurance company and agricultural reinsurance company. They undertake different agricultural insurance businesses, extending coverage to various areas of agricultural production, not limited to the narrow scope of agricultural insurance, and manage it as a unified system. Additionally, the company continuously innovates in business planning, strengthens risk management capabilities, and meets new demands for agricultural insurance. Through nearly

20 years of practice, the company's operating model has not only achieved "risk management through insurance" but also enhanced the operational capacity, greatly promoting the development of agricultural insurance in France. As of 2019, the group's net assets reached 4.5 billion euros, and premium income amounted to 12.2 billion euros.

The enlightenments from the experience of agricultural insurance policies: Firstly, the establishment of agricultural insurance relies on sound laws and regulations to ensure the standardized operation of the agricultural insurance system. Secondly, the government implements a subsidy system for farmers participating in agricultural insurance, effectively mobilizing their enthusiasm for agricultural production. Thirdly, there should be a well-established management and operational system for agricultural insurance to reduce operational risks. Fourthly, the government provides tax relief to insurance companies, thereby enhancing their operational motivation.

3. Strengthening agricultural science, technology, and equipment support

(1) Strengthening the innovation, implementation, and application of agricultural science and technology, promoting the development of agricultural technology, and improving production efficiency

Agricultural technology is the fundamental guarantee for ensuring the long-term and sustainable supply of agricultural products, achieving stable agricultural development, and accelerating the modernization of agriculture. The realization of a strong agricultural technology country relies on the promotion and implementation of policies for agricultural and rural technological innovation, including policies that promote scientific and technological innovation and policies that facilitate the application of technologies.

Countries around the world are actively promoting "digital agriculture" technologies. The European Union has proposed the "Partnership for Agricultural Productivity and Sustainable Europe" program, which promotes joint funding by governments and businesses for in-depth research on the application of agricultural big data by various research institutions. EU member states attach great importance to the widespread application of new technologies in agriculture and are undertaking an "agricultural digital revolution" by using digital technologies to improve the efficiency of agricultural technology service systems. The UK has established agricultural innovation centers to catalyze further research and market application of agricultural technologies. Among them, the Agricultural Information Technology and Sustainable Development Indicator Center has achieved outstanding achievements in constructing agricultural big data and promoting agricultural digitization. Germany is committed to promoting the development of "digital agriculture" by applying big data and cloud technology to upload data on climate, soil, and geographical location to the cloud for processing, and then sending the processed data to intelligent large-scale agricultural machinery to command precise operations. It invests heavily in the development of agricultural technologies and has large enterprises leading the research and development of "digital agriculture" technologies. Israel has achieved agricultural management informatization with its high level of informatization and digitization. The Israeli government attaches great importance to the promotion and application of agricultural data products in agricultural production. For example, its famous "water-saving farms" use technology to turn water-scarce Israel into an agricultural oasis.

　　Belgium places great emphasis on innovation and implementation of agricultural technologies. In Belgium, some agricultural colleges and agricultural research centers shoulder the task of promoting agricultural research and extension work. They maintain close contact with the government and farmers, providing technical guidance to farmers and promoting practical technologies. For example, in potato cultivation, agricultural research centers conduct in-depth research on late blight problems and assist farmers in potato cultivation. They establish databases to monitor real-time climate, soil, and crop conditions, and timely provide farmers with information on pesticide application timing and dosage to effectively prevent late blight in potatoes. This helps Belgian potato farmers achieve a yield of up to 20 tons per hectare.

Major agricultural technology powers around the world have introduced corresponding policies to promote scientific and technological innovation from the perspectives of legislation, financial support, and education. In terms of legislation, Japan has formulated the *Basic Law on Agriculture* to promote the innovative application of modern agricultural technologies from the aspects of production, pricing, and circulation. It has also established systems for popularizing research results and organizing institutions for promoting agricultural research achievements. France has enacted the *Charter of Agricultural Extension* established an agricultural technology promotion fund, and set up a committee for agricultural technology promotion and progress. In terms of financial support, the United States stipulates that the government must provide funds to each state to establish an agricultural extension system and continuously increase investment in agricultural technological innovation. In terms of education policy, France has established the Agricultural Development Agency to provide skills training for agricultural workers and promote the latest agricultural science and technology.

The enlightenments from the experience of strengthening agricultural technology innovation, implementation, and policy implementation are as follows: Firstly, strengthening the establishment of a legal system for agricultural technology. Most agricultural technology powers in the world define agricultural technology policies in the form of laws, which can enhance the implementation of agricultural technology policies under legal constraints. Secondly, strengthening the coordinated management of scientific and technological resources by coordinating various departments and institutions involved in agricultural technology, optimizing the division of responsibilities among organizations, integrating and coordinating scientific research project proposals, budgeting, and talent development to improve the utilization efficiency of scientific and technological resources. Thirdly, increasing financial support for agricultural technology. Stable financial support can effectively support research, implementation, and promotion of agricultural science and technology, while motivating enterprises' enthusiasm for agricultural technological innovation. Fourthly, establishing a user-oriented research and extension model, strengthening communication between research institutions and farmers, transforming practical problems in agricultural production into research questions, and applying agricultural technology to practical use, maximizing its benefits.

(2) Supporting the rural industrial chains by technology, promoting the expansion of agricultural product sales channels and the logistics system

The vigorous development of the agricultural industry chain is one of the core elements in realizing the rural industries. By integrating the primary, secondary, and tertiary industries, it drives the simultaneous development of agriculture, processing, tourism, and other industries, actively supporting the development of the entire industry chain, including production, purchasing, sales, processing, and distribution. Advanced technologies such as the Internet of Things (IOT), big data, and cloud computing can support the development of rural industry chains. During the agricultural production phase, an automated agricultural production system is constructed, integrating environmental monitoring, crop model analysis, and precise regulation. During the sales phase, real-time monitoring and transmission of agricultural procurement and circulation data are implemented. In terms of administrative management in the agricultural sector, the modernization of agricultural management is promoted, enhancing the decision-making capabilities of agricultural production management and bringing about new changes to the rural industry chain.

The United States utilizes IOT technology to carry out "smart agriculture" promoting the development of rural industry chains. A comprehensive agricultural information service system has been established to provide ample domestic and international market information for agricultural production, processing, sales, and other business entities. This assists agricultural business entities in making informed operational decisions. Additionally, e-commerce technology is employed in agricultural circulation, establishing online direct sales channels from producers to consumers for both agricultural products and agricultural supplies, fundamentally transforming the traditional agricultural circulation system. The French government focuses on creating a "big agriculture" data system, encompassing high-tech research and development, commercial market consulting, legal policy support, and internet applications in seemingly unrelated industries. The Japanese government places high importance on the development of agricultural IOT, advancing the efficiency of agricultural production and circulation, and plans to popularize the application of agricultural robots based on agricultural IOT technology. A comprehensive agricultural market information service system has been established for the sales of agricultural products, providing real-time networked dissemination of various agricultural product sales volumes, predicted production quantities, price trends, and formulating a strict legal support system for standardized operation.

The Netherlands' "Chain Strategic Action Plan" aggregates scientific and technological resources, integrating and coordinating the agricultural industry chain to construct an efficient integrated industrial system. This plan has played a crucial role in the Netherlands' journey to becoming a world agricultural powerhouse. Relying on technology, the plan closely integrates various links such as agricultural production, processing, transportation, and sales, forming a complete and interlinked production chain. Additionally, technological innovation has been invested across different links of the production chain. In terms of research and breeding, the Netherlands' agriculture places significant emphasis on selecting superior varieties, each of which is developed by professional breeding companies. For the production of vegetables and flowers, greenhouse cultivation techniques and soilless cultivation are employed, utilizing computer technology to control temperature, humidity, light, fertilization, watering, pest control, and other factors. Strict control of each parameter leads to high yields. The Netherlands also possesses advanced cold storage technology for storage and sales and has a well-developed air cargo logistics system for the convenient transport of agricultural products.

Furthermore, the Netherlands has made high-tech investments in production materials and agricultural equipment, resulting in high output and economic benefits from limited land resources.

Experience and insights from technology-supported rural industry chain policies include: Firstly, strengthening the product transformation of agricultural industrialized operating enterprises, integrating technological resources, and intensifying efforts to tackle key processing technologies for agricultural products. Secondly, perfecting the construction of information technology in the agricultural industry chain, with the government taking on the responsibility of agricultural informatization, establishing an information consultation system, and providing guidance in the construction of the agricultural industry chain information network. Thirdly, strengthening the construction of a scientific and technological innovation and training promotion system, establishing a comprehensive training mechanism for the vast rural population. Mature technological achievements that can generate significant economic and social benefits are demonstrated and promoted in an organized and planned way, enhancing the application capacity of technological achievements. Fourthly, accelerating the construction of modern agricultural infrastructure and the upgrading of agricultural equipment.

4. Providing strong talent support for the development of rural industries

(1) Establishing a training system for agricultural professional skills to enhance farmers' vocational skills

Countries around the world attach great importance to the training of farmers' professional knowledge and vocational skills, and have formulated different training policies based on their own national conditions. Agricultural education and training can be divided into three models: East Asia, Western Europe, and North America.

The East Asian model, represented by Japan and the Republic of Korea, has a relatively small per capita arable land area and a severe aging rural labor force. In this model, the government has established a legal guarantee system for farmers' vocational education, forming a multi-level education system led by the government, involving participation from universities and cooperation with enterprises. Taking Japan as an example, the Japanese government has established a system of agricultural education for young farmers, starting with vocational education to cultivate and support a group of young and promising agricultural practitioners. Different levels of agricultural education systems have been established for different training targets, including undergraduate education, farmer university education, agricultural college education, rural preparatory school education, and agricultural mentor education. These systems have developed various agricultural talent training and education models, encompassing theoretical research education, theoretical-practical training education, technical training education and short-term training.

The Western European model, represented by Germany, the United Kingdom, and France, focuses on the connection between different levels of farmer education, with family farms as the main operating entities. The government provides sufficient education funding to support farmers in receiving free vocational training and has established systems such as training qualification certificates to enhance the effectiveness of farmers' education. For example, Germany has established a distinctive agricultural vocational education system, including three stages: preparatory vocational education, intermediate vocational education, and vocational further education. In France, the government stipulates that farmers over 18 years old must participate in one year of agricultural knowledge training, while farmers under 18 years old need to undergo three months of training, followed by three years of farm internships, and finally obtain a certificate through assessment prior to engaging in agricultural production work. France also strengthens the construction of agricultural research institutions, utilizing agricultural idle periods to popularize agricultural scientific knowledge and promote agricultural technology. In terms of farmer training content, emphasis is placed on practicality, covering a wide range of topics.

The North American model, represented by the United States, has highly mechanized and large-scale agriculture. Its agricultural education and training focus on practicality and have formed a dual system of formal farmer education and short-term farmer training. Under this mechanism, agricultural education in the United States is flexible and diverse, emphasizing the transmission of professional planting skills, production skills, agricultural product marketing, agricultural enterprise management, and other knowledge through agricultural projects. At the same time, an educational system integrating teaching, research, and extension services has been established, with federal, state, and county governments jointly participating in funding, training, and feedback processes during farmer training. The U.S. government encourages agricultural schools to establish their own 4-H organizations (Head, Hand, Heart, Health) to cultivate the interest of rural youths in agricultural work and promote new agricultural technologies and knowledge. This organization has become the largest and most influential high-quality farmer training organization in the United States, nurturing a large number of talents for the development of agriculture. In addition, the U.S. Department of Agriculture has established many relevant agricultural institutions, such as four national research centers and ten regional centers, as well as comprehensive training, research, and extension integrated agricultural experimental stations. It is under such a high-level and systematic high-quality farmer training system that the United States can cultivate many highly skilled agricultural professionals, ensuring the development of its agriculture.

The experience and inspiration of agricultural education and training policies are as follows: Firstly, it is important to focus on macro-level legal construction and institutional guarantees, strengthen the close cooperation between the agricultural sector and the education sector, and establish a multi-level education system for agricultural and educational systems. Secondly, it is crucial to integrate theoretical knowledge and practical training, aligning education and training content with the practical needs of farmers' production processes, and providing targeted instruction based on the individual characteristics of different farmer groups. Thirdly, it is necessary to improve the agricultural training system, guided by the government, led by institutions, and with participation from enterprises and universities, further integrating various educational resources.

(2) Attracting talent to return to the countryside by providing support for entrepreneurship and improving social security

With the development of urbanization and industrialization, countries around the world are facing the challenge of rural talent loss. In order to change the problems of hollowing out and aging population in rural areas caused by the loss of rural talents, many countries have introduced relevant policies and launched movements to revitalize and develop rural areas, aiming to attract talents back to the countryside.

The Republic of Korea has implemented a "Return to Farm, Return to Village" plan as a policy to induce the return of urban residents to rural areas. It mainly includes the establishment of support systems for returning to farming and villages, online and offline education, entrepreneurship consulting and financial support, and settlement support in rural areas. Individuals interested in returning to farming and villages can apply for high-quality farmer training based on their professional expertise. Those whose applications are approved can receive educational support funds for returning to farming and villages upon completing the training and meeting the requirements. Additionally, they can seek entrepreneurial support from comprehensive rural centers and access entrepreneurship funds provided by the government of the Republic of Korea. The Korean government also emphasizes the training of young farmers, conducting training for those returning to farming and villages to cultivate high-quality farmers. With an annual investment of 81 billion Korean won, it promotes 360 demonstration projects, cultivates advanced examples of young farmers, and continuously expands the coverage of learning organizations. Under the guidance of policies, the population returning to farming and villages in the Republic of Korea has increased, leading to improvements in rural residents' income and the level of social services, thus promoting rural economic development.

Japan, a country with scarce natural resources and a severely aging rural labor force, considers the cultivation of new professional young farmers and the attraction of talent back to rural areas as the key to achieving high-quality and sustainable agricultural development. Therefore, Japan has implemented the "New Farmer" plan. Since 1968, Japan has introduced policies to attract urban population back to rural areas and integrate into rural life, continuously improving and enriching its policy system over the decades. The focus areas include initial financial investment, basic life assurance, acquisition of housing and farmland, agricultural management, and community integration. To attract the talents back, Japan provides financial subsidies to young people returning to rural areas. Since 2019, the age eligibility for this support has been raised from under 45 to under 50, providing specific support of 1.5 million yen annually to young people wishing to engage in agricultural operations. The Japanese government has also established a land management agency to provide information on land leasing and purchase for those interested in entering agriculture through a land navigation system, addressing their basic survival and development needs. Furthermore, a housing financial support agency has been set up to offer favorable loans to young people purchasing vacant houses, addressing the issue of housing for young returnees. The Japanese government not only promotes the agricultural operating income insurance to address the concerns of young farmers after engaging in the agriculture, but also provides the training courses in agricultural machinery and technology. Japan's "New Farmer" plan has been implemented for many years and has achieved significant results. It has led to a significant change in young people's perception of agriculture, with a noticeable increase in the proportion of "new entrants" and "newly employed in agriculture," as well as a year-on-year increase in agricultural employment, injecting a great deal of fresh energy into Japan's agriculture.

The experiences of policies to attract talent back to rural areas are as follows: Firstly, it is important to improve the incentive mechanism for talents returning to rural areas. Increase subsidies for young returnees and improve the service and support system for talent returning to rural areas by providing incentives in terms of funding and technical support, entrepreneurial venues, project incubation, financing guarantees, children's enrollment in schools, and social security. The second is to strengthen the construction of rural infrastructure and raise the level of rural public services. Increase public resource and fiscal investment in rural areas, fill the gaps in rural infrastructure construction, carry out rural environmental governance, narrow the urban-rural gap, and enhance the attractiveness of rural areas. The third is to construct a deep integration mechanism for the rural industry chain and talent chain. The development of the rural industry is the foundation for attracting talent back to rural areas. Promote the integration of the primary, secondary, and tertiary industries in rural areas, tap into the potential for rural industrial development, and create greater entrepreneurial space for returnees. Finally, improve the agricultural education and training for returnees. Training for returnees should not be limited to agricultural functional and technical education, but should also focus on agricultural awareness education, cultivating high-quality farmers who are "cultured, skilled, and business savvy."

III. Experience and enlightenment of rural industry development

1. Digging deep into the value of local resources and focusing on resource advantages to form a core industry

The most favorable condition for the development of rural industry is the rich resources that the villages have, including natural resources, biological resources, ecological resources, human resources, etc. The advantage of characteristic resources is an important basis for the differentiated development of industries. Scientific and orderly development and utilization of unique local resources are conducive to the formation of characteristic industries. With industry as the core, it pays attention to optimizing the resource structure, tapping and utilizing the resources advantages of the region, forming an industrial chain, and improving the overall level of the regional economy. For example, Japan's agricultural industry, while paying attention to the protection of the ecological environment, has created an international well-known brand by innovating the way of agricultural production, perfecting the industrial chain and continuously improving the product quality.

2. Innovating mechanisms to promote the model of integrated development

In the process of rural industry development, it is difficult for a single industry to sustain development, and innovation and integration development are needed. First of all, the extension of the agricultural industry chain, the development of agricultural products processing industry, and agricultural production to form a benign coordinated development, improve agricultural efficiency. Secondly, support the development of rural non-agricultural industries, encourage the rural population to engage in industrial and commercial activities, and form an industrial integration development model to increase the effective income of farmers and improve the quality of life of rural people. For example, the rural tourism in France organically combines elements such as culture, natural scenery, food and accommodation, forming a unique tourism experience and becoming a pillar industry of the regional economy.

3. Strengthening agricultural support and protection policies, and guiding the technology and capital invest in agricultural industries

Establishing sound agricultural support and protection policies, including policies on land and water resources protection, agricultural science and technology development, agricultural prices, income support, agricultural credit, agricultural taxation and foreign trade of agricultural products; strengthening government technical guidance and capital investment, including financial subsidies, tax incentives, technical guidance, standard setting and other means, to help enterprises succeed in the development of rural industries, enhance the competitiveness of enterprises, and lay a solid economic foundation for rural construction. For example, by virtue of its complete rural financial system and mature crop insurance business, the United States has long been in the leading position in the world in agriculture, thus effectively safeguarding rural development.

4. Improving the personnel training mechanism and enhancing the innovation ability of rural talents

Increase the investment in rural education, strengthen the training of rural teachers, encourage social resources to invest in education, encourage the establishment of private schools, promote the diversification of education investment and the diversification of education content, and then improve the urban and rural inequality in education. By continuously improving the technical level and management ability of the practitioners, and paying attention to the research and development of new products, services and technologies, the endogenous power is enhanced to accelerate the upgrading of rural industries and continuously promote the development of rural economy. For example, Japan has set up agricultural training institutions and coordination organizations to provide farmers with technical and marketing guidance and financial support, while at the same time improving farmers' agricultural knowledge and comprehensive quality.

5. Taking science and technology as a support, information technology as a driving force to promote the technological transformation of rural industries

Promote innovative agricultural technologies, promote all-round technological exchanges in agricultural science, raise the level of science and technology in the agricultural industry globally, and strengthen the empowerment of agricultural science and technology to improve agricultural productivity. Under the digital background, strengthening the digital support and fostering the construction of digital villages are the active adaptation and integration of rural construction to the digital era. Through technological empowerment, the seamless connection between supply and demand of rural products can be realized, which will drive the optimization and transformation of rural industrial structure, integrate rural resources and promote high-quality sustainable development of villages. In the process of building a digital village, attention should be paid to adjusting measures to local conditions and proceeding from reality, so as to avoid the adverse effects such as the increase of rural economic burden and the mismatch between digital construction and rural industrial base.

6. Paying attention to the protection of ecological environment, and promoting the development of green industry to achieve sustainable development

Based on the concepts of green and environmental protection, the combination of ecological value, cultural value, leisure value, tourism value and economic value of rural society is emphasized, so as to improve the quality of rural life and meet the needs of local development. A multi-faceted governance system for all sectors and entities in all economies should be built to work together to govern the rural environment and strengthen environmental protection. Utilizing scientific and technological innovation to enable rural environmental governance and protection. Establishing diversified investment and financing mechanisms to promote environmental protection and governance by introducing various financing methods.

◎ **Chapter II** **International Rural Talents Development**

Abstract

    The development of rural areas in the world cannot be achieved without the support and promotion of talents. However, due to the rapid development of cities, rural areas are limited by economic, social and ecological development difficulties, and a large number of rural labor forces work in cities. And problems such as rural hollowing, aging and feminization have become increasingly prominent. An in-depth analysis of global and major regional policies and practical measures for rural talent development can help better address issues such as insufficient endogenous driving force for rural development, low levels of rural agricultural production, and low levels of rural education in the context of rapid urban development. Due to the differences in rural economic, social and ecological conditions, different countries face different needs for talent development, and countries have implemented different models of talent development policies and practices for rural talent development. The main policy models of rural talent development are: policy support type, government led type, economic incentive type, technological cultivation type and facility improvement type. Looking forward to the future: Formulating relevant laws, focusing on the cultivation and introduction of new farmers, guiding multi-party cooperation by the government, improving infrastructure construction, and upgrading industrial structure are important ways to develop rural talents.

I. Current situation and model of rural talent development

1. Current situation of rural talent development

(1) The demand for information technology talents continues to rise

Under the impact of COVID-19, the integration of digital technology with various industries is getting better and better, and new business forms and models, represented by online office, online education and Internet health care, continue to evolve. At present, countries around the world are stepping up their efforts in digital transformation, and the demand for digital talents in the world's major economies is expanding. In European cities, the demand for digital talent in manufacturing, software and IT services has increased significantly. In the process of talent development, most countries have accelerated the pace of talent training to meet the needs of industrial talents and realize the matching of personnel and positions. In order to adapt to the changes of the job market, the following characteristics are displayed. The first is to speed up the development of new vocational training jobs, set up cross-enterprise joint training courses, and train high-quality talents suitable for industrial development. The second is to launch national training programs to improve basic scientific research and enhance personnel training. For example, to provide financial support to college students and new researchers, and attract young people to choose mathematics, informatics, natural science and technology majors, Germany has focused on three talent training and mobilization plans: "Taking off through education", "Securing jobs, boosting growth momentum and modernizing the State — the German Employment and Stability Package" and "The contribution of working migrants to securing Germany's professional talent base". In addition, emerging economies such as China are also vigorously boosting basic science research and strengthening the role of basic science as a pillar of future development. In particular, with China's transformation into a phase of high-quality development, the demand for innovation-driven development is increasing, and so is the demand for high-quality talent development.

With the increasing demand for information technology talents in various regions of the world, new requirements are also put forward for talent development in rural areas. In the process of the development of rural talents, all regions in the world have generally accelerated the pace of talent training to meet the needs of new industrial talents. Digital transformation in rural areas has ushered in broader opportunities, as digital technologies such as telecommuting and online education have been widely used in regions including vast rural areas, due to travel restrictions during the pandemic. The digitalization process in rural areas will also see deep integration for some time to come. Many developing countries are also taking advantage of the development opportunities of information digitization to drive the progress of agriculture and rural areas. This requires more professional talents to devote themselves to rural construction. For example, the Indian government has launched the "Digital India" program to bring digital technologies to rural areas to provide services such as Internet access and electronic payments. The implementation of the "Digital India" plan will include three main aspects: The first is to carry out the popularization of information technology, improve the level of infrastructure construction, and promote the construction of digital networks and data transmission. The second is to strengthen the security of digital services and information, establish a digital security mechanism to protect the data security of citizens and enterprises, and strengthen digital security awareness education and training. The third is to promote the development of the digital economy, strengthen the development of digital economy areas such as e-commerce and online transactions, and improve the level of integration of digital technologies and industries. Through the deep integration of information technology in rural construction, countryside strives to realize the upgrading of industrial structure, which also has great potential for agricultural development and rural construction. Moreover, in February 2022, China issued the *14th Five-Year Plan for the Development of Agricultural and Rural Informatization*, which clearly proposes to strengthen the construction of agricultural and rural informatization talent echelon and scientific and technological innovation team support, and cultivate leading talents in agricultural and rural informatization. Government would strengthen the training of agricultural and rural informatization technicians and related content, carry out technology demonstration and technical services, and cultivate a group of farmers who have mastered smart agricultural technology. Government would support enterprises, institutions, educational and training institutions in conducting targeted training, and speed up the training and introduction of practical personnel for IT application in agriculture and rural areas.

(2) The contradiction between supply and demand for rural personnel is intensifying

Aging population and low fertility rate have a great impact on rural labor supply. With the increasing demand for talents in rural areas, some countries and regions have begun to encourage young people to return to rural areas for development. Especially in the process of rural revitalization, there is a shortage of high-level talents for the development of agricultural resources. Talents should constantly adapt to the development trend of integrated informatization and digital agriculture to better serve industrial development. In France, the government has introduced the *Act for the Rural World* to encourage young people to return to rural areas to start their own businesses, while providing training and financial support. China has issued *the Opinions on Supporting Entrepreneurship and Innovation of Returnees and Promoting the Integrated Development of Primary, Secondary and Tertiary Industries in Rural Areas*. The policy aims to guide more young people to start their own businesses in rural areas and provide policy support in terms of capital and taxation, so as to attract them to take root in rural areas and make them the backbone of promoting the revitalization of rural industries.

For many emerging economies, the shortage of professional rural talents is also a major problem they face. Different from the developed countries, how do many developing countries train rural talents? How to give full play to the ability of talents? How to realize talent resident in rural areas? There are still big difficulties. Drawing on the advanced experience of developed countries, many countries are introducing relevant policies to support rural education and personnel training. In addition, the shortage of rural infrastructure construction is also a major problem plaguing talent retention. Infrastructure construction is an important starting point to promote agricultural and rural development. In many countries, the epidemic has exposed the lack of infrastructure in rural areas. In particular, many developing countries have been exposed to the shortage of public medical resources, emergency management capacity and medical personnel supply in rural areas during the epidemic. As a result, some governments have begun to increase investment in infrastructure construction in rural areas. For example, the Philippine government has launched the "Hot Sun Program" to improve the level of infrastructure in rural areas, including roads, bridges and public buildings. In September 2022, China jointly issued the Work Plan on Expanding Current Investment in Agricultural and Rural Infrastructure Construction, which will expand effective investment in agriculture and rural areas with rural infrastructure construction as the starting point. This plan will not only help short-term economic stability, but also improve the overall agricultural production capacity and promote high-quality development of agriculture and rural areas in the long run. Therefore, it is all the more important to focus on social forces to drive effective investment, fully stimulate the power and vitality of social investment, and continuously provide a solid guarantee for rural revitalization.

(3) The mobility of rural talents has continued to increase

A new round of scientific and technological revolution and industrial transformation is gathering pace. The global knowledge economy is developing in depth. New technologies, models and forms of business are emerging. In the face of the more personalized and changeable needs of consumers, as well as the fast-changing external macro environment, organizational capabilities are constantly transitioning to decentralization and flattening, and the individual value of employees is becoming prominent. The influence of the epidemic has led to a deeper adoption of remote work, and new employment forms have emerged continuously. Talents have also begun to seek personalized development paths under such structural changes. Therefore, in the process of talent management and development, organizations are bound to adapt to changes in order to ensure that individual development is consistent with the strategic direction of the organization. Especially under the continuous deepening of the contradiction between supply and demand of talents, countries have launched a series of measures to attract population migration in order to improve their competitive advantages.

Most countries took measures to close exchanges in the early stage of the epidemic, which led to the continuous influx of talents after the global pandemic, relaxed skilled immigration policies, and lowered the threshold for foreign senior talents to enter the domestic labor market. By strengthening international exchanges, they are encouraging the labor force to release more high-quality talent resources in their own countries. Many countries around the world are competing for the talents they need by introducing immigration-specific policies and measures. For example, Singapore has implemented the "Global Campus" program, which aims to attract overseas students and corporate employees to receive education or training in Singapore. The United States has reformed the random lottery for temporary occupational visas (H-1B) to enhance its efforts to attract highly skilled and well-paid talent in STEM (science, technology, engineering and math education) fields. The EU has relaxed restrictions on mobility and introduced the start-up visa to attract high-level talent for innovation and entrepreneurship. China has made great efforts to build its comparative advantage in international competition for talents, and gradually transformed itself from the world's largest source of overseas talent to a major source of returning talent. Japan has increased the number of highly specialized vocational visas and adjusted its points system to meet its target of attracting 20,000 high-level talents ahead of schedule. The UK has reformed its visa system to make it more attractive to outstanding talents and those who have studied abroad.

Rural revitalization is not about keeping people in the countryside. It is about enhancing the internal driving force for rural development, taking advantage of opportunities for consumption from cities to rural areas, increasing rural population flow and modern factors, and modernizing agriculture and rural areas. Rich farmers must "reduce" the number of farmers, and "leaving the countryside" is a step towards "gaining access, retaining and developing well". In recent years, some industrialized or post-industrialized countries and regions began to see population migration between city and town after the "rural-city" migration of surplus rural labor force to cities in the early stage of industrialization. Especially after a long period of epidemic lockdown or isolation, people began to pay more attention to health and wellness. Rural areas usually have a better environment and air quality, and in order to obtain a good health environment, people's mobility between urban and rural areas has increased significantly, which provides important opportunities for rural revitalization. In Italy, the government is promoting post-epidemic rural tourism and rehabilitation programs to attract more urban people to rural areas and promote the overall development of rural areas.

(4) The talent development gap in rural areas is widening

With the deepening of globalization, the differences between the world's economies are also expanding, and this difference is also fully reflected in rural talents. The north-south difference in global economic development is spreading to agricultural and rural talents. There is a great gap in the supply of rural talents between developed and less developed countries, which is not only reflected in the difference of economic development level among economies, but also in the difference of income, employment status and education level between urban and rural sectors in less developed countries in Asia, Africa and Latin America. In the United States, there are numerous agricultural professional schools and research institutes, a large number of personnel training, and the vocational salary of agronomy graduates is quite considerable. According to the Bureau of Labor Statistics, the average annual income of agricultural workers was $31,070 in 2014. The agricultural education in other developed countries has also continuously cultivated more professional talents, who are widely serving in the fields of agricultural professional production, scientific research and development, and agricultural machinery manufacturing, providing a huge internal driving force for their own agricultural development.

However, in many developing countries, especially in Asia, Africa and Latin America, the overall productivity of many countries is low, the industrial structure is single, and the agricultural development is highly dependent, and there is no scientific and technological support, and it is impossible to make more efforts in the cultivation and improvement of rural talents. What's more, local residents have a low level of education and face a huge urban-rural development gap. The employment rate in rural areas was only 57.9% in 2011, and average incomes in rural areas are much lower than in urban areas. Venezuela's 2011 rural population employment rate is only 57.9%, the average rural income also is far lower than the urban areas. The employment rate in Sri Lanka's rural areas was 46.8%, lower than that in urban areas, which was 49.4%. The average income in rural Sri Lanka is Rs 37,000 per month, lower than that in urban areas, which is Rs 64,000 per month. At the same time, education levels in rural areas are also lower than that in urban areas, with only 11.6% of rural residents having a high school diploma or higher compared to 23.5% of urban residents[4]. In 2017, the population of Pakistan's rural areas stood at 130 million, accounting for 63.6% of the total population. The employment rate in rural areas of Pakistan is 48.5%, which is lower than 54.9% in urban areas. The average income in rural Pakistan is Rs 14,000 per month, lower than Rs 26,000 per month in urban areas. Education levels in rural Pakistan are also lower than that in urban areas, with only 13.8% of rural residents having a secondary or higher degree compared to 32.7% of urban residents[5]. In Kenya, the unemployment rate in rural areas reached 35.5% in 2019. The backwardness of human capital undoubtedly restricts the development of rural talents in developing countries.

---

4 Sri Lanka Bureau of Statistics. http://www.statistics.gov.lk/.

5 Pakistan Bureau of Statistics. https://www.pcbs.gov.ps/default.aspx.

2. Main models of rural talent development

(1) Talent training: enhancing the endogenous vitality of rural areas

Developed countries continue to build a complete system of personnel training. The special training of rural talents has improved the hematopoietic function of agriculture development and rural areas. The experience from developed economies shows that the emphasis on higher education and vocational training can effectively improve the professional level of rural talents, and provide rural talents with a wide range of learning opportunities and resources. First of all, it is necessary to build agricultural higher scientific research institutions with complete specialties and rich educational resources. There are more than 70 agricultural universities in the United States and more than 40 in Japan, offering education in a wide range of specialized fields, from agricultural science to agricultural economic management. Second, they actively explore diversified vocational training methods and form a unique vocational training system that serves production. Such as agricultural experiment stations, agricultural cooperatives, agricultural consulting services, etc., provide rural talents with ways to improve skills, update knowledge, production technology and marketing consulting. Third, the country continue to increase research funding to provide sufficient material support for the whole process of personnel training. The French "Law on the Orientation and Planning of Scientific Research and Technological Development" clearly stipulates the proportion of national public scientific research funding in the GNP and its annual growth rate, and requires a reasonable division of the proportion of state funding used to support basic, application and development research, and the proportion of funding used to support major key areas of scientific and technological development. According to OECD statistics, from 2000 to 2015, the proportion of funding for basic research in France's GDP was higher than that of other countries, and remained stable at about 0.5%. It also keeps France's professional and technical personnel in the leading position in the field of technological innovation and application. Fourthly, through improving the legal system, effectively protect the rural talents' right to education. The Republic of Korea's policies such as "the Farmers' Continuing Education Act" and "the Farmers' Vocational Ability Development Act" have determined the rural talents' right to education and training through mandatory laws and regulations, and adopted policies and other ways in the training process to ensure that rural talents can get rich educational resources and incentive measures.

Developing countries are speeding up the professional training of their own talents. On a global scale, there are a large number of developing countries, and their development is highly uneven among all countries. In the process of rural development, emerging economies attach great importance to the training of rural basic education and vocational education, so as to improve the basic quality and employability of rural talents. This is because despite the rapid economic development of these countries, the requirements of rural modernization continue to expose the problem that rural talents are not professional enough to promote the leapfrog development of rural areas. The BRICS countries have provided rural talents with basic cultural knowledge and skills through the implementation of universal compulsory education, improving the quality of education and increasing investment in education. In India, due to the generally low level of education, the country's government has introduced and implemented policies such as the Education for All Act to provide free compulsory education for all children aged 6 to 14, which to some extent ensures basic education for the workforce. Brics countries have also provided rural talents with professional skills and knowledge adapted to market needs by conducting diversified vocational education and training. South Africa's policies, such as the *Technical and Vocational Education and Training Act* and the *Vocational Qualification Framework Act*, have provided rural talents with a full range of continuing education and training, from basic skills to professional skills to innovative skills. Many less developed countries in the third world, while actively exploring the development of agricultural industry, are also strengthening the training of rural talents. For example, Sri Lanka, Pakistan and other countries have included the training of professionals in their national development plans and tilted their policy resources. However, due to their relatively weak resources, there are great difficulties in various training methods and processes.

(2) Talent introduction: improve the blood transfusion capacity in rural areas

The policy system of developed countries serves the market mechanism. Talent is the main driving force for sustainable rural development, and all countries have implemented extensive policy measures to guide talent introduction. In developed economies, the introduction of talent resources to serve the development of rural areas is mainly through strengthening market-oriented and innovation-driven, as well as policy guidance and information support, to enhance the competitiveness and creativity of rural talents. First of all, countries attach great importance to the introduction of various types of talents into rural areas, and organically combine the exploitation and cultivation of human resource advantages in rural areas with the input of other factors such as capital, so as to give full play to the role of human capital as a factor of production in promoting rural economic growth. The second is to focus on improving the leading role of market mechanism in the process of talent flow. By establishing perfect market mechanism, European and American countries encourage rural talents to adjust production structure and mode according to market demand, and improve product quality and efficiency. By establishing a sound market information system, the UK has provided timely and accurate market information and signals for rural talents. France has set up an agricultural innovation fund to provide rural talents with conditions and support to carry out scientific and technological innovation and application innovation. The third is to link it links the training of talents with practical application. Germany has the most famous vocational education system in the world. In the process of village renewal, governments at all levels have set up vocational training schools for farmers in rural areas, and have also cooperated with colleges and universities to carry out training in village planning, ecological agriculture and non-agricultural employment skills. Cultivating multi-level market players, strengthening the training of professional farmers, and appropriately guiding all kinds of talent resources to flow to rural areas are a strong guarantee for promoting sustainable rural development. The practical experience of the Saemaeul Movement in the Republic of Korea shows that although the government's financial income was limited at that time, it carried out a nationwide movement for the development of rural talents, and in-depth education was conducted for the majority of farmers and social subjects, thus establishing the important position of agricultural development.

Developing countries pay attention to policy guidance. Although the market mechanism has strong guidance for the rational flow of factors of economic development, in developing countries, the relatively backward economic development level is difficult to achieve effective development under the guidance of the market. Different from the implementation of neoliberalism in developed countries, developing countries put more emphasis on the government to realize the flow of human resources in urban and rural areas through strong policies and regulations. Brazil, through the implementation of the Agricultural Credit Program, Agricultural Insurance Program and other policies provides rural talents from the city to the countryside or from the countryside to rural migration and employment with economic support. China, by combining rural revitalization with poverty alleviation, has adopted policy support measures to encourage urban professionals to provide fixed-point assistance to rural areas. And through the establishment of sound household registration system, social security system, labor market and other mechanisms, rural talents have been provided with migration and employment market opportunities from the countryside to the city or from the city to the countryside. Therefore, policy incentives are widely adopted in developing countries to increase the reserve and flow of rural talents. By implementing various forms of government subsidies, tax incentives, credit support and other measures, BRICS countries have provided economic support for the migration and employment of rural talents from urban to rural areas or from rural to rural areas. In less developed areas, talent introduction mainly focuses on attracting the transnational flow of rural talents, relying more on the assistance of international organizations and other international cooperation mechanisms to introduce specialized agricultural production technicians to help local scientific and technological development and improve the level of agricultural modernization.

(3) Talent retention: support the long-term development of rural areas

Developed countries continue to optimize market mechanisms. It is certainly important to attract talent to rural areas and to serve the countryside, but what's more important is to ensure they stay and take root in the countryside. For developed countries, despite the objective differences between urban and rural development, well-developed infrastructure and material incentives can meet the needs of talents. Firstly, in the process of modernization and upgrading of agricultural industry, the professional development of farmers has enabled talents to highlight their professional attributes in the process of serving rural construction. Moreover, in the process of talent development, urban and rural areas can be combined to achieve two-way development of talents. Secondly, due to the emphasis on the combination of various capital elements, developed countries have effectively released the asset function of land as a production factor and the capital function as collateral in the process of promoting rural development. Under the guidance of policies, a land system featuring equal rights and prices, smooth circulation and revenue sharing has been established[6]. A system of rural housing land that is acquired fairly in accordance with the law, used economically and intensively, and voluntarily withdrawn with compensation has been established. In this way, the organic combination of land value and human capital can be realized. By helping talents obtain land property rights in rural areas, the combination of people

---

6　Shao'an Huang, Jian Zhao. Land property, land finance and rural economic growth [J]. Jianghai Academic Journal, 2010 (6): 86-93, 238-239.

and land will keep more talents in rural areas. Thirdly, talents stay and work in rural areas for a long time, mainly focusing on improving rural culture and ecology, upgrading industrial structure, and improving rural talents' sense of belonging and happiness. Germany holds various forms of farmers' festivals, beer festivals and wine festivals every year, showing the local customs and customs of German villages. By establishing national parks, nature reserves and ecological corridors, the United States has provided a beautiful ecological environment and leisure space for rural talents. Japan's policies such as the "One Village One Product" movement and the six industrialization strategies have provided rural talents with diversified employment options and income increase channels. It has also provided an improved production and living environment for rural talents by implementing measures such as the construction of rural infrastructure, the provision of public services and the improvement of social security.

Developing countries have made efforts to improve policy guidance mechanisms. Rural construction in developing countries is more about getting rid of the backwardness of rural areas and narrowing the dual structural gap between urban and rural areas. In addition, it is necessary to improve the basic public services and social security system in rural areas to meet the most basic production and living needs of talents. First, developing countries pay attention to the modernization of agricultural production and the upgrading of industrial structure brought about by technological progress. Through large-scale promotion of agricultural mechanization and technological innovation in modern agricultural production, they will create more practical jobs for talented people and meet their basic needs. After the introduction of talents into rural areas, they can make use of their intelligent advantages to help achieve all-round improvement in agriculture. Second, the backward infrastructure in rural areas is being improved. Backward transportation conditions, medical and educational resources, and limited social security measures all hinder talents from taking root in rural areas. By implementing policies such as the *New Rural Construction Plan*, China is committed to improving the level of basic public services, narrowing the gap between urban and rural areas, and improving the working and living environment for rural talents. Third, China is committed to coordinating the contradiction between people and land, and constantly improving the policy mechanism that is appropriate for land use and human resources development. Although the market mechanism is not perfect, many developing countries are still exploring ways to revitalize the value of land resources and rationally allocate resources by releasing human resources under the continuous promotion of policies. For example, in the process of building new rural areas, China is constantly exploring the conversion of resources into assets, funds into shares, and farmers into shareholders, and actively exploring the participation of rural collective land use rights in the construction of urbanization, industrial parks and other projects by means of joint management and investment[7].

(4) Talent incentive: stimulate the motivation of social participation

Developed countries have complete incentive systems. As for talent motivation, it mainly stimulates the initiative and creativity of rural talents by advocating social participation and rural autonomy. In the process of rural development in various countries, human capital, as one of the main production factors, plays an irreplaceable role in promoting rural economic and social development. First of all, government should make use of our own technological advantages to continuously inject the endogenous growth impetus of technology into talent innovation and development. Science and technology, modern management methods and advanced experience in rural governance need to be transformed into real rural productive forces by strengthening farmers' learning, training and experience accumulation. This transformation process is the process in which human capital plays a role. France's strong agricultural cooperative system, which covers the whole industrial chain from production to processing to sales, provides opportunities for rural talents to share resources and benefits each other. By establishing a two-way cooperative

7 Zhaoyang Wang. Promote rual revitalization by urban and industrial reallocation [J]. Rural Finance Research, 2018 (6): 66-70. DOI:10.16127/j.cnki.issn1003-1812.2018.06.013.

relationship, the UK provides a mechanism for rural talents to participate in and collaborate with the government, enterprises, associations and schools. Second, let the role of rural elite talents be fully realized, and give the country gentry full space to participate in governance. To a large extent, the success of rural development depends on the active participation of farmers, especially the rural elite, that is, the squire class. Through the extensive social participation mechanism, the rural elite group on the one hand represents the full realization of the value of human capital and has a positive contribution to the development of local industries. On the other hand, by strengthening their full participation in local governance, rural talents can satisfy their governance rights and become the masters of the countryside. In the multi- participation of local management departments and social multi-subjects, the construction of smooth interest expression mechanism, participation mechanism, decision-making mechanism, etc., effectively safeguard and realize the interests of farmers, guide the new professional farmers to play their own subjective initiative, with the mentality of ownership more actively participate in the rural revitalization, improve the sense of honor and responsibility of rural talents. Third, developed countries in East Asia also release more emotional ties to rural culture, promote the identity of rural talents, and provide deeper spiritual incentives.

In developing countries, material incentives are the main ones. Giving full play to the market mechanism to effectively motivate rural talents is not applicable in the practice of most developing countries. First of all, government should improve laws and regulations, clarify the relevant incentive system for rural talents from the legal level, and gradually establish an effective incentive mechanism. In the process of promoting rural revitalization, China has established talent transfer mechanisms such as "special commissioner of science and technology", "rural revitalization commissioner" and "rural revitalization assistant", and has standardized incentives for talents to go to the countryside through clear systems. By giving priority to the employment support, material security, social welfare and development planning of talents, the career development needs of individual talents have been addressed, and the welfare needs of individuals have been ensured through institutionalized regulations. Thus, rural talents are encouraged to take root in the countryside and build the countryside wholeheartedly. Secondly, the protection of intellectual property rights should be clearly defined, and the transformation of technological knowledge should be accelerated. In the process of rural talent innovation practice, the issue of intellectual property is involved. For developing countries, the continuous promotion of reasonable intellectual property protection standards is related to the sustainability of technological progress. The policy explorations of China and Brazil are actively promoting the establishment of state-level guiding funds for the transformation of scientific and technological achievements, making use of the leverage of financial funds to promote the formation of diversified, multi-level and multi-channel financing mechanisms, and increasing financial support for rural talent-related enterprises. It is not only tilted in the policy, but also has a more far-reaching effect on the soundness of the future agricultural financial market. Third, most developing countries are agricultural societies, or agriculture occupies a large position in their own industrial structure. Therefore, due to the low level of agricultural machinery and automation, the work mode is mainly large-scale labor, so it is also a normal means to attract talents to return to their hometown to start a business. Although the effect is different, many countries have also attracted entrepreneurs, experts, scholars, doctors, teachers and other skilled talents in this way to serve rural revitalization by investing in rural areas, running medical schools and providing consulting services.

II. Policies and measures for the development of rural talents

According to the classification of developed countries, BRICS countries and less developed countries, the policies and measures that have achieved remarkable results in the introduction and development of rural talents in each region are selected, and in- depth case studies are conducted.

1. Policies and measures of developed countries and regions

(1) Japan: "One Village One Product" movement

After World War II, Japan concentrated on developing cities, and a large number of rural people moved into cities. According to the data of the World Bank, Japan's urbanization rate reached 63.3% in 1960 and increased to 75.9% in 1975. At the same time, the gap between urban and rural areas in Japan has gradually widened, and rural areas are facing the problem of capital and population outflow. From 1955 to 1975, the rural labor force dropped from 16.29 million to 7.34 million, and the proportion of agricultural labor force dropped from 41% to 19%. This led to a sharp decline in agricultural productivity and a widening gap between urban and rural areas. Problems such as wastage of cultivated land and lagging industries caused by population loss hindered the economic development of rural areas, and cities and villages were unable to improve local environmental facilities, which led to a vicious circle of further outflow of rural population, and the "One Village One Product" movement came into being.

In 1979, Morihiko Hiramatsu, former governor of Oita Prefecture, Japan, initiated the " One Village One Product " movement. In order to promote the coordinated development of agriculture and industry, the "One Village One Product" movement, under the slogan of "agriculture and industry go hand in hand", actively introduced new and high technologies, made full use of local resources and traditional technologies, which greatly promoted the economic development of Oita Prefecture. In the face of difficulties, the new governor Mr. Hiramatsu launched the "One Village One Product" movement, with the aim of developing leading products and leading industries with local characteristics based on the advantages of local resources, improving farmers' income and revitalizing the rural economy. Oita Prefecture in Japan, after advocating and promoting the "One Village One Product" movement, farmers' income continued to grow, farmers' income has reached 27,000 US dollars in 1994, and the rural outlook has been continuously improved, becoming a successful model of rural development, not only in Japan, but also in the world has attracted wide attention, many national leaders and government delegations to Oita Prefecture to study. For example, Ehime Prefecture has successfully developed a place-representative brand IP for "Ehime Citrus" through the "One Village One Product" initiative. Ehime leads Japan in both citrus yield and variety, producing over 100,000 tons annually (Figure 2.1). The "One Village One Product" movement has been promoted in some countries in Asia, Africa and Latin America, and has become an important way for rural revitalization in many countries, especially in less developed countries.

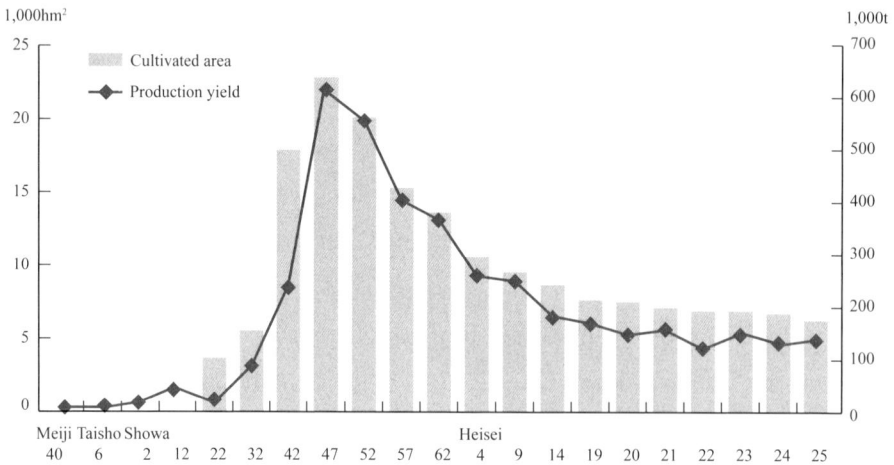

Figure 2.1   Citrus yield changes in Ehime Prefecture, Japan [8]

Data source: Japanese Ehime county. https://www.pref.ehime.jp.

The implementation of the "One Village One Product" movement in Japan mainly includes three aspects: "based on local and global vision", "independence, creativity" and "talent cultivation", among which the cultivation of local elites with an international vision and a challenging spirit is the key to the success of the movement.

Training activities are held to cultivate reserve talents. In view of the

---

8   Note: 1972 is the 47th year of Showa.

severe shortage of outstanding talents in rural areas, Oita Prefecture has made the cultivation of talents the ultimate goal of the "One Village One Product" movement, and has trained a group of regional leaders with global strategic vision and challenging spirit in agriculture, industry and service industries. In order to cultivate talents, Oita Prefecture relies on the government's Agricultural Improvement and popularization agency and the agricultural Association at all levels to hold personnel training workshops covering various fields and types, and pays attention to the combination of theoretical training and practical operation. The semester is set as two years, the first year is theoretical teaching and the second year is practical teaching. The theoretical teaching is mainly carried out in the way of evening school, and the learning content is the theory and technology of the revitalization of the relevant region. The real story of the "one village and one product" in the region is mainly taught; the practical teaching is mainly based on students solving local practical problems on their own[9]. These workshops started in 1983, and by 2005 had trained more than 2,000 outstanding talents, who were active in various regions of the county as leaders of the "One Village One Product" movement.

At the same time, special attention has been paid to the role of women in regional economic development. Women's groups or clubs have been set up, workshops have been held, and the voices of consumers can be directly heard to continuously improve production and management. This kind of entrepreneurial activity is very popular in Japan, and the number of participants is increasing. In Oita Prefecture alone, 278 business groups are organized by women themselves, ranking third in Japan.

A promotion fund has been set up to encourage talent cultivation. In order to develop the "One Village One Product" movement, Oita Prefecture established the "One Village One Product" Promotion Fund in Oita Prefecture with corporate donations in 1981, and formed an 11-member consultative council centered on talent cultivation. The Promotion Fund is mainly used to

9 GengXuan Li, Hui Liu, Danyu Shi, et al. The enlightenment and experience of "One Village One Product" in Japan [J]. Rural Economy and Science-Technology, 2016, 27 (11): 172-174.

commend persons and organizations that have made outstanding contributions and to dispatch personnel for further study. According to the regulations of the Promotion Fund, the Council selects people who are expected to play a key role in the "One Village One Product" movement, sends them to advanced areas in Japan or abroad for a month or more to learn production technology, processing, distribution and other experience, and reports the results after the completion of the training. In this way, a large number of outstanding talents are cultivated who want to revitalize their hometown with their own hands[10].

Clarify the government's position and guide policies in a scientific way. In order to promote the "One Village One Product" movement, the Oita County government has given great support in the production, development and expansion of sales channels of featured products. Multiple technical guidance institutions, including the Agricultural Technology Center, Livestock Experiment Station, Agricultural and Fisheries Products Comprehensive Guidance Center, Mushroom Research Guidance Center, Marine Fisheries Research Center, and the Industrial Science and Technology Center, aim to provide villagers with relevant product and technology guidance. The Oita County government conducts product exhibitions throughout the country, and establishes specialty stores and experience centers at important domestical and foreign cities to help villagers expand their markets and increase sales. What is rarer is that even the prefectural governor personally in the corresponding market to promote its special products, Oita Prefecture to the degree of attention to the activity. Oita Prefectural government's comprehensive and thoughtful service and guarantee provide a strong backing for the smooth development of its "One Village One Product".

Financial subsidies support the development of agricultural talents. Government needs to implement the policy of supporting successors to train agricultural successors. For young people under the age of 45, with an annual

---

10 Wei Chang, Wei Wang, Qingyun Que. The enlightenment of Japan's "One Village One Product" movement on rural revitalization in China–Based on the perspective of government function transformation [J]. Reformation & Strategy, 2020, 36 (5): 111-118. DOI:10.16331/j.cnki.issn1002-736x.2020.05.012.

income of less than 2.5 million yen, who are willing to operate agriculture independently, 1.5 million yen will be given a special support for the "Youth Farming Payment Fund". Set up a special fund for "Training New Farmers" to encourage young professional farmers to take the form of apprenticeship in middle school to study in large farming households or agricultural enterprises, and pay 150,000 yen a month as a living allowance to improve the ability of young professional farmers. For large farming households or agricultural enterprises that receive training for young professional farmers, the government will grant a one- time subsidy of 500,000 yen. For those who cannot study off the job, the National Rural Youth Education Promotion Association and other organizations will set up night schools to teach agricultural skills through distance education platforms[11].

The talent development needs facing Japan mainly include the shortage of young talents in the background of aging and the loss of rural population resulting in the lack of rural vitality. The lessons of Japan's "One Village One Product" movement are as follows:

Increase the enthusiasm of farmers to participate in the movement and attach importance to the training of outstanding personnel. From the successful experience of Japan's "One Village One Product" movement, its agricultural and economic development largely depends on the role of high-quality talents, therefore, to change farmers' thinking, enhance farmers' planting, processing and marketing skills and improve the overall quality of farmers for "One Village One Product" is of great significance. In the future development process, the government must control the input structure of agricultural support, appropriately increase the investment in the cultivation of farmers' professional skills, increase the opportunities for farmers to receive education, so that farmers' quality and professional skills have been comprehensively improved.

11　Xianming Lu, Qingquan Liu, Zhenghua Deng. Experience of talents training for rural revitalization in Korea and Japan and its enlightenment to China [J]. Journal of Hunan Administration Institute, 2021 (2): 106-114. DOI:10.16480/j.cnki.cn43-1326/c.2021.02.013.

The government guides and coordinates all social parties to support rural personnel training. The government has organized forces from all walks of life to form a complementary education system consisting of the government, schools and the private sector. Free training activities for farmers have been carried out at different levels, with a focus and as planned. Through agricultural colleges and universities such as senior high schools, agricultural science and technology training centers at all levels, agricultural technology extension service systems and improvement and popularization systems at all levels, agricultural association training centers at all levels, enterprises and various types of agricultural training service institutions to meet the needs of different farmers. The training courses are rich and practical, such as Marine aquaculture, commerce, agricultural production, computer training courses, farmers can according to their actual needs, free of charge to attend the course training.

The agricultural association organizes farmers to carry out production construction and technical exchanges. The Japan Agricultural Association covers the entire countryside and its members include almost all farmers. The JSA members include full members who are directly engaged in agricultural production and have the right to vote on the management policy of the JSA, and associate members who are not directly engaged in agricultural production but enjoy the services of the JSA but have no right to vote on the management policy of the JSA through investment. The grass- roots farmers' associations, the county economic federation and the central federation are the three level organizations that organically connect farmers with decentralized production and the large market that combines urban and rural areas, thus improving the degree of farmers' organization. In addition to the farmers' associations, there are also about 280,000 autonomous associations and town associations of different sizes organized voluntarily by villagers in cities and towns[12].

12　Xianming Lu, Qingquan Liu, Zhenghua Deng. Experience of talents training for rural revitalization in Korea and Japan and its enlightenment to China [J]. Journal of Hunan Administration Institute, 2021 (2): 106-114. DOI:10.16480/j.cnki.cn43-1326/c.2021.02.013.

Nearly 20,000 peasant instructors of the Nonghyup serve as the guidance for agricultural operation. After graduating from specialized agricultural schools and obtaining state-recognized qualifications, the instructors are specially hired by the NCAA. Their work scope includes farmland infrastructure construction, agricultural production, appropriate scale, fund management, technical exchange and training for each NCAA member, as well as long-term planning of regional agriculture.

(2) The Republic of Korea: Saemaeul Movement

In the 1960s, the Republic of Korean government implemented the export-oriented industrial development policy, which gave priority to the development of heavy industry. While the industrialization accelerated the urbanization process, it also caused the huge gap between the rich and the poor in urban and rural areas. In the 1970s, in order to solve the imbalance between urban and rural development caused by industrialization, the Korean government launched a national movement of "Diligence, self-help and cooperation" in 34,000 villages across the country, committed to rural modernization and farmers' poverty alleviation and income increase. Through the "government-led, villager participation" model, the government investigated and collected the problems that needed to be solved in more than 30,000 villages. Farmers' problems were solved by themselves, villagers' cooperation problems were solved by villagers' cooperation, and government programs were funded by the government and chosen by villagers[13]. The government divides the types of villages by building an index system with 10 items in five dimensions, including village roads, living environment, farmland facilities, community life and residents' income, including three categories of basic villages, self-help villages and self-supporting villages[14]. It determines development projects for different types of villages according to the type of policies, and innovates a

---

13   Qing Li.The characteristic and enlightenment of "new village" construction in eastern Asia of Korea and Japan [J]. Shanghai Urban Planning Review, 2012 (1): 89-94.

14   Jun Kim, Doyeon Kim, Min Zhao. Change of the content and organization of Korean Saemaeul Undong from the 1970s-2000s [J]. Urban Planning International, 2016, 31 (6): 15-19.

differentiated incentive mechanism of rewarding hard work and punishing lazy people to stimulate the enthusiasm of villagers.

1971-1973: Basic construction stage. The main goal was to improve the living environment and quality of life of farmers, guided by the government, the government provided cement, steel and other materials free of charge, and supported farmers to independently carry out infrastructure construction, including improving roofs, building roads, building bridges and erecting power facilities. In the process of policy implementation, the government will evaluate the efficiency of the utilization of resources in the early stage and grade the villages. For the villages with good performance, the government will increase its support to stimulate the enthusiasm of farmers to a greater extent.

1974-1976: Comprehensive development stage. The main goal was to increase farmers' income and promote economic development. The government has taken various measures to raise farmers' income, including optimizing the agricultural structure, promoting high-yield rice varieties, granting financial subsidies, increasing investment in rural areas, and providing loans and preferential policies to better- developed rural areas. At this stage, the implementation of Saemaeul Movement was directly managed by the Ministry of Internal Affairs of the Central Committee of Saemaeul Movement, and the Central Committee of Saemaeul Movement was set up to coordinate the relationship between various departments of the central Committee and organize cadres to go to the rural areas to guide the specific implementation of Saemaeul Movement. In addition, the Saemaeul Movement Research and Training Center was established to further train talents for the movement.

1977-1980: Enrichment and improvement stage. The main goal was to narrow the gap between urban and rural areas and promote the development of rural culture, which gradually shifted from government-led implementation to voluntary implementation by the people. At this stage, Saemaeul Movement mainly encouraged the development of animal husbandry, agricultural product processing industry and characteristic industries, and further narrowed the urban-rural income gap. At the same time, the government provided rural areas with building materials, built cultural houses and various cultural venues, and invited experts and scholars to conduct training and education in rural areas, so as to improve the quality of farmers and cultivate their pioneering spirit. At this stage, Saemaeul Movement gradually changed from government-led to spontaneous movement among the people.

1981-1989: The stage of the national spontaneous movement. The main feature of this stage was the establishment of private sector organizations to develop the national Saemaeul Movement, thus realizing the transition from government-led to civilian-led. At this time, the Republic of Korea clearly distinguished the responsibilities of the government and the private sector: the main function of the government was to make the overall plan to adjust the agricultural structure, while providing support in terms of resources; the private sector took the lead in the promotion, training and information work of Saemaeul Movement. At this time, farmers were encouraged to develop diversified business operations, so that the living standards of rural residents gradually approached the urban level.

1990-present: Self-development stage. After the first several stages of construction, the Saemaeul Movement became completely led by the private sector. With the rapid development of the Korean economy, the Saemaeul Movement became increasingly effective. In this stage, the government mainly devoted itself to the construction of rural civilization, including the education of national consciousness, the construction of democracy and the rule of law, and the strengthening of the education of farmers' collective consciousness. The functions of the previously established institutions gradually weakened, and many rural economic research organizations and rural education institutions emerged. These non-governmental organizations played an important role in inheriting the spirit of Saemaeul Movement and promoting agricultural development.

The Saemaeul Movement in the Republic of Korea was mainly carried out from the following aspects:

The construction of village hall. Saemaeul Movement usually takes place during the winter farming season, but it is difficult to find a place for villagers to gather and discuss activities at that time. Therefore, starting from the second year of the Saemaeul Movement, villagers' halls were built in various villages, which could be used to hold not only various meetings, but also various agricultural technology training courses and exchange meetings. The village hall collected all kinds of statistical data, including agricultural production statistics and agricultural income statistics, and often showed villagers their own village development plans and blueprints[15].

Utilize the organizing role of the government to its full extent. In 1970, the Republic of Korea's urbanization rate was about 50%, and small farmers were poorly organized and lacked organizational forms to express their own interests. They were affiliated to the government's National Agricultural Association. Since the implementation of Saemaeul Movement, governments at all levels have set up Saemaeul Movement promotion committees from top to bottom to organize and mobilize farmers. The first is to strengthen the concept of cooperation within the government. The Ministry of Internal Affairs will take the lead in coordinating the departments of economic construction, electronics, transportation, information, water conservancy, science, education, culture and health, and other departments, and governments at all levels will work closely together to break down divisions and form a cross-departmental management model. Second, the service concept of local officials should be improved. Each community should appoint a civil servant as the leader of Saemaeul Movement, increase the training of Saemaeul Movement leaders, and reform the political concept of local officials. While supervising the use of resources and mediating village conflicts, local officials should also act as evaluators to determine the type of village support, so as to better judge the future development direction of the village. On the other hand, village development has a direct impact on the

---

15　Shaojiu Chen, Bo Zhou, Weidong Tang, et al. The practice of the Saemaeul Movement in the Republic of Korea and its enlightenment for the construction of new countryside in China [J]. Issues in Agricultural Economy, 2006 (2): 72-77.

promotion of local officials[16].

The mechanism for training elite personnel will be strengthened. In order to publicize and implement the concept of Saemaeul Movement, the government set up the Central Research and Training Institute to conduct large-scale training of new village leaders through successful cases and group discussions, so as to solve village problems and stimulate new ideas for development through competition. In the process of new village education, the government and the people eat, live and work together, which strengthens the sense of responsibility of officials and promotes the improvement of rural governance ability.

The challenges of talent development in the Republic of Korea lie in: improving the endogenous power of village construction; the initiative of farmers to build new villages by themselves needs to be improved; improve the education level of farmers and improve the overall quality of villagers; the imbalance between urban and rural development has brought serious social problems, such as the hollowing out of rural areas and aging, which need to be solved urgently.

In the early stage of Saemaeul Movement, the Republic of Korean government mainly adopted the mode of providing construction materials such as steel bars and cement, and allowing villagers to plan and construct. Under this model, some villages created new sources of income through joint efforts without government financial support. During this period, most of the innovative cases that were identified as self- supporting villages were those villages that did not passively wait for the government's help. When the government extended the olive branch of support, farmers fully carried forward the spirit of self-help and seized the opportunity to actively change their poor and backward fate.

In the process of Saemaeul Movement in the Republic of Korea, rural

---

16   Yiqiang Liu. Rethinking the "Saemaeul Movement": A case study of the Republic of Korea crossing the critical stage of rural modernization [J]. Nanjing Journal of Social Sciences, 2017 (2): 83-90. DOI:10.15937/j.cnki.issn1001-8263.2017.02.011.

infrastructure, housing and ecological environment were improved, and farmers' income and living standards were greatly improved. As shown in Figure 2.2, during 1974-1978, the average annual income of rural households exceeded that of urban working households. In 1979, the average annual income of rural households reached 2.23 million won, an increase of more than 10 times compared with 220,000 won in 1969. Farmers saw room for development in the countryside, and some of the emigrants returned to the countryside. From 1975 to 1977, there was a great change in the proportion of rural and urban population in the Republic of Korea. The proportion of rural population rose from 40.8% to 48.8%[17]. It can be said that the development of the Republic of Korea's Saemaeul Movement slowed down the pace of rural population migration to cities in a short period of time, and retained a certain labor force for the social and economic development of rural areas at that time.

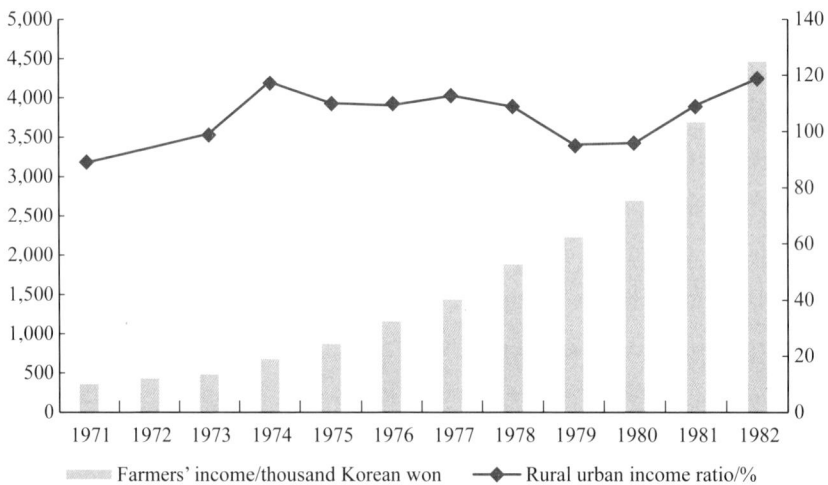

Figure 2.2   Saemaeul Movement and farm income in the Republic of Korea[18]

Data source: Daoxuan Han, Yang Tian. The experience and revelation from the Saemaeul Movement in the Republic of Korea [J]. Journal of Nanjing Agricultural University (Social Sciences Edition), 2019, 19 (4): 20-27, 156. DOI:10.19714/j.cnki.1671-7465.2019.0051.

17   Data source: National Statistical Network of Korea, http://kosis.kr/.

18   Note: Rural-urban income ratio = (annual income of rural households/annual income of urban households) *100%.

The experience and enlightenment of the Saemaeul Movement in the Republic of Korea are as follows:

Cultivate the spirit of modern farmers. Saemaeul Movement, an enlightenment movement based on the concept of "diligence, self-help and cooperation", inspired villagers to "work hard for a better life" to meet the requirements of the development of an industrialized society. Saemaeul Movement is a democratic movement. Women were given equal status with men, and each village elected a new village leader, one male and one female, independent of the village chief, to provide voluntary services. The new village leaders need to have a sense of market economy, pay attention to agricultural efficiency and dare to innovate, and play a key role in the process of rural innovation and development. Although new village leaders enjoy preferential treatment in agricultural loans and special employment for civil servants, they are unpaid volunteers who rely on dedication and exemplary leadership to create a national movement that is practiced by all. Villagers present their ideas for the construction of new villages at the village assembly and neighborhood meetings, and discuss the resolutions to form the village, which are implemented by the village development committee composed of the village head and the village elite, forming a democratic decision-making and implementation mechanism at the grassroots level.

At the same time, Saemaeul Movement is also a competition and cooperation movement. In the stage of village infrastructure construction from 1970 to 1973, the government first funded some materials such as cement and steel for public construction, and the subsequent funding was based on the implementation of each village in the previous year. Differentiated funding from equal quantification to basic village, self-help village and self-supporting village encouraged all villages to gradually set their own development goals, formed a competition mechanism among villages and stimulated the spirit of cooperation among villagers.

Attach importance to the cultivation of talents. The government and social organizations, including county, myeon[19] and local agricultural cooperatives, will identify new village leaders and nurture them through a new village training center under the leadership of Cheong Wa Dae[20]. The training focuses on practical results, with special emphasis on experience sharing and case exchange, including new village business courses, successful case education, field visits, etc., to cultivate entrepreneurial spirit such as initiative, self-help and modernization, so that they can master comprehensive skills in running village business. Excellent new village leaders can introduce successful cases at the monthly economic work conference of Cheong Wa Dae, stimulate their determination to actively participate in the new village business, and actively play an exemplary role. In 1973, the Saemaul Medal became a separate award in the government award system. Since 1975, the certificate of Saemaul Leaders has been issued in the name of the Minister of Interior. The National Conference of Saemaul Leaders has been held once a year to enhance the sense of honor, providing high social prestige and social recognition for Saemaul leaders. In the 1980s, the Republic of Korea established a national leadership organization "Saemaul Movement Headquarters" and set up local leadership organizations in municipalities, provinces, counties and cities to provide organizational support for the Saemaul Movement[21].

The Saemaul Movement implemented a system of volunteer instructors, with 3 million instructors mainly coming from college students. Through the voluntary application of students and the recommendation of the subject director, they apply for service projects according to their abilities and interests. The government calls on instructors to lead college students to serve as volunteer instructors in communities during winter and summer

---

19　One of the administrative divisions in the Republic of Korea.

20　Xianming Lu, Qingquan Liu, Zhenghua Deng. The experience of the construction of rural revitalizing talent team in Korea and Japan and its enlightenment to China [J]. Journal of Hunan Administration Institute, 2021 (2): 106-114. DOI:10.16480/j.cnki.cn43-1326/c.2021.02.013.

21　Meiying Xu. The international experience of rural revitalization and the Chinese road [J]. Agricultural Economy, 2020 (12): 30-32.

vacations. Many college students go to remote rural areas under the guidance of instructors and make contributions to the development of rural areas with what they have learned.

(3) Germany: Urban-Rural Equivalence

After the Second World War, Germany rebuilt its cities on a large scale, and the cities once again became industrial and economic centers. Rural population moved to cities, while cities moved factories to rural areas, constantly squeezing rural land, resulting in a widening development gap between cities and rural areas and a continuous reduction in the total agricultural area (Figure 2.3). In order to realize the balanced development of rural and urban areas, the Seidel Foundation of Germany first put forward the concept of urban-rural equivalence in 1950. In 1960, the *Promulgation of the Federal Construction Law* did not solve the contradiction between the state and the region, and the spatial planning became more urgent. In 1963, *Raumordnung Deutschland* was submitted to the upper house of the Government for consideration and was adopted in 1965. On this basis, the Bavarian combining target for the federal state planning and regional planning,

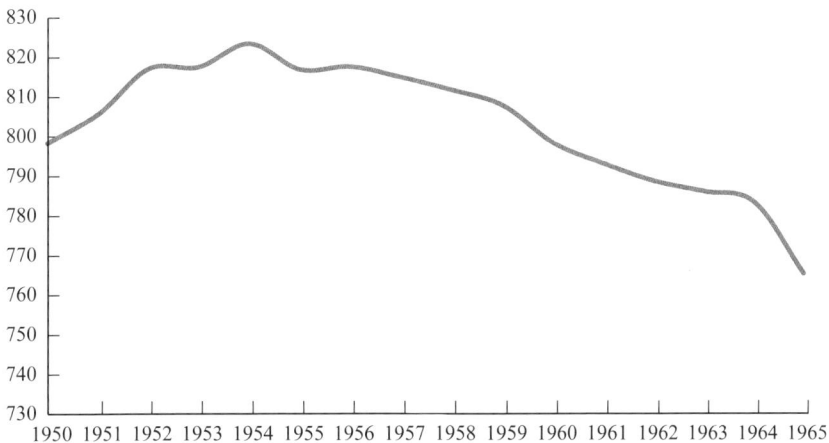

Figure 2.3   Changes in the total agricultural area of Germany from
1950 to 1965 (unit: ten thousand hectares)
Data source: German Statistical Office (https://www.destatis.de).

formulated the *Landesentwicklungsprogramm Bayern*, from the aspect of law for the equivalence between urban and rural areas will turn into the core values of regional planning and strategic objectives[22].

The goal calls for urban and rural residents to have the same living, working and transportation conditions, maintain and build equal public services, and protect natural resources such as water, air and land. The concept of coordinated development between urban and rural areas should be implemented by unifying the same quality of life and conditions for public facilities, employment and housing through spatial development planning. The equal development of urban and rural areas in Bavaria does not mean the disappearance of differences between urban and rural areas, industrial structure, economic production mode, culture, spatial landscape, etc. Nor does it mean the evolution of social regions from heterogeneous space to an absolute homogeneous space, But means gradually narrowing the gap in socio-economic development between urban and rural areas and improving the overall quality of life for rural residents, so as to promote more coordinated urban and rural development[23]. Make living in rural areas as comfortable and convenient as in cities, that is, "not of the same kind but equivalent".

Germany's urban-rural equivalence takes "the principle of sustainable development, the principle of adapting to local conditions, the principle of systematization and the principle of governance" as the basic principles, and "promoting social equity, developing urban and rural economy, and protecting natural resources" as the three major work objectives, aiming to increase the leisure, life, culture and ecological functions of rural areas, and ensure the attractiveness of rural areas as living areas and economic zones. As can be seen

---

22 Qijie Gao, Shu Zhang.The development concept of urban-rural equivalence in Germany with implication for China [J]. Ancient and Modern Agriculture, 2021 (4): 15-24.

23 Yushu Bi, Tianlai Gou, Qianzhi Zhang, Xinping Hu. The study on coordinated development between urban and rural areas of Germany and its implications for China: The case of the State of Bavaria [J]. Ecological Economy, 2012 (5): 99-102, 106.

from Figure 2.4, after 1965, the total amount of cereals in Germany increased significantly.

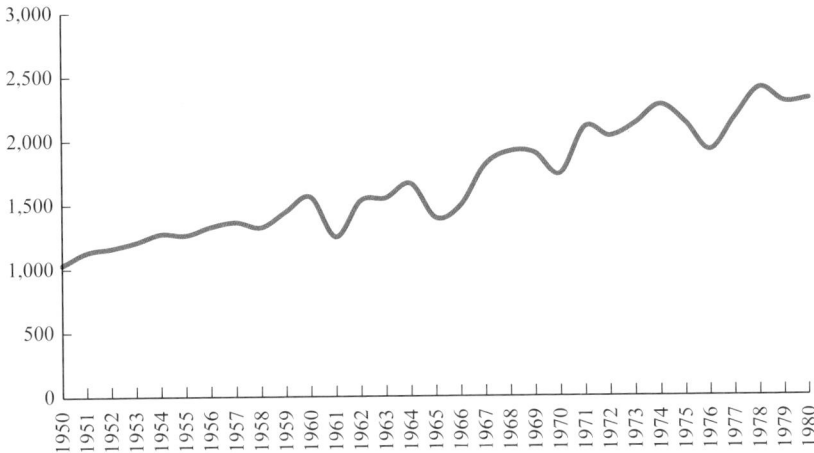

Figure 2.4　Changes in total cereals in Germany from 1950 to 1980 (unit: 10,000 tons)
Data source: German Statistical Bureau (https://www.destatis.de).

Improved rural infrastructure. "Equalization of urban and rural areas" requires that rural and urban residents enjoy public infrastructure services equally. In the 1970s, Germany proposed to rebuild the image of rural areas, repair and improve rural buildings. In the 1990s, it connected rural communities with the entire rural renovation and development, and intensified the construction of public infrastructure such as traffic roads, water supply systems, garbage disposal and rainwater drainage to ensure the daily needs of rural residents. With the development of diversified functions in rural areas, the needs of farmers have become increasingly abundant, and recreational, cultural and sports facilities have been improved.

Favorable rural education and training. The Bavaria government has set up three rural development training schools, and conducted trainings and seminars for township leaders and village representatives who apply for village renewal projects to enhance public awareness and ability to participate in them, so that villagers can understand the goals, contents and significance of village transformation, and enhance their sense of identity and responsibility for hometown development planning[24]. Promote the "dual system" teaching[25], combining the traditional apprenticeship training with vocational education. Before the training, farmers sign a labor contract for practical production with the relevant farms that have training qualifications, and engage in agricultural labor under the guidance of farm masters. In this mode, students can combine theory with practice and learn real agricultural skills in practice[26].

Effective financial fund support. First of all, the content of German financial support policies is rich and varied. The German federal government formulates different fiscal preferential policies according to different goals. For example, in terms of land transfer, it actively encourages farmers to transfer their land, giving incentives and compensation; in terms of ensuring the safety of employees working in agricultural enterprises, 30% of the government's social insurance funds are used for agricultural accident insurance. For rural households that need to expand their production and operation scale, the investment policy of providing low-interest loans is implemented.

Second, the federal government's financial support policy covers almost all rural residents, and is divided into multiple levels according to the identity or needs of farmers. For example, farmers in need of investment are provided with discount interest and preferential policies. Relevant enterprises can get financial incentives through direct application or tax relief; government needs to provide relevant social security for all residents to ensure the basic livelihood of farmers.

Rational industrial restructuring. Germany integrates and improves land through land consolidation, optimizes agricultural production infrastructure, cultivates new types of agricultural operators, and continuously expands the scale of farms. Through subsidies, credit and other preferential policies,

---

24　Yushu Bi, Tianlai Gou, Qianzhi Zhang, Xinping Hu. The study on coordinated development between urban and rural areas of Germany and its implications for China: The case of the State of Bavaria [J]. Ecological Economy, 2012 (5): 99-102, 106.

25　Yuer Wu. Urban Rural Equivalence in Germany [N]. Economic Daily (Rural Edition), 2006-12-22.

26　Huijing Li. Research on the Cultivation of Professional Farmers in the Development of Modern Agriculture [D]. Harbin: Northeast Forestry University, 2015.

the government encourages the flow of agricultural land and helps farmers find employment. At the same time, the structure of farmers' planting and breeding has changed, agricultural production activities have become more diversified, farmers' income has increased, and the risk of unilateral agricultural management has been reduced. In addition, due to the large-scale land management and the adjustment of agricultural production structure, the labor force required for agricultural production has decreased, and farmers have been promoted to transition from agricultural employment to non-agricultural employment. Some factories have moved from cities to rural areas, creating more jobs in rural areas and easing the employment pressure[27].

Germany's talent development is faced with the following challenges: after World War II, a large number of rural population flooded into the city, leading to the prominent problem of rural hollowing; the number of farmers engaged in agricultural labor decreased significantly after World War II; large enterprises in remote rural areas have not been able to enter the country, development opportunities are relatively lacking, young people cannot stay, and the phenomenon of aging of agricultural workers is serious[28]. The experience and enlightenment of Germany's urban-rural equivalence are as follows:

The development and expansion of rural economy is the basis of realizing urban-rural equivalence. Choosing projects suitable for local survival and development, supporting the development of local enterprises, and strengthening the rural economy are the basis for realizing urban-rural equalization. Only when the rural economy develops and grows, and farmers' income increases, can the villages truly retain farmers. Meanwhile, villages can have more sufficient funds for improving education, environment, transportation and other public utilities, so as to ensure that farmers' public service level, social security level, convenience of life and city people are roughly equal, and

27   Qijie Gao, Shu Zhang.The development concept of urban-rural equivalence in Germany with implication for China [J]. Ancient and Modern Agriculture, 2021 (4): 15-24.

28   Rongzhi Liu. The practice and enlightenment of rural development in Germany:Report on the training of standard system of rural construction planning in Germany [J]. Rural Work Communication, 2019 (6): 61-64.

really achieve "urban and rural equivalence".

Sufficient capital investment is the guarantee of realizing urban and rural equivalence. The adjustment of industrial structure, the improvement of rural infrastructure, the development of rural education, the improvement of rural environment, and the interaction between urban and rural areas all require a large amount of capital investment, and the improvement of farmers' social security system and the improvement of farmers' welfare level need a large amount of financial support. The introduction of funds requires element matching, and the biggest matching element in rural areas is land. The efficiency of non-agricultural land in land asset allocation should be improved.

(4) Canada: Rural Cooperative Partnership Program

Since 1996, there has been an increasing emphasis on the problem of lagging rural development in Canada. In the 1996 Government Work Report, the Government of Canada announced its commitment to revitalizing the rural economy and addressing the problems faced in a manner that meets the needs of rural areas. According to the study *"Considering Rural Areas"* provided by the Natural Resources Committee of the Canadian Parliament in 1997, the main factors restricting the development of rural Canada include the lack of basic education and skills, as well as insufficient funding for infrastructure and investment. Compared with urban areas, rural areas have limited access to education and training, infrastructure, funding, basic government services and decision-making. The report summarized the needs faced by rural development in Canada into seven aspects: better access to education and more effective training; improved infrastructure; strengthening resource development; developing more value-added industries; effectively promoting tourism; developing small enterprises in rural areas; and establishing a rational structure to handle rural development. In response to these basic problems faced by rural communities, 37 proposals were put forward, including adopting comprehensive rural policies, providing more effective government services, providing education and training opportunities, improving infrastructure, accessing the information superhighway, improving the energy mix, improving the investment climate, fostering research and development, and promoting sustainable development[29].

In 1998, the Canadian government introduced the Canadian Rural Partnership Program, which identified specific measures to promote rural development, help farmers access government programs and services, financial resources and health care, strengthen infrastructure construction, and increase employment and education opportunities for rural youth. In 1999, the Canadian government issued a Federal Framework for Action for Rural Canada, which identified 11 priority areas for the government to promote rural development: access to government programs and services; access to financial resources; opportunities for rural youth; human resource leadership development and community capacity building; rural infrastructure; rural communications and the use of the information superhighway; economic diversification; access to health care; access to education; community development partnerships; and promoting rural development[30]. As shown in Figure 2.5, there was a notable increase in gross cash receipts for Canadian farms after the implementation of the Rural Cooperative Partnership Program.

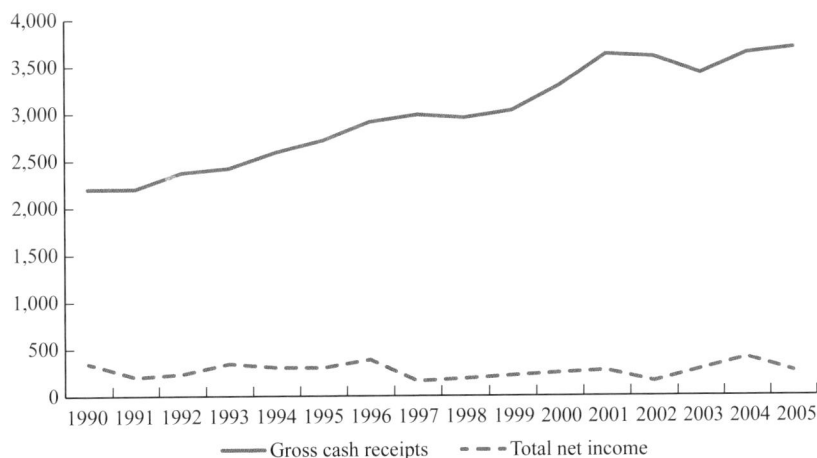

Figure 2.5   Changes in farm income in Canada, 1990-2005 (US $10,000)

Data source: Canada Statistics Bureau (https://www150.statcan.gc.ca) .

29, 30   Hua Wei, Haitao Li. Canada's measures to promote the development of underdeveloped rural areas [J]. Global Science and Technology Economy Outlook, 2001 (8): 21-23.

Provide development opportunities for rural youth and cultivate rural human resources. Human Resources Canada will help employers hire rural and remote youth as part of its youth employment program. These employers include business enterprises, non-profit organizations, public health and educational institutions, orchestras and ethnic councils, and municipal governments. In the areas of human resources, leadership development and community capacity building, the federal government is promoting rural economic and industrial development through community training programs to develop professionals. In addition, the National Secretariat for Access to Education of Canada has funded distance learning programs in 28 Northern Saskatoon communities, as well as literacy worker training programs in remote Northern communities.

Establishment of an interdepartmental Agriculture task force. Led by the Department of Agriculture, 32 federal agencies form an interagency working group to coordinate their work on rural development issues. It meets regularly to exchange information and ensure that federal agencies work together in the Canadian Rural Partnership Program. Provincial and municipal governments have also established "Rural Working Groups", composed of government rural affairs officials, to consult with other levels of government, agencies and organizations on major rural issues. At the same time, Canada has established a Coordinating Minister of Rural Affairs, who serves as the Minister of Agriculture, and a Rural Secretariat within the Department of Agriculture, which is responsible for coordinating and promoting the establishment and interaction of rural collaborative partnerships and promoting dialogue and communication between rural residents and the Federal Government[31].

It directly funds rural development projects and encourages individuals or organizations to start businesses in rural development. The Rural Secretariat launches and funds rural development projects on different themes each

---

31 Qing Zhao, Shilong Yang. The inspiration of foreign experience to China's new rural construction: The Canadian government becomes the partner of farmers' development [J]. Beijing Agriculture, 2006 (7): 44.

year based on the results of the "Rural Dialogue"[32]. For example, the Pilot Entrepreneurship Project, which was carried out from 1998 to 2002, focuses on the themes of financing rural residents and increasing employment opportunities for rural youth. With an investment of nearly C $12 million, it funded 307 projects across the country in four tranches.

An information service system for rural residents has been established and improved. Community information access sites have been established in rural areas to facilitate local residents' access to e-government websites and other business and service information networks of governments at all levels. In its 2000 budget presentation, the Government announced $160 million over two years to plan and launch programs in order to provide Canadians with online government services and to promote the use of electronic commerce. Through these online resources, rural residents can access general advisory services, including rural child health care, rural tourism, programs and services for rural youth, and starting a business in rural areas. On the other hand, they can also seek relevant information on specific issues or consult experts directly.

The challenges faced by Canada in talent development mainly include the following aspects: urbanization has led to a serious outflow of rural population; The proportion of young people in rural areas is low, the proportion of elderly population is large and the population aging speed is fast; while the market promotes the non- agricultural employment of a large number of rural people, it also causes the low-skilled labor force to stay in the countryside. There is a lack of training for the next generation of leaders in rural areas, the number of leading cadres is decreasing, rural residents have few means to develop their leadership abilities, and leaders who continue to be active in rural areas are facing increasing pressure; the development of modern agriculture in

---

32 "Rural Dialogue": In order to keep abreast of rural public opinion and development, Canada attracts residents from rural areas, especially the remote northern regions, to engage in "open two-way communication" with federal government officials through different forms of activities such as regular national rural conferences, rural youth dialogues, online discussions, opinion surveys and rural working group reports. To discuss the problems, challenges and opportunities facing rural development and identify the priority issues that need to be addressed by the Government.

Canada has also resulted in the inability of most farmers to adapt to the rapidly changing agricultural technology and market. In particular, due to the lack of necessary resources and capital, individual farmers are in an obvious weak position in the process of coping with agricultural marketization[33]. In terms of education, rural areas have difficulty in providing high-quality education to young people, lack of funds, and lack of attention to practical technology and knowledge.

2. Policies and measures of BRICS countries

(1) Brazil: Cultivation of professional farmers

Brazil's agriculture accounts for a large proportion of GDP and is dominated by the government. Brazil has formulated different support policies for agriculture and farmers in different periods. The development of relevant policies can be mainly divided into three stages: the first stage (1965-1985) and the agricultural subsidy stage. In this stage, the total investment of agricultural policy was 219.1 billion US dollars, which was used for agricultural subsidies and other support for investment in the market. In the second stage (1985-1995), subsidies to agriculture were reduced and prices of agricultural products were mainly supported. The third stage (beginning in 1995), in view of the WTO and the signing of the General Agreement on Agriculture, increased the degree of opening of the agricultural market. In this phase, two price support policies were introduced, namely the Product Selling Program (PEP) and option contracts. At present, the relevant policies of Brazilian farmer cultivation include the cancellation of "import substitution" policy, producer support policy, ecological subsidy model, rural insurance system, credit policy and rural infrastructure construction, etc., whose purpose is to protect and encourage farmers' production enthusiasm[34].

33　Dan Mao, Bing Peng. Market, Government and farmers:Implications from Canadian rural communities [J]. Journal of Zhejiang University (Humanities and Social Sciences), 2010, 40 (6): 33-40.

34　Yibo Li, Jin Zhou, Banghong Zhao, et al. Experience in the cultivation of professional farmers in BRICS countries [J]. World Agriculture, 2015 (1): 173-176. DOI:10.13856/j.cn11-1097/s.2015.01.037.

Perfect professional farmer cultivation organization system. Brazil has set up a management committee composed of the Ministry of Agriculture, the Ministry of Education, the Ministry of Human Resources and the National Farmers Union, which is responsible for the cultivation of professional farmers throughout Brazil. In 1991, the Brazilian government established a private education institution managed by the National trade association, the National Service for Agriculture Apprenticeship (SENAR), which was under the supervision of the Management Committee. Responsible for organizing, managing and implementing rural professional training and social promotion programs for youth and adults in agricultural areas throughout the country[35]. Its main functions include: (a) Organize, administer and implement rural vocational training and rural social development for farmers throughout the country. (b) Support employers in organizing and formulating workplace training programs. (c) Establish and disseminate rural vocational training and rural social development technology. To coordinate, direct and manage plans and projects for rural vocational training and rural social development. To support the federal government's work on rural vocational training and rural social development[36].

In 1995, Brazil's "National Plan for the Further Training of Workers" was implemented, funded mainly by employee taxes, and taught by higher agricultural education institutions. For employees of agricultural enterprises, members of non-governmental organizations, members of trade unions and ordinary farmers. In 2001, the total expenditure of the program was 272 million US dollars, accounting for 8.2% of the total expenditure, of which 12.3% of the trainees were from the agricultural sector[37]. The program has trained a large

35   Dahlman Carl, Rodríguez Alberto, & Salmi Jamil. Knowledge and Innovation for Competitiveness in Brazil [M]. World Bank Publications, 2008, 1-268.

36   Yibo Li, Jin Zhou, Banghong Zhao, et al. Experience in the cultivation of professional farmers in BRICS countries [J]. World Agriculture, 2015 (1): 173-176. DOI:10.13856/j.cn11-1097/s.2015.01.037.

37   Z M Liu, B Wu. International comparison of farmer vocational education and training policies in the process of "Three modernizations" [J]. Chinese Agricultural Education, 2013 (1): 1-6.

number of young farmers, injecting fresh impetus into Brazilian agriculture, and alleviating the problem of population outflow from rural areas to a large extent.

The Brazilian Agricultural Research Corporation (Embrapa) was founded in 1973 to lay the technical foundation for a true tropical agriculture and livestock model. And is one of the largest agricultural research companies in the world. Embrapa has 40 research centres across the country; among them, there are 11 national specialized research centers, 14 national agricultural research centers, 15 ecological regional or agroforestry research centers, in addition, there are three special service centers[38]. Among the more than 2,000 researchers of the National Agricultural and Animal Husbandry Research Corporation, 68% have a doctoral degree and 30% have a master's degree.

The Agriculture and Animal Husbandry Extension Corporation (E mater) was established in 1974 under the Ministry of Agriculture and is responsible for the promotion of new technologies in Brazilian agriculture under the supervision of the Management Board. With 23,000 employees (13,000 of whom are technicians) and more than 2,500 offices throughout the country, E Mater's main mission is to transfer new agricultural technologies and achievements directly to agricultural producers[39].

It develops training measures in conjunction with economic and social development. In the formulation and implementation of vocational training policies for farmers, Brazil will take into account the coordination of development with economic and social development. At the beginning of its establishment, the National Agricultural Vocational Education Service Agency anchored the goal of improving the skill level of farmers and promoting social progress, and linked farmer training to the overall development of society.

Government-led, multi-party participation and close cooperation.

38, 39   Derong Yue, Shuming Wang, Zhongxiao Guo, et al. Brazil's agricultural production and scientific research and popularization system [J]. Journal of Agricultural Science and Technology Management, 2008 (5): 5-7. DOI:10.16849/j.carol carroll nki issn1001-8611.2008.05.002.

In addition to the specialized agencies that coordinate vocational training for farmers, there are also organizations such as the National Federation of Agriculture, the Association of Agribusiness and the Brazilian Agricultural Cooperatives, which work closely with agricultural producers to impart the latest technologies and scientific achievements to farmers. As a "bridge" between the government and farmers, these organizations not only monitor the country's agricultural development, but also collect farmers' opinions and suggestions on agricultural production and trade to provide reference for government departments to formulate agricultural policies. Not only that, the government, the private sector and the market mechanism are organically integrated. SENAR is funded by taxes from the sale of agricultural products, and the quality of its training has an important impact on agricultural development and even economic stability. Fully linking training to market mechanisms can not only improve the effectiveness of training, but also promote the stable development of agriculture[40].

Introducing reasonable policies to ensure and support agricultural development. As a big agricultural country, Brazil's developed agriculture and high- level professional farmers are closely related to Brazil's current agricultural support policies, which mainly include rural credit, marketing, risk management and key industries[41]. Among them, in the key industries, the Brazilian government in order to save agricultural costs, increase farmers' income, constantly strengthen the construction of logistics and transportation network, the establishment of the national storage unit certification system (SNCUA), plans to provide 5 billion reais per year to support the construction of the national storage plan. Moreover, since coffee is the main engine of Brazilian agriculture, in order to support the coffee industry, Brazil has specially set up the Coffee Economic Protection Fund and the government-invested

---

40   Yayu Zhang. Rural Revitalization of the Horizon, the New Professional Farmers Cultivate Research [D]. Fuzhou: Fujian Normal University, 2019. DOI: 10.27019/,dc nki.Gfjsu.2019.001365.

41   Yi Luo, Ying Xiao, Laping Wu. Analysis of current agricultural support policies and support levels in Brazil in recent years [J]. World Agriculture, 2018 (6): 77-85.

Economic Protection Fund (Funcafe) to carry out coffee research programs. In addition, the Coffee Research Alliance, established in 1997, includes some 50 rural education, research and extension institutions.

The main challenges facing talent development in Brazil include: the overall quality of farmers needs to be improved; agricultural production technology is backward, production efficiency is low, and the utilization rate of resources is low. The training experience of professional farmers in Brazil is mainly as follows:

The government should take the lead and establish a system of cultivation suitable for agriculture. Government should give full play to the role of educational institutions at all levels, such as agricultural colleges and universities, vocational education and basic agricultural education, and improve the scientific and technological quality of farmers, especially the cultivation of young and high-quality agricultural talents. In addition, the government plays a leading role in the education, organization and management functions of the agricultural education and extension system, as well as in the raising, distribution and use of funds for the operation of the education system.

The combination of agriculture, science and education should play its role in training. Agricultural colleges and universities not only undertake scientific research tasks in the field of agriculture, but also train a large number of agricultural talents for the country. Agricultural scientific research institutions have been playing the main role in the research and development, promotion and popularization of agricultural technology. In practical work, agriculture, science and education are combined with each other and support each other. Only by combining them organically can they maximize their role.

Pay attention to the legislative protection of professional farmer cultivation. The enactment of corresponding laws is not only conducive to agricultural production, but also plays a significant role in standardizing farmers' education and training, guaranteeing the implementation of agricultural education and improving the efficiency of agricultural education.

(2) Russia: State program for "Comprehensive Development of Rural Areas"[42]

On January 1, 2021, the rural population of the Russian Federation was 35.956 million down from 36.375 million on January 1, 2020. Over the past seven years, the proportion of rural population in the Russian Federation had continued to decrease, from 25.70% in 2016 to 25.10% in 2022 (Table 2.1). Over the years, population polarization in rural settlements has continued to

Table 2.1   Ratio of rural population to total population at the end of
2016-2022 in some regions of Russia (unit: %)

Regions	Time							2022 compared to 2016
	2016	2017	2018	2019	2020	2021	2022	
Russian Federation	25.70	25.60	25.41	25.30	25.26	25.20	25.10	−0.60
Central Federal District	17.90	17.80	17.70	17.70	17.60	17.60	17.80	−0.10
Northwest Federal District	15.70	15.60	15.50	15.10	15.02	15.00	15.00	−0.70
Southern Federal District	37.60	37.40	37.30	37.20	37.04	36.90	36.80	−0.80
North Caucasus Federal District	50.90	50.20	49.90	49.70	49.57	49.60	49.40	−1.50
Federal District along the Volga River	28.30	28.10	27.91	27.80	27.71	27.60	27.70	−0.60
Ural Federal District	18.80	18.60	18.50	18.41	18.28	18.10	17.90	−0.90
Voronezh Oblast	32.70	32.50	32.20	32.00	32.04	31.91	31.50	−1.20
Ivanovo Oblast	18.60	18.50	18.41	18.30	18.21	18.10	17.90	−0.70
Kostroma Oblast	28.10	27.80	27.60	27.30	26.95	26.60	25.91	−2.19
Kursk Oblast	32.30	32.10	31.80	31.50	31.35	31.20	31.50	−0.80
Smolensk Oblast	27.91	28.10	28.20	28.20	28.00	27.80	27.30	−0.61
Tver State	24.41	24.20	24.00	23.91	23.73	23.70	23.70	−0.71
Vologda State	27.80	27.60	27.41	27.41	27.27	27.10	27.50	−0.30
Leningrad Oblast	36.00	36.20	35.70	32.80	32.68	32.80	32.91	−3.09
Murmansk Oblast	7.60	7.70	7.80	7.80	7.87	7.90	7.00	−0.60
Novgorod Oblast	29.20	29.00	28.70	28.50	28.33	28.10	26.91	−2.29
Pskov Oblast	29.30	29.10	28.91	29.10	29.06	28.91	29.10	−0.20
Volgograd Oblast	23.20	23.00	22.91	22.70	22.59	22.41	22.41	−0.79
Kirov Oblast	23.70	23.20	22.70	22.20	21.81	21.41	21.70	−2.00

Data source: the State Statistical Service of the Russian Federation (https://showdata.gks.ru).

---

42   Russia's federal government. «Комплексное развитие сельских территорий». http://gov.garant.ru.

increase, with an aging rural population, a declining birth rate in rural areas, a decline in the working-age population and a continuous migration of rural people to cities. The shrinking rural population is the result of both the fast urbanization process and the underdevelopment of the economy and infrastructure in rural areas. Figure 2.6 has demonstrated the distribution of people living in poverty by place of residence in the Russian Federation from 2013 to 2020.

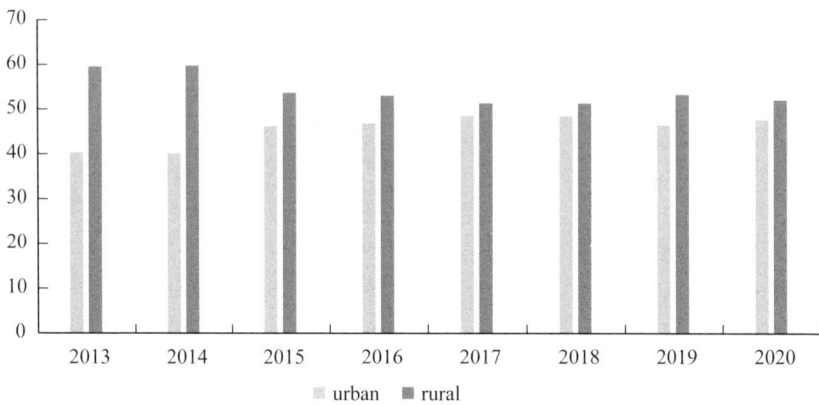

Figure 2.6   Distribution of people living in poverty by place of residence in the Russian Federation, 2013-2020 (%)

Data source: the State Statistical Service of the Russian Federation (https://showdata.gks.ru).

According to the statistics of the Ministry of Federal Affairs of the Russian Federation, the number of social infrastructure in rural areas is decreasing. For example, the number of cultural and leisure organizations decreased from 37,852 at the end of 2018 to 37,601 at the end of 2019. The number of municipal educational infrastructure information and medical prevention institutions decreased from 38,083 at the end of 2018 to 37,961 at the end of 2019, and the number of sports facilities decreased from 96,068 at the end of 2018 to 95,882 at the end of 2019. The number of sports schools for children and adolescents decreased from 1,277 at the end of 2018 to 1,228 at the end of 2019.

On May 31, 2019, the Government of the Russian Federation reviewed and adopted the *National Program for the Comprehensive Revitalization of Rural Areas for 2020-2025*, which will be implemented in 2020. The main tasks of the program include: Providing affordable and comfortable housing for the rural population, creating and developing infrastructure in rural areas, developing the labor market (human resources) in rural areas, providing analytical, normative and methodological support for the integrated development of rural areas, ensuring the implementation of the State program "Integrated Development of Rural Areas" of the Russian Federation, Ensuring educational guarantees for farmers, medical care, cultural services and other needs of the population.

By 2025, the plan aims to achieve three goals: (a) 25.2% of the total population of the Russian Federation is rural; (b) increase the proportion of resources at the disposal of urban and rural households to 72.8% per month; (c) the proportion of the total area of comfortable living areas in rural areas has risen to 48%.

State financial aid. The "Integrated Development of Rural Areas" program is financed in part by the budget of the Russian Federation, and the subsidies are mainly used to "protect people, health and well-being; development of human resources; to achieve a comfortable and safe living environment", among which "talent development" mainly includes the following measures: creation, reconstruction (modernization), reform of pre-school and general education organizations, cultural development centers and traditional handicrafts development centers, sports facilities, provision of primary health care; providing experts for the integrated development of rural areas, subsidies for educational institutions of the Ministry of Agriculture and for targeted training (Table 2.2).

Development of rural human resources. In order to promote the employment of people living in rural areas, the State provides support to entrepreneurs operating in rural areas, sharing with enterprises the costs of financing the implementation of integrated development measures. For apprenticeship contracts or internships, the Government reimburses 90% of the costs of contracts with university students of the Russian Ministry of

Table 2.2 Federal financial support for the "Integrated Development of Rural Areas" programme

Projects	Department objective plan, department project name	2020-2025 financial support amount
Analysis, standardization, and methodological guarantee of comprehensive development in rural areas	Ensure state monitoring of rural areas	400 million rubles (0.02%)
	Analysis and information support for integrated rural development	400 million rubles (0.02%)
Providing affordable and comfortable housing for rural populations	Developing housing construction in rural areas and improving the level of household improvement	1,058.5 billion rubles (46.26%)
Developing the labor market (human resources) in rural areas	Promote employment of the rural population	317.9 billion rubles (13.89%)
Establishing and developing infrastructure in rural areas	Modern rural landscape	690 billion rubles (30.16%)
	Development of rural transport infrastructure	90 billion rubles (3.93%)
	Improvements in rural areas	122.3 billion rubles (5.35%)
	Development of engineering infrastructure in rural areas	8.2 billion rubles (0.36%)
Ensure the implementation of the National Plan for the Comprehensive Development of Rural Areas in the Russian Federation	—	—

Data source:the Russian Government Комплексное развитие сельских территорий (http://gov.garant.ru).

Agriculture, the Federal Fisheries Service and the Federal Veterinary and Plant Quarantine Service, and 30% of the actual costs under contracts for agricultural students corresponding to the All-Russian Educational Professional Classifier[43]. By the beginning of 2026, ensure that 70% of the working-age population is retrained to increase the employment rate in rural areas; and reduce the unemployment rate of the rural working-age population to below 6.5%.

---

43 Ministry of Agriculture of the Russian Federation. https://xn- -j1amde.xn- -p1ai/.

Strengthen the construction and renovation of rural infrastructure. By 2022, no less than 1,480 kilometers of natural gas pipeline network will be laid; water mains will reach 1,300 kilometers; and at least 20 infrastructure projects will be implemented for rural populated areas in 2020-2021. By 2026, ensure that rural transport infrastructure is put into use or repairs rural roads that are part of the national road network, with a mileage of no less than 2,580 km maintained and put into use. By 2026, 31300 rural infrastructure renovation projects will be implemented.

The main challenges of talent development in Russia include: the loss of rural population, the shortage of rural human resources, and the unemployment rate in rural areas to be reduced; Russia's rural labor population education is generally not high, according to statistics, the current Russian total employment population, higher education accounted for 33.5%, secondary vocational education accounted for 45.1%, while Russia's agricultural employment population, the above proportion of 11.6% and 41.3%, in agricultural professional and technical personnel, The proportion of young experts is also relatively low[44]; insufficient investment in agricultural science, technology and education has resulted in shrinking agricultural research and education institutions, and a shortage of world-class modern agriculture and high-tech agricultural professionals. In 2013, for example, Russia's allocation for agricultural research was only 1/60 of that of the United States. The lessons learned from Russia's national program for the Integrated Development of Rural Areas are as follows:

Effective government financial support. The current level of socio-economic development in most rural areas of Russia is still very low, and the quality of life of rural residents is significantly lower than in cities. For decades, local self-government institutions have been unable to effectively address rural development issues due to insufficient financial and economic bases, while the allocation of large financial funds at the federal level can effectively address a wide range of rural problems.

---

44   China's rural research network. http://ccrs.ccnu.edu.cn/List/Details.aspx?tid=9243.

To promote the development of rural human resources and talents. Government is expected to promote the construction of rural infrastructure and provide guarantee for farmers' skills training. By subsidizing rural enterprises, government would create more internship training opportunities for farmers and promote employment for rural labor.

(3) China: Rural Technical Envoy

After the reform and opening up, agricultural science and technology plays an increasingly important role in the development of rural economy and farmers' poverty alleviation and prosperity. However, the past agricultural technology extension system is far from meeting the urgent needs of farmers for advanced agricultural science and technology, and also greatly limits the improvement of rural production efficiency and the development of modern agriculture[45]. In 1998, in order to solve the "rural, agricultural and farmer's problems" in northern Fujian, Nanping City of Fujian Province decided to send agricultural scientific and technical personnel directly to the countryside to serve farmers, providing them with technical guidance and skills training services. In 2002, Comrade Xi Jinping, then governor of Fujian Province, conducted a special research on the work of selecting the secretaries of the village Party branch, technology envoys, and township circulation assistants from Nanping City to rural areas. He pointed out that this approach in Nanping City is *"a beneficial exploration of innovative rural work mechanisms under market economy conditions, and is worthy of careful summary"*. In the same year, the Ministry of Science and Technology summarized the practical experience of the special commissioners in Nanping, Fujian Province, and carried out the pilot work of special commissioners in Ningxia, Shaanxi, Gansu, Qinghai and Xinjiang provinces and regions in Northwest China.

In June 2009, the Ministry of Science and Technology and other departments jointly issued the *Opinions on Deepening the Action of Technical Envoys*

---

45   Sufang Wu, Junfen Liang, Weixiong Luo, et al. Implementation status and development countermeasures of the system of Special Science and Technology Commissioners in rural areas of Guangdong [J]. Tropical Agricultural Engineering, 2021, 45 (2): 109-113.

in Rural Science and Technology Entrepreneurship, launched the action of Technical Envoys in rural science and technology entrepreneurship, and clearly put forward dual tasks. First, in the development of agricultural industry, encourage Technical Envoys to integrate all kinds of resources to start businesses. The second is to establish and improve the rural social science and technology service system to support entrepreneurship, and promote the science and technology ombudsman rural science and technology entrepreneurship action to carry out in depth across the country. In May 2016, The General Office of the State Council issued the *Several Opinions of The General Office of the State Council on In-depth Implementation of the System of Technical Envoys*, which is the first time to make institutional arrangements for the work of Technical Envoys at the national level. The policy clearly points out that rural Technical Envoys have three key tasks: Effectively improve the support level of agricultural science and technology innovation, improve the new agricultural socialized science and technology service system, accelerate the promotion of rural science and technology entrepreneurship and precision poverty alleviation[46]. In 2021, The General Office of the State Council issued the *Opinions on Accelerating the Revitalization of Rural Talents*, again pointing out that it is necessary to "improve the working mechanism of Technical Envoys, broaden the source channels of Technical Envoys, and gradually achieve full coverage of science and technology services and entrepreneurship of Technical Envoys at all levels".

The so-called Technical Envoys refer to professional and technical personnel who are selected and dispatched by local party committees and governments according to certain procedures, focusing on solving the "three ways" problem and the difficulty of farmers to see a doctor, and engaging in the transformation of scientific and technological achievements, the development of advantageous and characteristic industries, the construction of agricultural

---

46   Several Opinions of the General Office of the State Council on Deepening the System of Science and Technology Commissioners [J]. Bulletin of the State Council of the People's Republic of China, 2016 (15): 22-25.

science and technology parks and industrialization bases, as well as medical and health services according to the market demand and actual needs of farmers.

Improve the policy on selecting and appointing Technical Envoys. Colleges and universities, research institutes, vocational schools and other public institutions shall, within five years, implement the policy of retaining the salaries, benefits, posts, establishment and preferential promotion of the titles of the original scientific and technological special commissioners who provide public services for science and technology in rural areas, and incorporate their work performance into the evaluation system for scientific and technological personnel. For those who carry out scientific and technological entrepreneurship in rural areas, their personnel relations shall be retained within five years, and they shall enjoy the same rights to participate in the evaluation and recruitment of professional titles, post rank promotion and social insurance as other employees in the original unit. After the expiration of the term, they may resign and start their own business or return to the original unit according to their wishes. In combination with the implementation of the entrepreneurship guidance plan for college students and the employment promotion plan for unemployed college graduates, financial institutions, social organizations, industry associations, employment personnel service agencies and enterprises and institutions are mobilized to provide support for college students' Technical Envoys to start businesses, improve personnel, labor security agency services and other services, and those who meet the requirements shall be included in social insurance in time.

Improve the support mechanism for Technical Envoys. Universities and research institutes are encouraged to support Technical Envoys in transforming scientific and technological achievements and launching science and technology start-ups in rural areas by means of licensing, transfer and technology shares, so as to ensure that Technical Envoys obtain legitimate profits. Through the national Guiding Fund for the transformation of scientific and technological achievements, government should give full play to the leverage role of financial funds, promote the formation of a diversified, multi-level and multi-channel financing mechanism by means of venture capital guidance and loan risk compensation, and increase support for Technical Envoys to start their own businesses. It guides policy banks, commercial banks and other financial institutions to increase credit support within their business scope, carry out credit granting business and small loan business for science and technology special commissioners, improve the guarantee mechanism, and share start-up risks. Attract social capital to participate in rural science and technology entrepreneurship, hold well the China Agricultural Science and Technology Innovation and Entrepreneurship Competition, China Youth Agriculture-related Industry Entrepreneurship and Wealth Creation Competition and other competitions, encourage banks and venture capital institutions to establish market-oriented, long-term cooperation mechanisms, and support Technical Envoys with strong independent innovation ability and high growth potential to enter the capital market for financing. The country needs to implement the tax reduction policy for specialized farmers' cooperatives and other agricultural business entities, and provide entrepreneurship training and financing guidance and other services.

Technical training will be provided to farmers. Through effective communication with the villages, the rural Technical Envoys conduct various training courses at different levels and for different groups of people according to the different needs of the villages, so as to improve the scientific and cultural quality of farmers. Through technical training, efficient and smooth information exchange channels can be built. In the process of communication with farmers, the special commissioners can find some technical problems in agricultural production, and then explore and solve the technical problems of villagers in daily scientific research work. At the same time, farmers can obtain new skills, new technologies, new ideas into the actual production and life, and truly achieve increased production and income[47].

The talent development in rural China is faced with two challenges: first,

---

47 S X Xu. Thinking and countermeasures of promoting rural revitalization by rural science and technology commissioners [J]. Modern Agricultural Research, 2022, 28 (8): 22-24.

the traditional agricultural technology system can't meet farmers' demand for advanced agricultural technology, which greatly limits the improvement of rural production efficiency and the development of modern agriculture[48]. Second, the rural development lacks the support of scientific and technological services, and the technical bottleneck hindering the development of agricultural industry needs to be broken through. The experience and enlightenment of the system of rural Technical Envoys are as follows:

Strengthen organizational leadership. Play the role of the coordination and guidance group for Technical Envoys in rural science and technology entrepreneurship, strengthen top-level design, overall planning and coordination, and support policies, form an organizational system and long-term mechanism of departmental coordination and linkage, and provide organizational guarantee for the implementation of the system of Technical Envoys. All localities should take the work of Technical Envoys as an important starting point to strengthen science and technology work at counties and cities, establish and improve a multi-department joint working mechanism, formulate local policies and measures to promote Technical Envoys' entrepreneurship in light of actual conditions, strengthen supervision and implementation, and promote in-depth development of the work of Technical Envoys.

Meet the needs of rural development. The key to the success of Technical Envoys is the effective docking of science and technology personnel and grassroots needs. To this end, the key points should be highlighted to do a good job of supply and demand docking. The first is to select excellent personnel. On the basis of organizing and launching, the dispatched units shall implement individual registration and departmental recommendation, and propose their professional characteristics and intention to go to counties and townships for the selection of the organizations. Second, the township puts forward the request. According to the characteristics of local industries and

---

48   Sufang Wu, Junfen Liang, Weixiong Luo, et al. Implementation status and development countermeasures of the system of Special Science and Technology Commissioners in rural areas of Guangdong [J]. Tropical Agricultural Engineering, 2021, 45 (2): 109-113.

the need for the development of efficient ecological agriculture, the towns and townships put forward the requirements for the urgent selection of scientific and technological talents. The third is to implement two-way selection. The office of Technical Envoys shall, on the basis of the opinions of the dispatched units and towns, determine the plan for sending Technical Envoys through repeated contact and consultation[49].

The government shall increase its support. If the work of special commissioners of science and technology in rural areas is to achieve results and increase farmers' income, it needs long-term support of science and technology, and it cannot do without a large amount of funds as a guarantee. On the one hand, the government departments should continuously increase the financial support, on the other hand, the market mechanism and social resources should be fully introduced to give full play to the role of science and technology finance in the work of rural Technical Envoys.

3. Policies and measures of less developed countries and regions

(1) Sri Lanka: National Strategy on TVET Provision for Vulnerable People

In 2010, Sri Lanka's nearly 30-year ethnic conflict was peacefully resolved, and the economy was improving. The Government's "Mahinda Chinthanaya Vision" addresses the government's key concerns in reducing poverty, improving people's well- being, strengthening social capital formation and safeguarding vulnerable groups, and emphasizes the importance of vocational training. For young people in Sri Lanka, especially those from poor families, plantations and areas with high incidence of poverty, access to vocational training suffers due to the low level of education, barriers to the location of vocational training centers, and mobility restrictions. In 2010, The Tertiary and Vocational Education Commission Ministry of Sri Lanka introduced the *National Strategy on TVET for Disadvantaged Groups Provision for Vulnerable People in Sri Lanka Strategies and Action Plans*, which provides skills training

---

49   Xiangfa Ye. The practice and enlightenment of Zhejiang Rural Science and Technology Correspondent System in 10 years [J]. China Rural Science and Technology, 2013 (7): 64-67.

for six categories of vulnerable groups: "women, persons with disabilities, child labourers, the poor, war-affected and migrants" (Table 2.3). The strategy recognizes the training of vulnerable groups as a priority for countries achieving inclusive economic and social development, through the establishment of information systems to coordinate action and performance evaluation, Ensuring adequate funding, establishing vocational guidance and counselling, expanding the coverage and range of courses offered, adopting flexible and innovative approaches to training, providing livelihood and life skills training, integrating training with support for employment, and developing an inclusive culture within training institutions.

Table 2.3   Six categories of vulnerable groups targeted for vocational training in Sri Lanka

Vulnerable groups	Key underlying causes of vulnerabilities
Disadvantaged Women (Heads of single parent households; young unemployed women; women in informal sector employment)	Gender; family status; socio-economic constraints; poor educational attainment
Persons with disabilities	Disabilities (physical, mental)
Disadvantaged youth; young people disengaged from education and unemployed; employed in informal sector	Age, unemployment, socio-economic marginalization, low educational attainment
Poor (People in urban, rural, plantations areas); workers in informal sectors	Proximity/Geographic constraints; poor educational attainment
Displaced people and those affected by war	Affected by Armed Conflict and natural disasters; minority-language; geographic marginalization
Migrant workers	Employment type; absence of vocational qualifications; non-recognition of competencies

Data source: TVEC. National Strategy on TVET Provision for Vulnerable People in Sri Lanka (Strategies and Action Plans) [EB/OL].(2016-07-13)[2023-06-20]. http://www.tvec.gov.lk.

According to the Census and Statistics Bureau of Sri Lanka, 15% of the population is below the official poverty line, and rural areas are the hardest hit areas of poverty in Sri Lanka. More than 80% of the poor live in rural areas. Due to the uneven geographical distribution of vocational training centers, the higher the incidence of poverty, the fewer vocational training centers there will be. Vocational training centers located in areas with a higher incidence of poverty also tend to have a limited range of courses, which results in temporary employment/primary vocational training having less of an impact on poverty reduction. In addition, financial difficulties are also a key factor in the withdrawal of trainees from vocational training courses, and some vocational courses with higher earning potential (such as information technology) run by state and private vocational training centres are fee-based and also directly limit access for the poorer segments. As a result, most of the poor are excluded from primary and secondary education and have low levels of education.

Increase the number of rural vocational training centers. In particular, government needs to ensure that all economically disadvantaged areas have access to vocational training. Introduce and improve the quality of courses relevant to the labor market, where vocational training centers are available, and increase the chances of finding high-paying jobs in the surrounding areas.

Institutionalize training methods for poverty alleviation. There needs to be a shift in the culture and approach of vocational institution management and decision-makers to meet not only the specific training needs required by sectors of the formal economy, but also those of the informal labour market. Livelihood skills and entrepreneurship development services, in particular, help the poor to engage in employment in the informal sector and micro-enterprises through partnerships between mainstream vocational training centres, chambers of commerce and non-government sector training and entrepreneurial enterprises.

Flexible and innovative training courses targeted to the plantation labour market and beneficiary groups. Increase opportunities for plantation youth to participate in vocational and technical training to meet plantation job vacancies through alternative training models such as apprenticeships, workplace-based training, and especially the introduction of courses related to the mechanization of plantation work. Provide living allowances, such as transportation, food, accommodation, etc., to youth who participate in plantation vocational training.

The challenges facing talent development in Sri Lanka mainly include: the urgent need to improve the education level of young people in poor areas; the number and quality of vocational training institutions need to be increased; the early free education policy favored basic education, with fewer opportunities for higher education and professional skills. The experience and enlightenment of the national strategy of vocational education for vulnerable groups are mainly as follows:

Inclusive perspective: object determination and strategy formulation of vocational education. In terms of the determination of vocational education objects, Sri Lanka does not limit itself to the international standard of "per capita annual income", but defines the poverty alleviation objects of vocational education from the relatively broad perspective of "vulnerable groups", thus expanding the beneficiaries of vocational education and ensuring the inclusion of vocational education objects.

Exerting joint efforts: the coordination and cooperation of relevant institutions of vocational education. The collaborative mechanism of vocational education in Sri Lanka can be summarized as "multi-level and cross-ministerial". The so-called "multi-level and cross-ministry" refers to the vocational education management structure composed of three levels and main ministries: "National Coordinating Committee—project management committee—special working group". Among them, the National Coordination Committee is at the top of the management structure. It is responsible for coordinating various project management committees, and mainly performs several duties such as making poverty alleviation decisions, approving project planning and supervising project execution. Through the establishment of a resource sharing network, the project management committee effectively integrates the resources of multiple relevant ministries and commissions to ensure the coordinated promotion of poverty alleviation projects. The special working group is responsible for more specific poverty alleviation affairs, mainly including formulating specific vocational education programs, providing detailed project implementation suggestions, and submitting the plans and suggestions to the National Coordinating Committee and the project management committee for reference. The "three-level, cross-ministerial" coordination mechanism enables synergy to be transmitted from top to bottom, and is fully demonstrated at the level of the implementation framework (Table 2.4).

Table 2.4 Ministries directly relevant for TVET provision and support services for vulnerable people

Ministry	Project management committee				
	Vulnerable women	The disabled	Disadvantaged youth	The poor	Migrant workers
ILO	✓	✓	✓	✓	✓
World University Services of Canada	✓	—	—	—	✓
Centre for Women's Research	✓	—	—	—	—
Ministry of Labour Relations and Manpower	—	✓	✓	—	✓
National Apprentice and Industrial Training Authority	—	✓	✓	—	—
Disability Organizations' Joint Front	—	✓	—	—	—
Ministry of Social Services and Social Welfare	—	✓	—	—	—
National Child Protection Authority	—	—	✓	—	—
Ministry of Community Development and Social Inequity Eradication	—	—	—	✓	—
Consortium of Humanitarian Agencies	—	—	—	—	—
Department of Technical Education and Training	—	—	—	—	—
Ministry of Resettlement and Disaster Relief Services	—	—	—	—	—
Secretariat for Coordinating the Peace Process	—	—	—	—	—
Vocational Training Authority	—	—	—	—	✓

Data source: TVEC. National Strategy on TVET Provision for Vulnerable People in Sri Lanka (Strategies and Action Plans) [EB/OL].(2016-07-13)[2023-06-20]. http://www.tvec.gov.lk.

(2) Pakistan: education for all program

Pakistan is a developing country that is steadily transitioning from an agricultural- based economy to an industrial and services-led development model. In the past development, as most of the budget of Pakistan is devoted to meeting the challenges of national security and interest on loans, it has led to a lot of efforts in promoting economic growth and meeting the basic needs of the people. Relatively little investment in infrastructure such as education, health, social services, etc., has led to a series of serious development problems. At the same time, the rapidly growing population has exacerbated the shortage of public resources, illiteracy, rapid population growth and slow economic development have aggravated unemployment and hindered the normal economic and social operation. There are big differences in education indicators among provinces, between urban and rural areas, and between men and women. In 1998, the literacy rate for males over the age of 10 in rural Pakistan was 46.4%, compared with 20.1% for females (Table 2.5).

Table 2.5   Literacy rates in Pakistan aged 10+, 1998 (unit: %)

Region	City		Rural		Nationwide		
	male	female	male	female	male	female	both
Pakistan	70.0	55.2	46.4	20.1	54.8	32.0	43.9
Islamabad	83.2	69.7	75.1	48.8	80.6	62.4	72.4
Punjab	70.9	57.2	50.4	24.8	57.2	35.1	46.6
Sindh	69.8	56.7	37.9	12.2	54.5	34.8	45.3
North West Frontier Province	67.5	39.1	47.7	14.7	51.4	18.8	35.4
Balochistan	58.1	33.1	25.8	7.9	34	14.1	24.8

Data source: Pakistan Population Census Report (1998).

In 2000, the Dakar World Education Forum, convened by UNESCO, USAID, UNFPA, UNICEF and the World Bank, brought together participants from 182 countries, as well as major development agencies, to commit to achieving education for All(EFA) by 2015. In response to Qatar's action, the Government of Pakistan launched the *Education for All (2001-2015)* in 2003. The plan has three main objectives: basic education, adult literacy and early childhood education. The specific contents are: To help vulnerable groups in rural and urban areas, with a focus on out-of-school girls, illiterate girls and women; promoting participation in and access to basic education by grass-roots communities; and improving the learning performance of children, youth and recognition, and improving the relevance and quality of basic education. The plan is clearly linked to Pakistan's poverty reduction and development strategy, thereby creating a link between basic education and strategies that focus on skills development[50].

A comprehensive and systematic education policy. Considering The new trend of modern Education and the new needs of the country, the Pakistani government implemented the *Current National Education Policy (1998-2010)*. It calls for improving the quality of basic education, effectively using and increasing educational facilities and services to increase access to basic education, reducing the urban-rural imbalance, increasing the diversity of funding sources for basic education, improving adult literacy, institutionalizing primary education, etc. In 2001, the National Economic Council of Pakistan approved the *National 10-year Vision Development Plan (2001-2011)*, which focuses on four areas: economic growth framework, poverty reduction and human development, revitalization of agriculture to overcome drought, and public sector investment. Among them, poverty reduction and human development are the priority areas of the plan, which has been targeted by detailed strategies: poverty reduction strategy, employment policy, education and training, science and technology, information technology, etc. Moreover, based on the country's objective conditions, Pakistan has also undertaken education sector reform (2001-2005), which aims to increase access to education at all levels, promote equity and improve quality. Reflecting extensive

---

50　Ministry of Education. National Plan of Action on Education for All (2001-2015): Pakistan. https://planipolis.iiep.unesco.org/2003/national-plan-action-education-all-2001-2015-pakistan-3617.2003:7-13.

consultation between the Ministry of Education and cross-sectoral stakeholders, the reform resulted in more than 600 partners and initiated a team drive process to fully engage provincial governments, the federal Ministry of Finance, provincial education, provincial planning and development departments, non-governmental organizations, and the private sector.

Free education and incentives. In 2004, Pakistan began abolishing tuition fees and providing free textbooks to students in public schools (both formal and non-formal), an approach that has since been followed in all provinces/territories; monthly scholarships or grants to female students in middle and high schools in a few selected rural areas; cooking oil for female students with high attendance and their teachers to motivate them to pursue education; and providing free meals at select schools.

Focus on working with relevant authorities. The involvement of other relevant government departments, civil society organizations, community leaders and the international development partners strengthens partnerships between different sectors and creates opportunities for other stakeholders to voice their views and examine the feasibility of new measures (Table 2.6).

Table 2.6 Stakeholders of the EFA Programme in Pakistan

	Examples
Government departments	Relevant ministries, such as Ministry of Women's Development, Ministry of Social Welfare, Ministry of Planning and Development, Ministry of Finance and Ministry of Inter-Provincial Coordination, etc.
Civic organizations	NGOs, media and experts, etc.
International development partners	EFA International Development Partners Forum, etc.

Data source: Ministry of Education, Education for All 2015 National Review Report: Pakistan. https://unesdoc.unesco.org/ark:/48223/pf0000229718.2014:10-11.

Improving equity in education. First, highlighting gender inequality, improving women's access to education, increasing the number of girls' schools in rural areas, and providing incentives to encourage women's education have increased the importance of women's education among educators, civil society organizations and communities. Secondly, attention should be paid to the improvement of education conditions in rural areas, through increasing the number of teachers, education subsidies, education quality in less developed areas, strengthening education supervision and other ways to increase rural education opportunities and enrollment rates.

The problems Pakistan faces in talent development mainly include the following aspects: insufficient government investment in education, insufficient supply of rural education facilities and services; the lack of educational opportunities and the great demand in rural areas for high-quality education, especially skills education; eliminating gender disparities in school enrolment; inadequate and poorly paid teachers, and inadequate pre-service and in-service training for most teachers. The main lessons from Brazil's EFA experience are as follows:

Legislation on the right to free primary education. The adoption of a constitutional amendment recognizing free and compulsory primary education for all children as a fundamental right is also an important result of Pakistan's promotion of education for all. Some provinces have already enacted laws to implement this constitutional provision, while others are in the process of enacting them. The legislation has helped send millions of out-of-school children to school.

Put educational incentives in place. All provinces in Pakistan abolished tuition fees in 2000 and began distributing free textbooks to all public school students. This was an important milestone and historic success in Pakistan's Education for All strategy, contributing directly to an increase in primary school enrolment as the direct cost of attending school was reduced for poor parents. Cooking oil was used as a motivational tool to increase girls' enrolment and attendance in poor families and primary schools in remote areas in Baluchistan, Sindh and Sindh provinces.

Create organizations that evaluate the quality of education. Pakistan agreed to establish the National Education Assessment System (NEAS) with its provincial counterpart, the Provincial Education Assessment Centres. The new agency, established in 2004, conducted a series of surveys and studies to measure the quality of learning among students in different subjects and how it varied by gender and in different parts of the country.

(3) Kenya: Youth Empowerment Project

In the late 1990s, the World Bank launched the *Education Strategy* to illustrate the importance of education for poverty reduction: Developing countries need more educated people, and individuals need more skills and information to compete and grow, in order to better meet the needs of changing labour markets[51]. In 2005, the World Bank launched a new international assistance strategy, which identified education as the foundation for national economic development, job creation and building harmonious societies. The Bank should help developing countries, especially those in Africa with high rates of extreme poverty, maximize the role of the education sector in economic growth and poverty reduction, while strengthening education's support for the knowledge economy[52]. Kenya's economy began to improve between 2003 and 2007, but there are still large numbers of poor and unemployed people, mainly young people, and youth unemployment has become a major challenge in Kenya, such as high unemployment and underemployment. The overall youth unemployment rate is twice as high as the average for adults, at about 21%. In 2006, the poverty rate for households with at least one unemployed youth in Kenya was 55%, compared with 46% for all households, the data show[53]. According to the results of the World Bank's Poverty and Inequality Assessment survey in Kenya between 2005 and 2010, unemployed youth are one of the main vulnerable groups in Kenya, and a large proportion of the extremely poor are unemployed youth[54]. As a result, the World Bank has

---

51　Wenle Yan. Research on World Bank Education Assistance: Characteristics, Causes and Influences [D]. Shanghai: East China Normal University, 2012: 63.

52　Min Yin. Research on the World Bank's Aid Policy for Education in Africa [D]. Jinhua: Zhejiang Normal University, 2011: 25.

53, 54　The World Bank. Implementation Completion and Results Report [EB/OL]. https://documents.worldbank.org/curated/en/710301471883981006/pdf/ICR00003730-08042016.pdf/2018-12-12.

prioritized its assistance to youth in Kenya.

On May 20, 2010, the Kenyan government launched the Kenya Youth Empowerment Project (KYEP) in Nairobi, Mombasa and Kisumu with the support of US $17.03 million from the World Bank. This is a vocational education and training project implemented by the Kenyan government to solve the poverty and unemployment situation in the country, strive to improve the employment environment for young people, increase employment opportunities for young people, meet the needs of young people in skills development, and improve the employability and adaptability of young people.

According to the data, the KYEP project has benefited 20,384 young people (47% of them women) who have received training, and by the end of the training in 2016, 78% of the young people have completed the internship and been employed or started their own business[55]. Compared with the youth without KYEP training, the employment growth rate of the youth participating in the program is as high as 14.2%[56], and the average income has increased by 90% (Table 2.7).

Skills training for young people. KYEP's training targets are mainly unemployed youths aged 15-29, and those who have received higher education but have been unemployed for a long time. The training was carried out in a total of eight rounds between 2011 and 2016, each lasting six months, consisting of three months of vocational skills training and three months of internship. The skills training consists of three main stages:

The first phase aims to enhance the Life Skills Training, which lasts for three weeks and includes experiential training to enable young people to focus on self- awareness, self-esteem, decision-making, communication, leadership, interpersonal skills, personal management skills and coping skills, occupational health, first aid, interview, resume writing skills, work ethics, etc.

---

55   The World Bank. Implementation Completion and Results Report [EB/OL]. https://documents.worldbank.org/curated/en/710301471883981006/pdf/ICR00003730-08042016.pdf/2018-12-12.

56   KEPSA: The Voice of Private Sector in Kenya–Kenya Youth Empowerment Project [EB/OL]. https://kepsa.or.ke/kyep/2018-12-3.

Table 2.7   Completion of KYEP indicators in Kenya

Indicators	Initial target value	Actual finished value
Indicator 1:	Percentage who complete an internship and are immediately hired by the internship employer or new employer, or start a business	
value	35%	78%
accomplishment date	2010/05/05	2016/02/28
Notes	Overfulfill. The rate was 83% for men and 74% for women, with an overall average of 7%. The actual finished value was 153% of the initial target value.	
Indicator 2:	Proportion employed or self-employed 6 months after the end of the internship	
value	50%	76%
accomplishment date	2010/05/05	2016/02/28
Notes	Overfulfill. The rate was 82% for men and 70% for women, with an overall average of 76%. The actual completion value was 52% higher than the initial target value	

Data source: Kenya - Youth Empowerment Project (English). Washington, D.C.: World Bank Group. http://documents.worldbank.org/curated/en/710301471883981006/Kenya-Youth-Empowerment-Project.

The second phase focuses on core business skills training, lasting three to five weeks, providing a total of eight modules of learning content, including information and communication technology, customer care, communication, business practice, etiquette, marketing, human resource management and finance. Through core business skills training, young people can be equipped with business, financial and management skills. The focus of these skills training is to develop young people's proficiency in the application of theoretical knowledge.

The third phase is dedicated to sector-specific skills training. After life skills and core business skills training, youths will receive five weeks of technical skills training, including two weeks of entrepreneurship skills training, including business plan development, competition and mentorship, to enable youths to acquire technical skills that match the labour market and specific positions. At the end of the training, the youth are offered a 12-week work placement in the formal and informal sectors to gain relevant work experience. Interns are placed in the priority development sectors identified in *Kenya Vision 2030*, such as energy, finance, tourism, information and communication, manufacturing and small and medium enterprises[57].

Policies have been put in place to ensure the effective implementation of the plan. The national youth policy and youth policy planning in Kenya is primarily the responsibility of the Ministry of Youth Affairs and Sports. The relevant policies include: first, the development and implementation of training programmes for the staff of the Ministry of Youth Affairs and Sports, especially local youth development officers; the second is to develop and implement social audits to increase transparency and accountability in the training and internship component of KYEP; the third is to carry out communication activities to raise awareness of KYEP among youth; and the fourth is to support youth policy development by providing technical assistance to the National Youth Council and conducting analytical work. After the reorganization of KYEP in 2011, the following related contents have been added: The first is to strengthen the training of master craftsmen; second, by increasing the participation of officials in project management, it will enhance the support for the execution capacity of the private sector alliance; the third is to transfer the budget for exchange activities carried out by PFP from the Ministry of Youth Affairs and Sports to PFP; fourth, the Ministry of Youth Affairs and Sports assumed the exchange activities related to the whole project; fifth, the social audit was cancelled because the training and internship component had already included some additional monitoring and evaluation activities in the implementation process; and the sixth is to increase research on policies[58].

Joint training "international organizations-governments-rofessional organization". KYEP Training is managed in collaboration with a public-

---

57   The Kenya Youth Empowerment Project [EB/OL]. https://kepsa.or.ke/kyep/2021-08-28.

58   Jia Qi. The historical development and training model of vocational education under the Belt and Road Initiative: A study based on the World Bank's Kenya Youth Empowerment Project [J]. Tianjin business vocational college journal, 2021, 9 (6): 10-18. DOI: 10.16130/j.carol carroll nki.12-1434/f 2021.06.002.

private partnership of the World Bank-Government-Professional Organization collaboration. The World Bank conducts macro-management of KYEP in the aspects of training project evaluation, selection, preparation, negotiation, supervision and verification; the Kenyan government shall conduct macro-supervision and regulation at the level of KYEP implementation and operation, and form regular reports on the implementation and evaluation of training to the World Bank; professional organizations include KEPSA, NITA, third-party training institutions, private sector employers and artisans. Among them, KEPSA is specifically responsible for the organization, implementation, management and monitoring of the entire training and internship process, including selecting participants, hiring qualified third-party training institutions, mobilizing private enterprises to participate in training, supervision and management, and tracking and evaluation after each training cycle. The third party training institution is mainly responsible for the implementation of the three-month vocational skills classroom training and the training execution report. Private sector employers mainly provide internship positions for youth[59].

Kenya faces many problems in talent development, such as widespread youth unemployment in rural areas, lack of job opportunities and skills; the agricultural population is aging seriously; poverty exacerbates the lack of rural education and training opportunities; lack of access to land, capital and information technology mentoring opportunities; and inadequate policies to support youth agricultural entrepreneurship, with existing policies fragmented and low coverage. The lessons learned from its youth empowerment programs are as follows:

The training model of "international organization-government-professional organization" is adopted. For the World Bank, on the one hand, helping Kenya solve the problem of youth unemployment through the vocational education and training model integrating industry and education is

---

59　Jia Qi. The historical development and training model of vocational education under the Belt and Road Initiative: A study based on the World Bank's Kenya Youth Empowerment Project [J]. Tianjin Business Vocational College Journal, 2021, 9 (6): 10-18. DOI: 10.16130/j.carol carroll nki.12-1434/f 2021.06.002.

an important practice to promote its goal of poverty eradication and common prosperity. On the other hand, the success of KYEP has created a new model for the World Bank to implement similar training programs in other countries in Africa and the world in the future to achieve poverty reduction.

For the government, on the one hand, solving the problem of youth employment is an issue that cannot be ignored to balance social, economic and cultural development. It is also one of the priorities of the government at this stage and in the future. On the other hand, the government can play a key role in supervising and guiding the formulation of policies, and the government has enough leadership and regulation ability to ensure the continuous implementation of youth employment training and internship.

For private enterprises, on the one hand, young people are the main force in the labor market. Private enterprises attach great importance to whether the young people who enter the labor market have the qualities and skills that match the job positions. They also need high-quality young people to enter the labor market, so as to improve their credibility. On the other hand, private enterprises can quickly adapt to the changing market demand, make it clear what qualities and skills the market needs, and motivate employers in all walks of life to join youth training and internship programs. They are willing to participate in the implementation of youth employment training, expand the impact of training and internship, and feedback the results of youth employment training and internship.

Focus on the effectiveness of the implementation of the program. First of all, before the launch of KYEP, the World Bank has conducted a lot of analysis and survey on youth employment in Kenya, obtained a lot of data on youth employment, and is working with the United Nations Development Program, the International Labor Organization, the United States Agency for International Development and other development partners active in Kenya to jointly prepare youth employment training projects.

Secondly, KYEP design has learned some lessons from similar projects in other countries and regions as well as the implementation of projects in Kenya.

For example, attracting employers and the private sector to define skills is the key to ensuring the quality of training activities; using market competition mechanism to introduce training institutions flexibly; the introduction of life skills in vocational and technical skills is the key to the success of the project. Thirdly, during the implementation of the project, the Kenyan government, in collaboration with the private sector alliance, will match the employability of the young people after training with the preferences and conditions of the enterprises, so as to timely convey the market employment information to the young people in need of employment and reduce the employment information barriers. Finally, after the completion of the project, practical experience will be summarized to provide policy services for youth employment and development more effectively.

(4) Ethiopia: Education and Training Policy

When Ethiopia emerged from a 13-year civil war in 1991, the new government immediately launched a program of macroeconomic reforms that helped stabilize the economy. At this time, education in Ethiopia faced a number of problems, such as declining quality of education, high dropout and repetition rates, inefficient administration of education, inadequate funding for education, and uneven distribution of educational opportunities. In 1995, the national primary enrollment rate was 26.2%, the secondary enrollment rate was only 7.4%, and there were only 17 vocational education schools[60]. To this end, the Government of Ethiopia has adopted the *Education and Training Policy 1994-2016 (ETP)*, which focuses on improving educational equity, access to education and the quality of education. In 1997, in order to implement the ETP, the government introduced the *Education Sector Development Program (ESDP)*, a five-year program aimed at achieving universal primary education by 2015, which has been implemented to ESDP-6. Its strategies include: the gradual introduction of the new curriculum to improve the quality of education with an emphasis on developing basic skills in literacy, numeracy and communication

---

60 Ethiopia Sector Development Program I (ESDP-I).

in the mother tongue in primary education; devolving control of schools to district education bureau to improve coping capacity and efficiency and increase investment in construction; improving teaching facilities, with a focus on rural areas and primary education, to increase access to education and mitigate regional imbalances; and promoting private sector investment in service delivery (Table 2.8, Table 2.9).

Table 2.8   Changes in relevant education indicators in Ethiopia, 1997-2002 (%)

		1997 (base year)	1998	1999	2000	2001	2002
Education spending	Education as a share of the national budget	16.7	19	19.3	19.6	19.9	20.2
Admission opportunities	Number of people receiving vocational and technical training	94,592	137,625	243,009	265,044	304,058	312,826
	Enrollment rate (1-8)	79.8	87.7	94.6	100.2	105.5	109.7
	Ratio of qualified teachers (5-8)	55	63	69	74	87	95
Quality and efficiency	Percentage of qualified teachers (9-12)	41	51	61	66	71	88
	Student/faculty ratio (1-8)	71	69	65	61	58	54
	First grade dropout rate	22.4	19.1	15.9	12.7	9.5	6.3
	Eighth grade graduation rate	34.34	38.72	41.65	44.59	58.17	62.79
Equity	Gross primary school enrollment in the two most underserved districts (1-8)						
	ALPHA	20.9	37.4	60	70	80	90
	Somalia	23.3	38.6	60	70	80	90

Data source: Ethiopia Ministry of Education.the Federal Democratic Republic of Ethiopia Education. Sector Development Program III (ESDP III) 2005/2006-2010/2011 (1998 EFY-2002 EFY) [Z]. Addis Ababa:Ministry of Education. 2005:78-79.

Table 2.9   ESDP II expenditures for relevant years (million USD)

Items	2002	2003	2004	Three years total
Primary education	264.04	276.42	275.07	815.53
Preschool	234.54	245.15	253.03	732.73
Adult and non-formal education	6.19	6.45	6.45	19.09
Teacher training	13.04	14.54	10.20	37.77
Special education	2.21	2.34	2.29	6.84
Distance education	8.07	7.93	3.09	19.09
Secondary education	41.01	42.43	39.42	122.86
Vocational skills and technical training	132.72	84.33	61.65	278.70
Higher education	119.26	131.06	151.71	402.03
Capacity building	6.02	7.45	4.26	17.74
Administrative and other	37.43	41.58	40.65	119.66
Total	600.48	583.28	572.77	1,756.53

Data source: Federal Democratic Republic of Ethiopia (FDRE) and Ministry of Finance and Economic Development (MOFED). Ethiopia: Sustainable Development and Poverty Reduction The Program [EB/OL]. http://www.imf.org/External/NP/prsp/2002/eth/01/073102.pdf.2022:97-98.

Increase and improve educational facilities. The country should increase access to education, raise the school enrollment rate, increase the number of schools in rural and disadvantaged areas and provide corresponding teaching facilities, reduce and waive some grade tuition fees, and ease the financial burden of rural families.

Strengthen the capacity building of teachers. The country should provide on- the-job training for teachers, such as summer training and distance education training, and increase training for principals to improve the quality of education and the efficiency of school management.

Increase funding for education. Increase government funding, international aid and social donations, and increase private investment in education.

Government-led. The government plays an important role in pre-school policy development, curriculum setting, standard setting and provision of oversight, for example, by encouraging the participation of the private sector, NGOs and community organizations in pre-school education; review and revise curriculum and facility standards; providing technical assistance and teacher training; close monitoring to ensure the quality of pre-school education; establish a pre-school preparation strategy paper for all primary schools; and establishing regular communication platforms.

The main problems facing talent development in Ethiopia are: (a) Lack of practical talent education policies and targets, low level of education of farmers, high illiteracy rate and low level of agricultural technology. (b) The backward economy, the serious shortage of educational funds, and the continuous decline of educational quality and standards. Many years of civil war led to a financial strain in the country, and the investment in the field of education was seriously insufficient. All kinds of schools were in poor condition, the school buildings were insufficient and extremely simple, and the basic teaching equipment and facilities were incomplete. (c) Uneven distribution of educational resources, a small number of schools in rural areas, low enrollment rates, high dropout rates. The uneven development of education in Ethiopia is mainly manifested in urban and rural areas, between regions and between genders. In 1995 only 8% of primary-school-age children were enrolled in AFAR, compared with 85% in some developed areas (such as ADDIS)[61]. (d) Teachers are in short supply and poorly paid. According to statistics, 97.06% of Ethiopian teachers in the first stage of primary education (grades 1-4) have reached the national standard and obtained qualifications, while in the second stage of primary education (grades 5-8), only 54.6% of these teachers are qualified[62]. The lessons learned from Ethiopia's Education and Training Policy are as follows:

---

61   Ethiopian Ministry of Education. https://moe.gov.et.

62   Ethiopia Ministry of Education. the Federal Democratic Republic of Ethiopia Education. Sector Development Program III (ESDP III) 2005/2006-2010/2011 (998 EFY-2002 EFY) [Z]. Addis Ababa: Ministry of Education. 2005: 78-79.

An effective education management system. To build a scientific and effective macro quality management system is the basis for improving the quality of agricultural vocational education in Ethiopia, which provides clear requirements for teaching syllabus, textbook development, teaching mode, teaching conditions and teacher quality, and stimulates vocational education and training institutions to strengthen quality management.

Strong financial support for education. Although the Ethiopian government has limited financial capacity, it still pays attention to financial assistance in the field of education. At the same time, a large part of the implementation funds of ESDP programs come from international assistance.

(5) Venezuela: Centro Interamericano de Educación Rural[63]

In the 1930s, Venezuela gradually focused on its educational development, especially teacher training. In 1940, Venezuela promulgated the "Education Law" to legislate teacher training, formalized normal education, and divided it into urban and rural areas, respectively for the training of teachers in the two regions. The headquarters of ENRI, Centro Interamericano de Educación Rural (CIER), was established in Venezuela.

In 1954, the Organization of American States (OAS) and UNESCO began establishing the Escuela Normal Rural Intermericana (ENRI) in the Latin American region with the aim of providing specialized training and improvement for rural teachers. In 1967, CIER was merged with the "Gervasio Rubio" Normal School, the "Carlos Rangel Lamus" secondary school, the Institute of Agricultural Technology, etc. CIER provides teacher education, agricultural, industrial technical training, and teacher training and development in the field of secondary and higher education. To become a professional development program for rural educators in Venezuela. In 1972, this educational complex was officially named the CIER Educational Unit.

It provided teacher training for villages. The CIER model has the following characteristics: (a) The development and advancement of rural

---

63 Mora García, J. P., (2019). La historia de la Educación Rural en Venezuela. Caso: Centro Interamericano de Educación Rural (CIER). Educere, 23 (76): 811-829.

lifestyles, especially those stimulated by land reform, requires a school dedicated to training teachers in order to effectively assist this progress. (b) The rural education program and the schools that promote it require teachers who, in addition to having the specific skills and knowledge of their profession, also have an understanding of the techniques of rural work and an attitude of empathy and appreciation for the way of life of rural residents. (c) Training a good rural teacher requires a teacher training institution with facilities, organization, programmes and operations commensurate with its purpose. (d) Rural normal students must have every opportunity to continue their higher education in teaching. (e) The State must develop a programme for the establishment of adequate rural normal schools to provide farmers with the professionals needed for teaching. (f) The training of rural teachers must be linked to the training of other middle-level professionals working in rural areas.

The educational institutions of CIER are primarily responsible for training the following types of talents: professional technical personnel, rural center directors, model teachers, and principals of farm schools and advanced rural schools. In addition, they also provide further training for the following personnel: teachers of rural single schools, centralized and advanced rural schools; multifaceted activity guidance teachers in farm schools; professional teachers and lecturers; administrative staff and teachers of rural normal schools; and educational material production personnel, including those involved in the production, printing, distribution, and use of teaching materials.

The main problems facing talent development in Venezuela are: insufficient teacher training, poor teaching quality, and poor teacher salaries; the high dropout rate of students. The main lessons learned from the practical operation of the Inter-American Centre for Rural Education are as follows:

The production of teacher teaching is close to agriculture. Restricted by economy, geography, history and other factors, the supply side of rural teacher training presents difficulties in terms of supply structure, system and management. Venezuela's rural teacher education pays attention to the training of rural teachers, to a certain extent to alleviate the gap between urban and rural teaching quality, at the same time, rural teachers are required to understand agricultural work, close to agricultural production and farmers' lives, so that teaching can serve rural agriculture and farmers.

Departments cooperate in teacher training. Limited rural resources are often one of the difficulties in the development of rural teachers. Venezuela CIER has merged with other normal schools, secondary schools, agricultural technical colleges and other institutions to integrate educational resources and provide professional teacher education, agricultural and industrial training and development conditions for rural areas.

III. The experience and enlightenment of rural talent development

On the basis of the first two parts of policy research and practical case studies, the paper summarizes the similarities and differences, characteristics and achievements of talent development in major regions of the world. Through horizontal and vertical comparative analysis, the experience, trend and enlightenment of general rural talent development are sorted out and summarized with the economic development period as the axis.

1. Comparison of rural talent development institutional system in different countries

(1) **Comparison of policy types in different economies**

(a) **Similarity of policies through law**

The policies and regulations established by developed countries have achieved remarkable results. How to implement effective rural revitalization policies to continuously empower rural development and promote sustainable agricultural development is of paramount importance to all countries. In the process of policy formulation, laws have been enacted to strengthen the effectiveness of policies, which has been unanimously recognized by all countries. In this regard, many examples have been given by developed countries, which were the first to legalize policy guidance. Germany continues to explore legal protection and policy support to create a good environment for the development of rural talents. Germany's *Agricultural Law*, *Forestry Law* and *Land Reform Law* have all effectively regulated agricultural production and operation activities, and in this process, the rights and interests of farmers have been defined through legislation, so that rural talents have a great sense of gain and achievement in the process of agricultural employment. Germany has also implemented a series of policy measures, such as the *Urban-rural equivalence Plan*, *Agricultural Structural reform Plan* and *Rural Development Plan*, to provide rural talents with funding, technology, training and other aspects of support, improve the employment protection and support of professional farmers.

Japan attaches great importance to the in-depth integration of legal policy guidance and information technology support, and adopts a policy-technology development model. Since the 1960s, Japan has entered a stage of rapid growth. The income gap between industry and agriculture has widened, and surplus agricultural labor has transferred to non-agricultural or non-agricultural sectors, resulting in a decrease in the number of rural households. The growth of consumption demand and the change of consumption demand structure put forward new requirements for agricultural development and agricultural product supply. In 1961, Japan promulgated the *Basic Law of Agriculture*, which aimed to promote the concentration of cultivated land and the expansion of the scale of agricultural operators under the background of the outward transfer of agricultural labor force, so as to improve agricultural productivity. And cultivate agricultural management talents, improve the income level through agricultural development, and narrow the income gap between agriculture and other industries. Since then, Japan has also issued the *Agricultural Structure Improvement Plan* and *Agricultural Comprehensive Development Plan* and other policy documents, focusing on improving agricultural productivity, stabilizing agricultural prices, increasing the income of agricultural producers, and greatly expanding the scope of agricultural production and operation, leading to the establishment of modern agriculture development. In addition, along with the progress of information technology in Japan, the Japanese government has also applied technology into the process of supporting agricultural development. It has established information service systems such as "Agricultural Information Network", "Agricultural Talent Network" and "Agricultural satellite" to provide rural talents with information support for the whole process from production to sales to management.

In addition, other developed economies in the world have also continued to help rural revitalization and rural talent development through legal protection and planning support. The Russian government has formulated and implemented a series of laws, regulations and policy measures, such as the *Land Reform Law*, *Agricultural Development Strategy* and *Agricultural Structure Improvement Plan*, providing all-round policy support for rural talents from training to introduction and retention. The Russian government has also implemented a series of planning projects, such as the *Return of Farmers*, the *Employment of Farmers* and the *New Rural Construction Plan*, to provide rural talents with migration and employment planning support from the city to the countryside or from the countryside to the countryside. The Russian government has also provided improved production conditions and living standards for rural talents by strengthening the construction of rural industries and infrastructure. Through the implementation of the *Leisure Agriculture Development Plan*, rural talents are encouraged to develop tourism-related leisure agriculture projects and provided with a stable source of income through measures such as infrastructure construction, public service provision and market promotion.

Developing countries have been establishing and improving their legal and regulatory systems. In exploring the development of rural talents, developing countries have constantly paid attention to the important role of law, and realized the key role of policy in the training and development of rural talents through government leadership. The *Agricultural Credit Program*, *Agricultural Insurance Program* and *Agricultural Quality Management Law* issued by Brazil have provided standards and guidance for rural talents to guarantee product quality and improve product added value. The Brazilian government has also provided guarantees and incentives for rural talents to enhance product competitiveness and meet consumer demand by strengthening product quality supervision and certification. For example, through the implementation of the *Agricultural Brand Plan*, Brazil encourages rural talents to develop high-quality agricultural products that meet consumer needs and improve their market share and profit margins through certification and publicity. In addition to guaranteeing rural talents in all aspects of agricultural production, many countries also pay attention to the perfection of the legal system in the process of talent training to ensure that the rights and interests of rural talents have laws to follow. China has promulgated the *Agricultural Law*, *Agricultural Support Protection Law* and *Agricultural Science and Technology Promotion Law* to encourage rural talents to adjust their production structure and methods according to market demand and improve product quality and efficiency. Through the implementation of the Six Industrialization Strategy, the Chinese government has continuously increased investment in science and technology, supported rural talents to carry out scientific and technological innovation and transformation, and promoted the modernization and diversification of agriculture. Rural talents are encouraged to develop diversified industries related to agriculture, such as processing, service and tourism, and improve their added value and competitiveness through scientific and technological innovation and transformation. Through the implementation of the *National Rural Employment Guarantee Program*, India encourages rural talents to participate in rural infrastructure construction, production mode reform, lifestyle improvement and other activities, which has enhanced the initiative and creativity of rural talents.

Most of the later-developing economies in Asia, Africa and Latin America still rely on agriculture as their main pillar industry. This is due to the slow process of local industrialization, the inability to form a strong industrial system, and the inability to support the joint development of agriculture. Therefore, how to guide the development of rural talents through the formulation of policies and regulations has become an important means. In 2005, the second African Science and Technology Ministers' Conference formulated the *African Science and Technology Joint Action Plan*, aiming to form a plan for science and technology development and progress through regional cooperation. The program holds great hopes for lifting all countries out of poverty through scientific and technological development and cooperation. Most of these science and technology programs focus on agricultural science and technology, seeking to guide production technology with scientists, train more rural talents, increase investment in agricultural production, and use science and technology to increase production. However, in the process of law implementation in many African countries, the irrationality of institutional changes has led to the duality of rural production, that is, the coexistence of the relatively backward livelihood agriculture engaged in by a large number of farmers and the relatively advanced modern commodity agriculture controlled by a few foreign investors or foreigners. With the basic goal of maintaining family livelihood, livelihood agriculture is small in scale and has low input level of capital, technology, equipment and fertilizer. It often relies on increasing land area and labor force to achieve expanded production. It is not only inefficient, but also prone to land waste and environmental damage. Modern commodity agriculture has the characteristics of large scale, advanced technology and high degree of intensification. It not only has high production efficiency and good quality of agricultural products, but also has advantages in processing capacity and sales channels. However, there is no effective policy coordination to realize the intensification and refinement of production. Nor can it provide complete and effective policy support for talent training and development. It can be seen that no matter what kind of development process, countries all over the world attach great importance to the effective guidance of laws to the realization of policies for the development of rural talents, so as to ensure the development rights and interests of talents and realize rural revitalization. However, there are still differences among countries in the aspects of law formulation and policy measures.

(b) Differences in the construction of talent training systems

The specialized training systems of higher education in developed countries have become more and more complete. The special training of rural talents is instrumental in increasing the hematopoietic function of rural areas, and many countries have paid great attention to the cultivation and development of rural talents. However, it must be admitted that due to the large differences in the level of economic development among countries, the spatial and temporal distribution of educational resources is extremely unbalanced. There is no consensus on the policy system for the development of rural talents. How to build a training model suitable for the actual development of the country is the key to the cultivation of rural talents. Developed countries have a long process of industrialization in history, basically built a complete industrial production system, and the exploitation and utilization of resources have been at a high level. In the field of agricultural development in particular, agriculture has a high degree of mechanization and advanced production technology. Some developed countries also have the characteristics of both resource-based countries and developed countries, such as Australia and Canada, which have experienced a rapid development process in the process of agricultural development, and the training of rural talents is very complete. Developing higher education and vocational training is the key to enhancing the professional skills of rural talents. Through various forms of vocational training such as agricultural experiment stations, agricultural cooperatives, agricultural consulting services, as well as a comprehensive range of continuing education and training policies covering basic skills, professional skills and innovative skills. However, these are inseparable from the advanced characteristics of economic development in developed countries, where the per capita years of education are longer and human capital is abundant. In particular, the integration of urban and rural areas has resulted in the integration of urban and rural areas and the mutual promotion of workers and farmers. What developed countries are faced with is how to upgrade specialized education and refine training at the existing level.

Developing countries urgently need to build multi-level training systems. In the short to medium term, developing countries are in the process of economic catch- up, with a weak foundation for economic development and a poorly educated workforce, which leads them to engage in simple tasks with low returns. In particular, many developing countries are still agricultural countries with a low degree of industrialization, unable to drive the progress of production technology, and naturally unable to popularize mechanization on a large scale in the field of agricultural production. This requires local governments to give more consideration to the practical needs of consolidating the production base and improving the refinement of labor when formulating policies. At the same time, it is also necessary to walk on two legs, that is, personnel training and practical application should be closely linked. Therefore, different from the reform and development of higher education in developed countries, developing countries must continue to promote the widespread popularization of basic education while considering the popularization of higher education, and form a positive development characteristic of education training and social participation. A representative case comes from India. Through the formulation and implementation of a series of laws, regulations and policy measures, such as *Education for All Act* and *Salvo Shiksha Abyan Plan*, the government has provided all-round education and training services from basic education to higher education, and from vocational training to continuing education for rural talents. The Indian government has also established and improved a series of social organizations and civil groups, such as self-help groups, cooperatives, village committees, etc., to provide a platform and organizational form for rural talents to exchange and cooperate. The Indian government has also promoted rural talents to participate in public welfare activities such as community building, public services and environmental protection, thus enhancing their sense of social responsibility and citizenship. Sri Lanka's *National Development Plan for Vocational and Technical Education and Training (2023-2027) (NDP)* emphasizes the importance of quality and targeted skilled human resources for the country's economic progress. The vocational and technical education and training (TVET) sector, in particular, is given top priority in rural revitalization, which will support the development of various industries and service sectors and reduce unemployment and underemployment. The plan's emphasis on developing the TVET sector will further address the informal labor market and ultimately recognize their skills in the formal certification process.

(c) Differences in rural talent introduction and retention measures

Developed countries: market mechanism dominates. Faced with the development of industrialization, the urban-rural dual system has gradually become a problem that all countries must face in their development. Thanks to the development of industrialization and urbanization, many countries have experienced the process of rural human resources flowing into cities to meet the needs of industrial production. This leads to the lack of high-quality talents in rural development, so how to introduce human resources to serve the countryside has become a key issue. Policy guidance is one of the important ways to attract talents. Most developed countries have provided preferential policies in tax policy, talent evaluation mechanism, and transformation of scientific and technological achievements to lower the threshold for talents, especially high-end talents, to migrate to rural areas. The country should pay attention to the role of market forces, lower information barriers to farmers' employment, and increase support from social employment funds. The country should strengthen the personnel management system and give special treatment, priority support and incentives to outstanding personnel. In addition, these countries generally pay attention to professional technical support and introduce more technical talents to rural areas. Agricultural technical talents mainly include university professors, researchers in scientific research institutions, technical consultants and engineers. These talents are encouraged to set up science and technology demonstration sites in rural areas, lead farmers in scientific and technological experiments and popularization, and improve the efficiency and quality of agricultural production. At the same time, cooperation between universities and rural economies should be strengthened, and the transformation and promotion of scientific research results should be strengthened to provide better technical support for rural agricultural development. Infrastructure construction carried out in rural areas not only retains the natural features of the countryside, but also meets the needs of talents for quality of life. At the same time, the construction network of roads and transportation facilities between urban and rural areas is strengthened, which solves the worries of rural talents in the process of development.

Developing countries: Policy-led talent to serve rural areas. For developing countries, the backward rural development has seriously affected the willingness of talents to enter the countryside, and the backward professional technology is also in urgent need of talent introduction to achieve leapfrog development. This drives more countries to adopt policy incentives to directly guide more talents into rural areas. For example, Brazil's agricultural credit program, agricultural insurance program and other policies, and China's continuous improvement of the household registration system, social security system, labor market and other mechanisms have provided rural talents with market opportunities for migration and employment from the countryside to the city or from the city to the countryside, providing more employment support for rural talents. In order to strengthen the strong support of talents for rural revitalization, China has also introduced policies and measures such as "sending cadres to the countryside" and "pairing support" to realize the pairing help of developed areas and less developed areas. These include special Technical Envoys selected from universities, research institutes, vocational schools and other public institutions to carry out public welfare services in rural science and technology. By meeting the daily needs of talents and combining effective policies and measures, they have not only solved their worries, but also injected a strong impetus into rural revitalization. In other words, different from the developed countries to achieve talent introduction through the establishment of free market mechanisms, developing countries choose to achieve talent introduction through policy leadership.

(d) The difference of rural talent incentive methods

Developed countries: advocate talents to participate in rural governance. As mentioned above, the incentive of rural talents plays a great role in promoting talents to root in rural areas, serve and benefit the countryside. Most developed countries are inseparable from the characteristics of free market development, especially emphasizing the free market mechanism and effective government guidance in economic development, and at the same time, the democratization of governance goes deep into every link. As for the incentive of rural talents, more exploration has also been carried out from the political demands of talents. Through advocating social participation and rural autonomy, talents have more sense of ownership and participation in the process of rural construction. After the Second World War, the process of urbanization in France went deeper and deeper. Jean Fourasti, a famous French economist, described France from 1945 to 1975 as "thirty glorious years". During this period, the urbanization rate of France increased rapidly from 53.2% in 1946 to 72.9% in 1975, making France a developed industrial country in the world. However, a large number of farmers continued to emigrate, the problems of rural hollowing out, population aging, and population imbalance between urban and rural areas became more and more serious. Since then, France has realized the road of sustainable rural development through various policy interventions. In this process, France also links rural autonomy with talent development, forming a two-way coordinated policy guarantee mechanism, which can not only combine specialized farm production with enterprise management to form industrial advantages, but also realize the participation of talents in rural governance through rural autonomy. In addition, many developed Asian countries pay more attention to the combination of rural culture and talent feelings.

In developing countries, the government takes the lead to achieve effective incentives. Drawing on the successful experience of developed countries, many developing countries have also imitated in the process of talent incentive. India has leveraged the dominant role of rural communities by establishing various forms of community organizations, such as self-help groups, cooperatives and village committees. Skilling Pakistan's *2008-2012 National Skills Strategy Vision* is also highly motivating in the process of skills training for rural talents. Based on extensive international experience, it emphasizes consultation and cooperation among industry, private and public training providers, government and the public to promote talents to serve rural communities. In the process of exploring talent incentive methods, China has highlighted the successful experience of policy-led, such as the system of Technical Envoys. These practical policy tilting and guiding mechanisms are of great help to the legal income generation of rural talents and the protection of intellectual property rights, and further improve the fundamental guarantee for this group to serve the countryside.

(2) Comparison of different countries' policy models

According to the cases of rural talent development in various countries, rural talent policy can be divided into five policy models: policy guarantee type, government-led type, economic incentive type, technology cultivation type and facility improvement type (Table 2.10).

Policy support type. There are some similarities in the policies formulated by different countries to develop rural talents. For example, Kenya, Pakistan and Sri Lanka all pay attention to rural education and farmer skill training, especially Kenya also emphasizes education quality, education supervision and management, training and publicity. In addition, China's unique system of Technical Envoys also has relevant policies and support mechanisms for selecting and appointing rural Technical Envoys. Brazil's policies pay more attention to rural credit, marketing, risk management and agricultural support in four key industries to promote the development of professional farmers and agricultural modernization.

Government led type. Some countries play an obvious guiding and organizing role in the process of rural talent construction. For example, the Republic of Korea, Japan and Brazil all emphasize the close cooperation between governments, different departments, and between the government and the market, providing farmers with technical guidance and scientific and

Table 2.10   Comparison of talent policy models in different countries

Country	Policy support type	Government led type	Economic incentive type	Technological cultivation type	Facility improvement type
Japan		Clear government positioning, scientific policy guidance	Establish a promotion fund to stimulate talent cultivation; financial subsidies to support the development of agricultural talents	Organize training activities, cultivate reserve talents	
The Republic of Korea		Play the organizational role of the government		Strengthen the training mechanism for elite talents	Construction of village hall
Germany			Effective financial support	Favorable rural educational training	Improve the rural infrastructure construction
Canada			Direct funding of rural development projects, encourage individuals or organizations to start businesses in rural areas	Provide development opportunities for rural youth	Establish and improve the information service system for rural residents
China	Selection and appointment policy, support mechanism of technology special envoys			Technical training for farmers; cultivate rural talents; enhance endogenous human resources	
Brazil	Reasonable policies to ensure & support agriculture	Government-led, multiple participation; close cooperation		Perfect professional farmer cultivation organization system	

(Continued)

Country	Policy support type	Government led type	Economic incentive type	Technological cultivation type	Facility improvement type
Russia			State financial subsidies	Develop rural human resources	Strengthen the construction; upgrading rural infrastructure
Sri Lanka	Institutionalized training in poverty alleviation methods			Flexible and innovative training courses aimed at the plantation labour market and beneficiaries	Increase the number of rural vocational training centers
Pakistan	A comprehensive and systematic education policy		Free education and incentives		
Kenya	Relevant policies to ensure the effective implementation of the plan			Skills training for young people	
Ethiopia		Government led	Increase funding for education	Strengthen teachers' capacity building	Increase and improve educational facilities
Venezuela				Rural teacher training	

Source: The author collated according to relevant literature.

technological guidance for agricultural production, and improving management efficiency. In addition, Ethiopia's model also shows that the government plays an important role in the formulation of educational policies, curriculum setting, teaching standards setting, and supervision of educational management.

Economic incentives type. The funds used to stimulate the development of rural talents are from a wide range of sources, such as government finance, social donations, international aid and so on. In some countries, such as Russia, Pakistan and Japan, the funds are directly used to encourage rural residents to receive education, training or awards in the form of scholarships, grants, funds, etc. Or the funds are used to improve rural education facilities, increase employment opportunities for rural youth, and provide financial incentives for farmers, such as Germany and Canada.

Technology cultivation type. Technology cultivation is the most widely used of the five policy models. The government and relevant departments hold training courses, seminars and other activities to improve farmers' agricultural production technology, especially Japan and Germany not only emphasize theoretical knowledge, but also pay attention to practical skills training. In addition to technical education directly aimed at farmers, the Republic of Korea, Brazil, China and Germany also focus on the training of rural leaders and agricultural technology researchers, while Ethiopia and Venezuela also focus on the training of rural teachers.

Facilities improvement type. It is common to improve rural education facilities and services, such as increasing rural schools, corresponding educational facilities and introducing employment-related courses, so as to improve the educational opportunities, enrollment rates and employment opportunities of rural residents, such as Germany, Russia, Sri Lanka and Ethiopia. In addition, Canada has established and improved an information service system for rural residents to help farmers obtain information and consultation channels on rural youth projects and services, rural entrepreneurship and business, and reduce the information barriers to farmers' employment.

2. National and regional trends of rural talent development

(1) The construction of rural talent training system pays attention to actual needs

Talent is the main guarantee to realize rural revitalization, and the key is the cultivation and education of human resources. Existing experience shows that countries need to establish a complete system of rural talent training, including relevant vocational training and regular special training programs. It can realize the organic combination of agricultural theory and production practice, use scientific means to train high-quality farmers, and drive rural talents to become knowledgeable, scientific and professional. By comparing the talent training methods of different types of countries, it can be found that the greater heterogeneity determines the future development trend. Developed countries are committed to building various agricultural education and training institutions to improve farmers' professional literacy and technological capabilities. Farmers should not only learn the theory of agricultural production, but also engage in practical teaching. Among them, the practice is more mature in Japan and Germany. Japan's talent training workshops under the "One Village One Product" movement include one year of theoretical teaching and one year of practical teaching; Germany's "dual system" teaching system requires the combination of school education and enterprise practice, market-oriented, to cultivate professional farmers with broad agricultural knowledge and skills, as well as professional skills. Rural talents training in less developed countries and developing countries should focus more on consolidating agricultural basic education and quality education.

(2) Policy incentives and market mechanisms continue to integrate

It is not difficult to find that the development strategies of rural talents in various economies around the world can be roughly divided into two categories: building a complete policy system and giving play to the dominant position of the market. However, in the actual development process, the roles of these two can't be completely separated, but increasingly emphasize the integration of each other. How to achieve the cultivation, introduction, retention and incentive of rural talents should consider the development needs of talents, which can not only be achieved by the unified public policy type led by the government. In particular, with the diversification of economic development, talents' yearning for a better life also brings the diversification and diversification of demand, and the government is likely to fall into the "fatal conceit" situation by its own strength. Extensive social participation has become the common governance experience of all countries in the process of rural revitalization. The establishment of a government-society-enterprise-individual collaborative governance mechanism can effectively promote a better fit between rural talent development needs and labor supply. In addition, a free and flexible market mechanism has always been a development requirement emerging in depth under the background of economic globalization. However, in the global context, different economies have different levels of economic development. The market-oriented and innovation-oriented approach adopted by developed countries cannot be separated from the long-term accumulation of cutting-edge technologies and high human capital. It is obvious that these advanced experiences cannot be fully applied to developing countries. Therefore, in these countries, government policy guidance should be given full play. A strong policy system, combined with multiple and effective implementation measures, plays an extremely important leading role in the rapid realization of agricultural modernization and rural revitalization in developing countries. At the same time, the combination of the two can better realize the optimal allocation of resources at the national and regional levels and release the value of factors to the maximum. Focusing on countries around the world, a key path is to deeply build a "community of human destiny" for rural talent development. In the process of rural revitalization, countries should strengthen cooperation, establish a wide range of collaborative governance mechanisms for rural development, and effectively allocate human resources.

(3) Focus on equity in education

On the whole, countries at different stages of development pay attention to equity in education. First, equity in education for both sexes, and second, equity in education for urban and rural areas. Less developed countries, such as Sri Lanka, Pakistan and Ethiopia, place great emphasis on women's access to education while focusing on the improvement of rural education facilities, services and conditions. These countries have improved the quality of education for women by increasing the number of girls' schools and courses in rural areas and encouraging women to receive education. In addition to increasing women's educational knowledge through training, developed countries also emphasize the status of women in rural development. For example, Japan has set up women's business groups or clubs for mutual exchanges and discussions to improve the quality of production and management. The Republic of Korea emphasizes the equal status of women and men in the leadership of new villages.

(4) Supervision of teaching quality

Less developed countries, such as Pakistan, Kenya and Ethiopia, pay special attention to teaching quality supervision because their rural economies are more backward, leading to inadequate teaching facilities and services and poor pay for teachers, which in turn leads to low quality of teaching in rural areas. In these countries, while improving the quality of teaching, they also pay attention to teaching quality supervision. For example, Pakistan has established the Education Quality Assessment Organization, Kenya is supervised by the World Bank for training, and Ethiopia is supervised by the government for education policy making and curriculum development.

3. Policy implications for the future development of global rural talents

(1) Formulate relevant laws to ensure and encourage the development of rural talents

Whether it is Canada, Germany and other developed countries with advanced agricultural production, Brazil, Russia and other BRICS countries, or Sri Lanka, Pakistan and Kenya and other less developed countries, all have formulated relevant farmer education and training laws or policies to ensure the smooth progress of rural talent training. Therefore, China should also issue laws and regulations on farmer education and training as soon as possible, build a sound legal system and corresponding supporting policies, such as talent training, talent introduction, talent retention and talent incentive, and promote the development of rural talents through the guidance of laws and policies. Among them, the talent incentive can adopt political incentive, honor incentive, salary incentive, financial incentive, title evaluation incentive and other means to motivate talents to participate in rural construction and enhance the sense of pride and honor of rural talents.

(2) Pay attention to the cultivation and introduction of new farmers, and enhance the endogenous development power of rural areas

From the practice of various countries, on the one hand, foreign countries improve the quality education level of farmers by increasing rural basic education facilities and services, and cultivate and improve farmers' basic reading, writing and arithmetic abilities; on the other hand, through the development of agricultural skills training courses, cultivate farmers' agricultural knowledge and life skills, especially the cultivation of agricultural practice and production capacity. With the development strategy of rural revitalization, the development of new farmers has added vitality to the development of agriculture and rural areas. Therefore, China needs to build a new concept of agricultural talents to promote the development of rural talents. First, government should improve the opportunities, quality and efficiency of rural basic education, and take reasonable incentive measures to encourage rural residents to receive education. Second, government should pay attention to the professional training of farmers. While increasing the introduction of talents in the agricultural field, government should also pay attention to the training of local professional farmers to improve the ability of rural development.

(3) Establish a multifaceted and integrated farmer training system, with the government facilitating collaborative efforts among various stakeholders

Throughout the experience of rural talent training in developed countries, institutionalized and standardized farmer education and training systems have played a vital role. The department management mode which is isolated from each other is easy to reduce the efficiency of rural talent training and lead to the disconnection with the labor market. Therefore, China needs to strengthen farmer training and build a farmer education and training system with multi-level goals and diversified functions, which is planned by the government and coordinated by social organizations such as agricultural colleges, farmers' cooperatives and agricultural enterprises. The government should give full play to its functions of overall planning, coordination, supervision and financial support in rural personnel training. The training subjects should give full play to their comparative advantages, with clear responsibilities and powers and clear goals. And develop diversified training methods, teaching according to local conditions and aptitude.

(4) Optimize the environment for rural talent development and improve the quality of public facility services

Firstly, providing a superior living and working environment for rural talents is crucial, as it strengthens the region's soft power in attracting and retaining these individuals. Villages are expected to accelerate the construction of rural public infrastructure, promote the improvement of rural living environment, improve the livability of rural areas, narrow the gap between urban and rural life, and provide a good living and working environment for rural talents. Secondly, raise rural talents' sense of satisfaction for rural public services, and improve rural education, transportation, medical and other basic public services. Also, it is necessary to improve rural talents' satisfaction with rural public services, and give rural talents more welfare benefits in terms of salary, post establishment, title evaluation, so that talents can feel at ease to stay and work, as well as make more contributions to rural development.

(5) Create employment positions and opportunities catering to the skills and needs of rural talents

Long-term development of talents in rural areas hinges on the availability of more job positions and opportunities. Optimize the rational allocation and strategic integration of rural resources, and reshape the value chain of rural industries. The transformation from outdated farming methods to modern agricultural production requires a substantial pool of skilled talents, and the pace and quality of agricultural advancement necessitate expert guidance. Furthermore, upgrading the industrial structure can spur the emergence of new industrial models, generate additional employment opportunities, and empower more rural talents to secure "quality employment" and "satisfactory jobs".

◎ Chapter III International Rural Cultural Revitalization

Abstract

The revitalization of rural culture is an important element and strong support for rural revitalization. The proper protection and utilization of agricultural cultural heritage can stimulate the vitality of rural culture. China's public cultural construction in rural areas has laid a good and strong humanistic environment and cultural foundation for the development of grass-roots society in rural areas. Relying on the construction of key villages, localities have realized the creative transformation and innovative development of high-quality cultural resources in the countryside, driven the integration of rural industries, and become a typical example leading the upgrading and development of rural tourism. Many places have stepped up their efforts to build unique rural public cultural spaces, and the spiritual outlook of farmers has continued to improve, while the cohesion and attractiveness of villages have continued to rise. Rural festivals are an effective carrier for displaying agricultural civilization and folk culture, and a booster for developing rural tourism and booming rural economy. To deepen the construction of rural civilization, it is necessary to fully mobilize the enthusiasm and initiative of the majority of farmers to participate in it, to form a consciousness from the ideology, norms from the system, and atmosphere from the culture, so that the new civilized style will continue to nourish the happy life of the villagers. Taking into account the practice of various countries in rural cultural revitalization, insights can be drawn from the following: cultivating and expanding rural cultural subjects, establishing a multifaceted linkage mechanism, strengthening project construction and financial support, coordinating the protection of rural cultural resources, and strengthening rural cultural and artistic training.

I. Current status of rural cultural revitalization

The revitalization of rural culture is an important element and strong support for rural revitalization. To promote rural revitalization, it is necessary to both shape and forge the soul, continuously enrich the people's spiritual world and strengthen their spiritual power, better cultivate civilized rural customs, good family customs and simple folk customs, raise the level of civilization in rural society and bring about a new civilized atmosphere in the countryside. Therefore, it is of great significance to analyze the current situation and characteristics of rural cultural revitalization in major countries of the world according to the different fields of international rural cultural governance, in order to develop the practice of international rural cultural revitalization.

1. Protection and utilization of important agricultural cultural heritage

Globally Important Agricultural Heritage Systems (GIAHS), are conceptually equivalent to World Heritage Sites. The Food and Agriculture Organization of the United Nations (FAO) defines it as "the unique land use systems and agricultural landscapes formed under long-term synergistic evolution and dynamic adaptation between rural areas and their environments, which are rich in biodiversity and can meet the needs of local socio-economic and cultural development, and are conducive to the promotion of regional sustainable development". The proper protection and utilization of agricultural cultural heritage can stimulate the vitality of native cultures, transform rural cultural resources into cultural dividends, promote the deep integration of rural culture and tourism, promote the construction of rural civilization and the construction of ecological civilization, as well as maintain food security and food safety, and protect the diversity of species, food varieties and cultures, and thus provide a strong boost for the comprehensive revitalization of the countryside as soon as possible.

In recent years, China has made great progress in the top-level design of the protection and utilization of agricultural cultural heritage, with the *Measures for the Management of China's Important Agricultural Cultural Heritage (for Trial Implementation)* formally implemented in 2014, the central government's 'Document No.1'in 2016 explicitly proposing to "carry out a census of the agricultural cultural heritage and its protection", and the *Opinions on Promoting the Cultural Industry to Enable Rural Revitalization* in 2022 proposing to "support the construction of farming cultural experience sites at eligible sites". In 2022, the number of globally important agricultural cultural heritage sites recognized in China will be the highest in the world, and the Ministry of Agriculture and Rural Development has recognized six batches of 138 important agricultural cultural heritage sites in China, and the heritage sites of GIAHS have made full use of this "Golden Signboard", and on the basis of effective protection, fully explored the biological resources, cultural heritage, and landscape advantages of GIAHS, and transformed the green water and green mountains of GIAHS into "golden mountains and silver mountains". Diebu County in Gansu Province has strengthened the infrastructure construction of agricultural and cultural heritage sites, carried out the construction of tourism infrastructure such as roads, viewing platforms, toilets, and trestles in Zagana Scenic Area, and established stone monuments and signboards for the protection of the GIAHS to clearly define the scope of protection and content. Aohan Banner in Inner Mongolia vigorously develops dry farming, forming a specialty miscellaneous grain industry, while relying on the huge production of cereal grass to feed meat donkeys to create a donkey industry. Shandong Xiajin in-depth exploration of the development of mulberry resources, research and development and production of mulberry fruit wine, dried mulberry fruit, mulberry leaf tea and other specialty food, health care products, attracted a large number of mulberry product processing enterprises to invest in the plant. At present, the domestic GIAHS heritage around the policy support, brand building, industrial development, publicity and promotion, digital construction and other aspects of the formation of a distinctive development model.

2. Situation of public cultural service system in villages

Looking around the world, the Communist Party of China has always attached great importance to the construction of rural culture, and in the process of switching from the construction of a new socialist countryside to the strategy of revitalizing the countryside, the only consistent requirement and goal has been the "civilization of the countryside". Against this background, the Party has always attached great importance to the construction of rural public culture, placing it in the strategic context of the modernization and development of national governance. The report of the Twentieth National Congress of the CPC pointed out the implementation of a national digitalization strategy, the improvement of a modern public cultural service system, the innovative implementation of cultural projects to benefit the people, the improvement of the level of public services, and the enhancement of the balance and accessibility of public cultural services. At the same time, the Outline of the Fourteenth Five-Year Plan states that priority should be given to the development of agriculture and rural areas, and that the revitalization of the countryside should be promoted in a comprehensive manner.

At present, under the guidance of the cultural construction policy set out in the No. 1 Document of the Central Government in successive years, the construction of public culture in rural areas of China has continued to develop, laying a good and thick humanistic environment and cultural foundation for the development of grass-roots society in the countryside, cultivating the spiritual and cultural homeland of the peasants, and enriching the daily lives of the peasant masses and their norms. At the same time, it has become an integral part of the country's overall cultural construction, providing better modern rural spiritual and cultural resources for the country's modernization. Firstly, the rural public cultural service system has been gradually improved. The rural public cultural service system is a comprehensive system consisting of cultural supply institutions, cultural benefit policy programs, and cultural service mechanisms.

According to a field survey of a number of townships in Henan Province, after a series of policies and measures such as cultural poverty alleviation policies and rural cultural revitalization and other sustained construction, each township has built a grassroots comprehensive cultural service center capable of completing public cultural projects at all levels and providing public cultural services such as exhibitions and activities for party members and the general public. The villages under the jurisdiction of the townships have basically built cultural activity rooms and cultural squares for villagers' recreational activities. The construction and improvement of the basic public cultural service system at the village and township levels has greatly enriched the amateur cultural life of villagers. Secondly, the innovation of public cultural services in villages is rich and diversified. First, in the form of service innovation. The public cultural service mechanism of mass ordering, team ordering, and government ordering is operated more effectively through cultural digitization, and has begun to give birth to new cultural spaces, where rural residents can obtain all kinds of cultural resources through the Internet; in addition, the organizational form of the service has also changed, and a large number of mass cultural organizations have been established under the guidance of the government to gradually provide public cultural services. Secondly, in terms of innovation in service content. The most obvious embodiment of public culture and traditional culture, local culture, national culture and other innovative exploration of integration and development, effectively cracked the "pan-ideological" thinking limitations, not only to promote the main theme, but also to achieve the depth of the local culture excavation. Both the form and content of the service innovation, to varying degrees, have enriched the connotation and social value of rural public culture services, to protect and realize the cultural rights and interests of the villagers, but also effectively responded to the strategic demands of the rural cultural revitalization and the national governance of the public order and morals of the countryside[64].

---

64   Xiaojing Han. Development status and optimization path of rural public cultural services [J]. Rural-Agriculture-Farmer (A Edition), 2022 (4): 63-64.

3. Development of rural cultural tourism industry

Rural cultural tourism is a new model of rural industry for the integrated development of rural culture and tourism industry, which has changed the traditional growth mechanism and method, realized the leapfrog development and innovation of the industry, and can effectively promote the integration of one, two and three industries and drive the development of rural economy. Promoting the high-quality development of rural cultural tourism is an inherent requirement of rural industrial development and an important hand in realizing rural revitalization and development. In recent years, many countries have relied on local ecology, agriculture, native culture and other resources to develop special products and routes, and constantly enhance the charm of rural tourism. Returning to nature and experiencing local customs, the countryside is becoming an increasingly popular tourism space for tourists from all countries.

Foreign rural tourism from the 1960s began to develop to the present, has tended to mature and accumulated successful experience, many foreign developed countries have formed a relatively rich system of rural tourism types, and its rural tourism products cover a rich content, involving a wide range[65]. The town of Grasse, the perfume capital of France, named after the novel *Perfume*, has a developed perfume industry, with the oldest perfume processing plant of Flora, as well as famous perfume processing plants such as Molinar and Jalima, which is an important origin and raw material supplying place of French perfume. The origin shopping experience and special customized service have laid the foundation for Grasse to build a deep perfume experience route; the perfume museum and perfume factory have made Grasse a real perfume experience center. Daesau Village, Jingshan County, the Republic of Korea,highlights the local flavor of Korean kimchi and daejang bibimbap as its core signature. Utilizing local indigenous materials and adopting traditional craftsmanship to make healthy food to manufacture dashi, it is in line with

---

65 Hongguo Tian. Research on rural tourism development practice at home and abroad [J]. Science and Technology Information, 2014, (1): 242-243.

the modern health science, and also allows visitors to visit the original living condition of dashi village and inherit the folk culture characteristics. France Provence organically combines agricultural production with ecological agriculture construction as well as tourism, leisure and sightseeing, and establishes a multifunctional tourism area integrating production, processing, commerce, sightseeing, entertainment, culture and vacation, etc. The core tourism projects and tourism products include idyllic scenery sightseeing tours, wine winery experience tours, perfume workshop experience tours, and so on.

Domestically, rural tourism is also increasingly popular among tourists and has become a consumption hotspot, which has strongly driven villagers around the country to get rich and increase their income, and has also become a major pillar industry to pull the revitalization of the countryside. On the one hand, the number of rural tourists and tourism revenue is growing rapidly, beautiful scenery, ecological beauty of the countryside attraction gradually enhanced; on the other hand, relying on the rich cultural resources of the countryside, various types of rural tourism brands continue to emerge, a picture of a hot and vivid rural tourism scroll is slowly unfolding. Domestic rural tourism has entered the era of "legalization", and the leading role of planning in the development of rural tourism has been highly valued, with the formation of a policy system that includes guiding the direction of development, solving bottlenecks, and promoting poverty alleviation in many dimensions. At the same time, the significance of "ruralness" and "localness" in rural tourism has been gradually highlighted, emphasizing the importance of accurately grasping the local characteristic elements, fully exploring the folk culture mainly based on the residence, costumes, food, rituals, amusement, etc., and based on which to promote innovation, increase the number of accompanying products and derivatives, and build a tourism brand with strong regional characteristics to ensure the "shape" of rural tourism. Rural tourism "shape" and "spirit" at the same time. In fact, the national rural tourism key villages cover a large number of traditional villages, historical villages, characteristic ethnic villages and other resources. Relying on the construction of key villages, localities have realized the creative transformation and innovative development of rural high-quality cultural resources, driven the integration of rural industries, and become a typical example to lead the development of quality upgrading of rural tourism.

4. Construction of cultural spaces with international rural characteristics

The *Opinions on Promoting the High-Quality Development of Public Cultural Services*, jointly issued by the Ministry of Culture and Tourism, the National Development and Reform Commission and the Ministry of Finance, suggests that "based on the characteristics of urban and rural areas, we should create public cultural spaces with distinctive features and taste, and expand the coverage of public cultural services to enhance their effectiveness." Many places have stepped up their efforts to build distinctive rural public cultural spaces, with farmers' spirits improving and the cohesion and attractiveness of villages continuing to rise.

In many rural areas of China, revolutionary culture, national culture, historical culture is rich, and these are important resources for upgrading public cultural spaces. Whether it is Henan Mengzhou City, the old seedling bookstore, or Zhejiang Wenzhou City, Longxi Art Museum, are to remember nostalgia to create a new cultural carrier, culture and history in this condensed, the space carries the story, the building can also be read. At the same time, distinctive public cultural space to play "cultural tourism" effect, can be for rural tourism, red tourism, traditional cultural experience to enrich the rich content. Different regions have adopted different approaches according to local conditions. Some areas will be on the verge of disappearing rural farming equipment, folk skills, folk rituals, customs and people to dig out, in a living way to inheritance and innovation, not only to produce considerable economic benefits, but also the protection, inheritance and revival of traditional culture; some areas of the overall planning of the public cultural space theme, the content of the different spaces are both differentiated and through the intrinsic link, so as to create a bead into a chain of rural tourism and red tourism routes; some regions have launched "four-and-a-half-point classrooms", summer and winter vacation custodial classes and other services to address the pain points of caring for left-behind children. Based on their own characteristics, localities are actively promoting the upgrading and upgrading of public spaces in rural areas, making public cultural spaces with value and content the cultural landmarks and spiritual homes of villages, continuing the cultural lineage, and fostering a civilized countryside, a good family culture, and a simple folk culture.

In Germany, cultural life is more active in the countryside, where cultural diversity and richness can be found everywhere. Rural areas have their own crafts, industries and services, and can also provide space for natural beauty and cultural recreation, and their settlement characteristics and cultural landscapes have shaped a unique German image. The German government supports the development of rural culture and the enrichment of the supply of cultural products in a number of ways. The German Council for Cultural and Media Affairs launched the "Culture in the Countryside" promotion program in 2019, which provides financial support for cultural infrastructure located in communities with a population of less than 20,000 people, and uses cultural venues as public spaces for gathering and interaction. In the aftermath of the new pneumonia outbreak, the agency also supported the operation of rural cinemas, libraries, folklore museums, and cultural centers through its Emergency Assistance Program. In addition, mobile models have been developed to enable cultural provision to reach rural populations, as in the case of the State Museum System in Berlin, which has brought the neighboring Brandenburg countryside closer to the museums of the big cities through the provision of services.

Japan has further improved the construction of rural culture through the "town-building movement". In the "town-building movement", first, emphasis is placed on the promotion of traditional culture. For example, in the case of architecture, traditional architectural features are adhered to, and no anti-traditional or oddly shaped buildings are allowed. Therefore, the architecture of houses in every village in Japan has a strong traditional flavor. At the same time, almost every village has a few or a dozen old residences recognized by the government as cultural protection units, and the government provides subsidies for repairs and protection. Secondly, public cultural services are emphasized. In Japan, every town has a civic hall, equivalent to a public cultural service center, where a large number of public cultural and educational services are provided. In addition, most villages now have their own village museums. Thirdly, they emphasize the provision of culture at different levels. In the "town-building movement", rural social pensions have been transformed from a purely financial support type to a care-service type, so that rural elderly people not only receive pensions, but also receive all-round life care and spiritual and cultural comfort, with life care becoming more specialized and cultural services more targeted. The "town-building movement" has promoted the improvement and upgrading of Japanese villages on multiple levels, including the environment, industry, public services and spiritual culture.

5. Construction of international cultural festivals with rural characteristics

Rural festivals have gradually become an indispensable part of rural tourism, and it can be said that rural festivals are the seasoning in rural tourism and the most intuitive way for tourists to feel the rural life and culture. Rural festivals are based on idyllic scenery and traditional culture, moderately developing entertainment projects, integrating entertainment, leisure and sightseeing into a new tourism project, promoting rural revitalization through festivals, inheriting traditional rural culture, and their local characteristics are remarkable.

Rural festivals and activities is to show the agricultural civilization and folk culture of the effective carrier, but also the development of rural tourism, prosperous rural economy booster. Shandong binzhou jujube festival has become famous for the province and abroad "gold medal festival", in the festival tourism successfully organized, not only enhance the popularity of shandong jujube, but also promote binzhou at home and abroad attention, at the same time drive the development of the whole region's tourism industry. Zhejiang watermelon lamp festival is Pinghu's traditional folk culture celebration, in order to celebrate the local watermelon harvest, every year at the end of September and early October to hold a large-scale watermelon lamp cultural tourism festival. During the watermelon lamp cultural festival will not only set up the traditional ornamental projects, but also organized "thousands of people carve melon lamp competition", watermelon creativity "beautiful feast race", cultural and creative exhibition, show and so on activities, attracting a large number of tourists to come to watch and play. Foreign countries also have many activities and festivals dedicated to celebrating the harvest, and through these rural festivals for the destination to attract a large number of tourists, driving the development of local tourism, such as Mexico's carrot festival, Polish Harvest Festival, the French Lemon Festival and so on. In addition to festivals developed with agricultural creativity, there are also many festivals developed based on local characteristics and cultural resources to further utilize the advantages of local characteristics and resources to attract more tourists.

6. Construction of international rural customs and traditions

Rural revitalization, rural civilization is a guarantee. To deepen the construction of rural civilization, we should fully mobilize the enthusiasm and initiative of the majority of farmers to participate in the ideological formation of self-awareness, the formation of norms on the system, and the formation of an atmosphere on the atmosphere, so that a new civilized style of civilization continues to nourish the happy life of the townspeople.

In the country, in recent years, with the rural customs to build a civilized countryside work to promote a solid, civilized countryside around the trend is growing stronger. Nowadays, many villages are cluttered with unauthorized buildings, abandoned fences into a well-designed micro-garden, micro-vegetable gardens, micro-orchards; countryside stage to a good play "sent" to the countryside, "planted" into the hearts of villagers; farm bookstore to knowledge of the people, benefiting the people, enriching the people! The rural bookstore is a cultural "granary" in the countryside; "civilized families", "ten-star civilized households", "ten filial piety stars", etc. are selected to make advanced models emerge frequently. Selection so that advanced models emerge frequently, civilized countryside constantly renewed new atmosphere. Feixiang District, Handan City, Hebei Province, each village has formulated a detailed and clear village rules and regulations, for star civilized households and other honorary villagers can enjoy free medical checkups, entrepreneurial loans, and many other preferential policies, such a clear standard of the village rules and regulations, operability, and effectively improve the enthusiasm of the farmers to participate in the construction of civilized countryside style. Heshui County in Gansu Province pays attention to the realistic needs of farmers, and helps age-appropriate rural youth broaden their circle of friends by organizing youth fellowships and other means, which are widely welcomed by young people. Aiming at the realistic problems in the lives of rural folks, practical and effective approaches have been consistently adopted to do practical things, promote reforms and make up for shortcomings, gradually relieving them of their worries and promoting their more proactive participation in the construction of a civilized township.

II. Typical modes of rural cultural revitalization

1. Cultural tourism-enabled rural revitalization mode

(1) New Castle Village, Portugal - Protecting traditional villages and passing on cultural heritage

New Castle Village is located in the city of Fontaine, Brancuburg District, Portugal, and is situated in the Galdunia Mountains. Overlooking the village from the top of a lush hill, the many gothic buildings made of granite create a picture of serenity and beauty. 2022 New Castle has been selected as one of the "Best Villages for Tourism" by the United Nations World Tourism Organization, an award that recognizes the village's strong commitment to tourism and the preservation of the village's architectural, natural and cultural heritage. and cultural heritage.

In recent years, Portugal has vigorously developed rural tourism, and the Portuguese Historical Village Network has played an important role in it. In 2007, the Portuguese Historical Villages Network was established and managed by the Portuguese Historical Villages Tourism Development Association. It includes 12 ancient villages with unique historical and cultural heritage in the Bella region, with the aim of restoring and promoting the region's historical heritage, promoting investment in tourism infrastructure, developing tourism products with local characteristics, and improving the living standards of village residents. Due to the presence of two important archaeological sites - the ancient Roman Bathhouse and the defensive fortifications left over from the Bronze Age, the new castle village has also been included in the Portuguese historical village network.

With the support of the Network of Historic Villages of Portugal and the Municipality of Fondão, the village of Novo Châteauneuf launched in 2014 a social, cultural and educational project called "Creative Storytelling", with the creation of a Creative Workshop, which will help local children to learn about the history of the village and will attract more tourists to visit it. In April 2022, the Network of Historic Villages of Portugal in April 2022, the Network of Historic Villages of Portugal launched a pilot project on "Inclusive and Sustainable Transport" in the village of Novo Castelo, making it the first village in Portugal to achieve 100% zero-emission transport. Since the launch of the project, the village has installed electric vehicle charging stations and a fleet of electric vehicles to provide train station connections and mobility services for visitors and residents.

(2) Wales, UK-Developing specialty farm tourism according to local conditions

The tourism experience program of the "Good Day" farm in Wales, United Kingdom, combines local characteristics and develops rural activities such as shepherding sheep, bathing animals and weaving wicker baskets, which have been well received by many tourists. When affected by the epidemic, the farm also developed a new online business - according to customer demand, remote display of the farm's animal life scene.

In the United Kingdom, most of the rural tourism relies on farm resources, with some focusing on sightseeing agriculture and others on in-depth experience. Since the 1960s and 1970s, farms have become an important choice for British urban residents to travel and relax on vacation. After the 1980s, the infrastructure and public services in the British countryside were gradually improved, and rural tourism developed towards standardization and specialization. In the mid-1990s, 1/4 of the British farms carried out tourism business or provided tourism-related services, and agricultural attractions, together with theme parks and industrial attractions, became the three most popular attractions in Britain at that time. In order to better realize the sustainable development of rural tourism, in recent years, some natural scenic spots in the countryside have taken measures to limit the flow of traffic, designated nature reserves and regularly inspected and restored, and the local authorities also plan to further invest in new energy transportation to reduce environmental pollution.

(3) Bali, Indonesia - Organic combination of nature and humanity

Ubud is a major painting and art town in Bali. The town has a unique style of architecture and is dotted with various types of art stores and museums. For example, Mario Blanco, the Spanish painter who pioneered the Balinese oil painting genre, lived here for a long time, and his early studio and showroom have been converted into an oil painting museum. The town is surrounded by rice paddies, with a patchwork of green seedlings and quaint village houses. Tourists from all over the world enjoy themselves on foot or by bicycle. The quiet idyllic scenery and the ubiquitous artistic atmosphere make this place a desirable place for many tourists and artists. Not only Ubud, Bali as an island mainly for tourism and agriculture, many places have better preserved the countryside and historical and cultural monuments, which is also an important reason why tourists from all over the world prefer Bali.

Since the 1990s, the local government has launched a "sustainable development plan" to increase the promotion of rural tourism, emphasizing that preserving cultural characteristics is the basis for sustainable development. The government has attracted tourists to the countryside to experience the local culture through the development of villages with special characteristics such as painter's villages, batik villages and wood carving villages. Currently, 146 villages in Bali have developed rural tourism.

2. Rural festival triggering mode

(1) Japanese Rice Planting Festival

In Japan, the culture of rice cultivation is deeply rooted. Rice-planting is an important agricultural activity for rice cultivation. A grand ceremony has long been held throughout Japan during the rice-planting season to welcome the god of grain and to pray for a good harvest. At the beginning of the 12th century, this ceremony evolved into an important local festival, the Rice Planting Festival. Today, rice-planting festivals (also known as "Oshida festivals") are held every year during the rice-planting season in many parts of Japan, and although the content of the festivals varies from place to place, they generally include welcoming the god of the valley and rice-planting. The rice-planting festival of Shima City in Mie Prefecture, the rice-planting festival of Sumiyoshi Taisha Shrine in Osaka, and the rice-planting festival of Katori Jingu Shrine in Chiba Prefecture are known as the three most famous rice-planting festivals in Japan, and they have been inscribed on the list of Important Intangible Cultural Properties of Japan.

The Rice Planting Festival of Shima City in the southern mountains of Japan is held in June every year. There are four celebrations:

The first is the welcoming of the god of rice, in which villagers dressed in traditional Japanese costumes, wearing masked flower crowns and hats, dance traditional folk dances to welcome the god of rice in an ancient ceremony; the second is the grand parade of oxen, whose backs are decorated with colorful flags representing each household, and which walk slowly through the main market; and the third, which is also the highlight of the rice-planting festival of Shima, is the "fetching bamboo god event" that takes place before the rice-planting. The third event, which is also the highlight of the Shima City Rice Planting Festival, is the "Bamboo Taking Event," in which men engage in mud fights, learn to leap frogs, and snatch fans from bamboo poles in the rice paddies bare-chested, which is a lively event; and after the comical mud fights, the next event is the elegant and dignified rice-planting ceremony. In the sound of drums and music, the villagers ignite the rice straw in the paddy field, the oxen start to pull the plow to plow the field, and people pray loudly for the coming of the God of the Valley while planting rice seedlings in the field; after planting the rice seedlings, they send off the God in unison, praying for the God of the Valley to bless a good year.

Rice-planting Festival is to develop the traditional farming activities in the countryside into an agricultural festival, and on the basis of retaining the original juice and leaves of the ceremony, it also incorporates humorous performance components, making the festival more ornamental, so as to achieve the purpose of attracting tourists.

(2) California Strawberry Festival

California, with its unique coastal climate and sandy loam soil, is considered to be the world's most suitable region for growing strawberries, and up to 90% of the strawberries produced in the United States come from the state. As early as 1983, in an effort to promote the region and showcase its uniqueness, an Oxnard City Councilman proposed holding a strawberry festival in Oxnard and organized a team to co-program the festival, design a logo, and name it the "California" Strawberry Festival, reflecting California's growing reputation. In 1984, the new California Strawberry Festival debuted in Channel Islands Harbor. The goal was simple: to honor the local strawberry crop by inviting the public to join in the festivities, generate revenue to ensure next year's festival, and give as much back to the community as possible. The inaugural event was so well received that the first year's proceeds benefited 30 nonprofit organizations. Since then, the California Music Festival has become a local tradition, an annual event that has grown in size and variety, and in 1991, the festival was moved from the Channel Islands Harbor to Strawberry Fields in University Park, providing more space for the ever-increasing number of guests. In 2001, the festival evolved into a public benefit nonprofit with an all-volunteer board of directors, an organization established exclusively for social, educational, recreational or charitable purpose. The charity is a group of like-minded individuals from all walks of life who continue to contribute their ideas to the Strawberry Festival.

Now one of the top 10 events in the nation, the California Strawberry Festival is held annually on May 18 and 19. With more than 50 food and beverage booths, 200 crafts and a variety of performances, and cooking demonstration booths, you'll enjoy everything about strawberries for food and drink and the arts. It attracts more than 50,000 people each year and, as of 2019, is in its 36th year, raising more than $4.5 million for local charities in fundraising events that benefit more than 20 southern regional organizations.

3. Creative design empowering rural revitalization mode

In recent years, the way in which art contributes to rural revitalization is changing from "blood transfusion" to "blood creation", and high-quality cultural resources are constantly being transformed into kinetic energy for the sustainable development of the countryside.

(1) Transforming beautiful and livable spaces

Rooted in native traditions and intermingled with rural life, in recent years, the concept of art and design to help revitalize the countryside has been maturing and the practice has become richer, promoting the countryside to become a civilized and harmonious space with richness of things and heart, and a beautiful and livable space.

Systematic design and renovation, so that the traditional village "live" up, "fire" up. After systematic combing, restoration, reconstruction or new construction, Guizhou Province, Qianxinan Buyi and Miao Autonomous Prefecture, Ceheng County, Banwan Village, now becomes the province's rural tourism key village. The staggered hanging footstools, blending with the green hills, are picturesque; new public spaces such as pavilions and small squares enhance communication among villagers; the Buyi Opera Cultural Heritage Base, theaters and earthenware kilns inherit the vernacular veins and enrich the cultural life of the countryside... Designer remodeling has stimulated the vitality of the ancient villages. Like Songyang County, Lishui City, Zhejiang Province, "Save the old house action", Luoqi Town, Yubei District, Chongqing municipality Yangjiacao traditional village protection and development projects, the ancient villages jumped into suitable for travel and livable new rural villages, and the villagers' quality of life has been greatly improved.

(2) Stimulating the vitality of local culture

The pace of revitalizing traditional crafts has been accelerated, and an innovative trend of "local manufacturing" has been formed. With the deepening of the concept of "productive protection", hundreds of "national demonstration bases for the productive protection of intangible cultural heritage" have come into being, and more than 10 traditional craft workstations have been set up one after another, so that rural crafts have been better protected and inherited. At the same time, representative inheritors of intangible cultural heritage projects have played a leading role, not only in promoting the creative transformation and innovative development of traditional crafts, but also in actively helping to build villages. Some other regions have formulated relevant policies and taken positive measures to promote the docking of non-legacy to modern life and highlight the new charm of non-legacy. In Guizhou, some enterprises have adopted the "company + farmers" mode of operation, with farmers as the main body of creation, so that traditional handicrafts such as Miao embroidery and batik have become fashionable, and some of the products have been put on the stage of fashion, which has led to local employment. In the 2022 Beijing International Design Week "China Traditional Crafts Revitalization Theme Design Exhibition" and the "Connecting Modern Life, Blooming Charming Brilliance" themed non-legacy publicity and display activities, the excitement of integrating traditional skills and patterns into daily life is on display everywhere.

4. Rural handicraft revitalization mode

(1) Minakami-machi, Japan - A town of artisans with "one village, one product"

Located in Gunma Prefecture, Japan, Minakami Town is surrounded by mountains, which give it a beautiful landscape, but also make farming difficult, and intensive agriculture cannot be carried out here. In 1990, the Minakami Town government proposed the "Rural Park Concept", where the whole town would become a wide-area park, maximizing local tourism resources and integrating agriculture with tourism and leisure. The entire town of Minakami will become a wide-area park, maximizing local tourism resources and integrating agriculture with tourism and recreation.

When Minakami-machi began planning for the construction of the "Craftsmen's Village," the basic policy was to preserve historical sites, inherit craft traditions, and promote Japanese food culture. In addition, the tourism program was divided according to the characteristics of the area, and the "Artisan's Village" was created by uniting the tourism experience areas that exhibit rural culture and pass on traditional rural crafts, and by inheriting and promoting the traditional crafts culture of the area, more than 20 traditional crafts workshops were established, including pecan carving and painting, straw weaving, wood weaving, and ceramics.

Minakami-machi, which closely combines agriculture and tourism, has taken a new path of independent development in the face of the shrinking of traditional agriculture, and the "Craftsmen's Village," which focuses on experiential tourism, has been widely acclaimed and recognized by the Japanese government, winning various awards, including the Excellence Award for the Comfortable Countryside Competition held by the Japan Land Agency and the Craftsmen's Award for Excellence from the Ministry of Construction. It has been recognized by the Japanese government with various awards, including the "Award of Excellence in Comfortable Rural Competition" by the Japan Land Office and the "Award of Excellence in Handicraft Production" by the Ministry of Construction.

5. Digital culture-enabled rural revitalization mode

(1) Jizhou District, Tianjin City - Bringing rural cultural tourism to the cloud

Over the years, the rural cultural and tourism industry in Jishui District of Tianjin has been continuously strengthened. China Unicom has fully leveraged its advantages in network, technology, products, and services to support the construction of a digital countryside, creating a new quality productivity for the development of the cultural and tourism industry in Jishui District and contributing intellectual and digital strength to the revitalization of the countryside, illuminating a new card for a smart cultural and tourism town.

Tianjin's Jishui District has a long history and a profound cultural heritage, known as the "thousand-year-old county, city of mountains and waters, and the garden of Beijing and Tianjin." In spring, enjoying the scenery, strolling through the fields, staying in bed-and-breakfasts, and going for picking have become the highlights of tourism in Jishui. However, looking back a few years ago, there were still issues with the rural tourism in Jishui, such as single promotional methods, inefficient management platforms, and weak service capabilities. China Unicom assisted Jishui in building a digital rural platform to consolidate the information foundation for the development of agriculture and rural areas, and officially launched the "Cloud Shangjizhou" project in 2022 to help solve the pain points in the development of Jishui's countryside and to create a smart tourism card for Jishui.

"Yun Shang Jizhou" is based on the Edge Intelligent Business Platform independently designed by China Unicom, fully integrating the cultural and tourism resources of rural tourism and related industries, building a tourism industry database, and achieving multi-dimensional, three-dimensional, and highly accurate promotion. It provides tourists with professional tourism information, personalized product services, and cutting-edge technological experiences, creating a one-stop, comprehensive smart tourism service covering "food, accommodation, transportation, touring, shopping, and entertainment." The platform not only offers convenience to tourists but also provides digital and intelligent management tools for merchants, covering areas such as scenic spots, hotels, cultural and creative industries, boutique bed-and-breakfasts, farmhouses, picking gardens, agricultural product sales, and Jishui specialties. At present, the local life module of "Yun Shang Jizhou" has covered more than 500 stores in various industries, making a positive contribution to the revitalization of the local rural economy and the increase of farmers' income.

(2) Shandong - Digital technology helps rural intangible cultural heritage enter the market

The emerging digital formats, including online live streaming, are bringing huge attention and considerable economic benefits to rural intangible cultural heritage in Shandong. In response to the trend of digital technology development, the cultural and tourism departments in Shandong province are doing a good job in exploring and organizing intangible cultural heritage resources, and on the other hand, building platforms, facilitating sales, and expanding influence, making intangible cultural heritage an important helper for rural cultural revitalization.

Since 2019, the Shandong Provincial Cultural Museum (Shandong Intangible Cultural Heritage Protection Center) has upgraded its "Shandong Public Cultural Cloud" platform, making the exhibition and broadcasting of rural intangible cultural heritage an important part of the platform. In recent years, Shandong has conducted multiple large-scale surveys of intangible cultural heritage resources and found that many intangible cultural heritage projects in rural areas have high market attention, but the promotion and promotion are not in place, and the combination with digital creativity is not strong enough. To this end, the "Shandong Public Culture Cloud" integrates various resources, links with cultural centers at the city and county levels throughout the province, promotes the entry of representative local intangible cultural heritage projects into the platform, regularly showcases and plans online experiential activities, and the effect is very good.

The old area of Zaozhuang Cultural Museum has become a window for the external dissemination of local rural intangible cultural heritage after design and exhibition in the past two years. With the assistance of the digital live streaming platform of the Zaozhuang Cultural Museum, the intangible cultural heritage workshop operated by Zhang Yong, the inheritor of the Peach Blossom Micro Sculpture Intangible Cultural Heritage, has achieved significant results. Not only has the order volume of the workshop been increasing year by year, but it has also successfully attracted students from all over the country to join in learning. The development of digital technology is an important opportunity for the creative transformation and innovative development of intangible cultural heritage resources. Currently, the application of digital technology in the field of intangible cultural heritage mainly focuses on dissemination and promotion, effectively expanding the influence and awareness of intangible cultural heritage. With the continuous progress and innovation of technology, digital technology may be more deeply integrated into various aspects of intangible cultural heritage protection and inheritance. Especially, it will play an increasingly crucial role in the research and development design of non heritage cultural and creative products, as well as the census, recording, and digital archiving of intangible cultural heritage resources. This not only provides strong technical support for the creative transformation and innovative development of intangible cultural heritage, but also opens up new possibilities for the comprehensive protection and inheritance of precious cultural heritage of humanity.

6. Rural farming culture revival mode

(1) Agricultural systems in the oases of the Algerian wadi - maintaining the original ecological attributes of the countryside

The village of Doud, located in the southern region of the Sahara Desert in Africa, the oasis built by the people of Doud is known as the Algerian Wadi Oasis Agricultural System, which has been around since the 15th century. At that time, the nomadic people of the desert adapted their unique water management methods to the local conditions and combined them with their knowledge of the desert by digging more than 10-meter-deep ditches around areas with shallow groundwater sources and planting date palms in the ditches. Herders planted fruit trees, vegetables, medicinal herbs and shrubs under the 30-meter-high date palms, gradually forming an agro-ecosystem with a multi-layered structure. The researchers found that the Wade Oasis agricultural system not only addresses the needs of the local population, but also plays an important role in protecting local biodiversity.

Since 2011, when the Food and Agriculture Organization of the United Nations (FAO) officially inscribed Algeria's Wadi oasis agricultural system on the list of Globally Important Agricultural Cultural Heritage, the Algerian Government has stepped up its efforts to protect it. On the one hand, it has supported the development of local agriculture, commerce and tourism in order to stabilize the livelihoods of oasis inhabitants and avoid overexploitation; on the other hand, it has taken measures to maintain the original ecological attributes of production and life in the oases. The Government has sent agricultural experts to be permanently stationed in man-made oases to provide scientific guidance on living and production activities, such as eliminating the use of chemical fertilizers and pesticides and limiting the number of animals raised, in order to avoid damaging the ecological environment of the oasis.

(2) Development and utilization of the Spanish agricultural cultural heritage

Spain's agro-cultural heritage is diverse, involving the salt industry, viticulture, the olive industry, irrigation and agro-forestry-pastoral complex systems. The Spanish Government has taken a number of measures to develop agro-cultural heritage tourism, further protect the agro-cultural heritage and develop the local economy. Firstly, it has strengthened the construction of policies and regulations and financial guarantee, formulated and adopted the Natural Heritage List, the Strategic Plan for Biodiversity, Natural Heritage and Biodiversity, the Natural Resources Management Guidelines, the Orta Conservation Act and many other regulations, and provided financial support through the establishment of foundations and other measures. Secondly, tourism routes have been developed according to local conditions. In order to enable people to have rich travel experiences, the Spanish management has designed various travel routes according to local characteristics, including ecological tours, cultural tours and agricultural tours. Thirdly, to enhance the added value of products through geographical indications, the Ministry of Agriculture, Fisheries and Rural Development of the Andalusian region of Spain has successfully applied for the "protection of origin" of "Málaga raisins". In addition, the "Málaga" geographical indication is used for local liqueurs and wines. The Sierra de León Agroforestry and Livestock Complex involves the certification of 16 high-quality food products, contributing to the development of the local tourism industry with a focus on gastronomy[66].

III. Experiences and insights in rural cultural revitalization

1. Fostering and expanding rural cultural mainstays

Strengthening the construction of rural cultural industry talents. In terms of policy support, cultivate and grow market players, support localities to cultivate and introduce backbone cultural enterprises, support the development of small and micro cultural enterprises and studios in villages, individual creators, etc., and encourage enterprises in other industries and private capital to invest in the rural cultural industry through various forms. At the same time, culture and tourism administrations at all levels should establish effective mechanisms to guide cultural industry practitioners, entrepreneurs, cultural workers, cultural volunteers, teachers and students of colleges and universities specializing in arts to go deep into the countryside for docking support and investment, and drive culture to the countryside, capital to the countryside, and industry to the countryside. Encourage localities to explore the implementation of a special commissioner system for the cultural industry in the light of the actual situation,

---

66 Zhang Yu. Spain attaches importance to the development and utilization of agricultural cultural heritage [N]. China Social Science Journal, 2023-04-17 (007).

and build a talent pool of cultural industry-enabled rural revitalization. It will implement the cultural and tourism creator action, create a favorable environment for innovation and entrepreneurship, and support the innovation and entrepreneurship of cultural and tourism practitioners, graduates of relevant colleges and universities, returning entrepreneurs, and local talents. Focusing on the leading role of rural cultural and tourism experts, industry leaders, representative inheritors of intangible cultural heritage, arts and crafts masters, folk artists, etc., it has tapped and cultivated local cultural talents and fostered a new team of professional farmers. Encouragement is being given to schools of higher education, vocational schools and research institutions to set up cultural and tourism internships and training bases in villages.

2. Establishing multiple linkage mechanisms

Adhering to the principle of "linking agriculture with agriculture" and integrating development, exploring the establishment of multiple benefit linkage mechanisms according to local conditions, promoting the integrated development of the agricultural industry, effectively driving farmers to increase their income and get rich, and adding color to rural revitalization. Adhering to the development of industry to drive the masses to increase their income as the fundamental policy of poverty alleviation, vigorously implement industrial poverty alleviation, build multiple benefit linkage mechanisms, and tie the poor masses firmly to the industrial chain.

Establishing a mechanism for linking capital and dividends to increase income. It has established a sound system for the utilization and management of funds for industrial poverty alleviation, and is exploring a mechanism for linking interests that is in line with the actual development of national industrial poverty alleviation.

Building employment linkage mechanisms to increase income. Enterprises are encouraged to give priority to absorbing the population with documented card status to participate in industrial construction, and to develop long-term jobs for the population with documented card status in conjunction with the actual development of industry, so that the population with documented card status can be transformed into industrial workers.

Building order-acquisition linkage mechanisms to promote income generation. By vigorously promoting the construction of planting, breeding, processing industry and other poverty alleviation industries, guiding enterprises and the masses to sign order-type raw material purchase agreements, and using the minimum protection price for purchase.

Building a land transfer and linkage mechanism to promote income generation. Vigorously promoting and deepening comprehensive rural reform, accelerating the reform of rural land and forest rights, and revitalizing land and forest resources and bringing rural assets to the market by means of land equity, mortgages and loans, as well as transferring operations.

3. Strengthening project construction and financial support

Facing the reality, rural revitalization must solve the problem of "money", and solve the problem of "money" in a scientific and long-term manner. The creation of a rural financial system will solve the problem of lack of "money" for rural revitalization from the perspective of institutional mechanisms.

Strengthen project construction and financial support. In accordance with the principles of voluntary declaration, dynamic management and key support, a number of key projects for rural revitalization empowered by the cultural industry will be selected, and support and services will be strengthened to promote the implementation of the projects. The State Development Bank, in compliance with national policies and regulations, credit policies and under the premise of market-oriented operation, will provide comprehensive and high-quality financial service support for rural culture and tourism projects, including long-term and low-cost funds, in accordance with the principle of "preserving the capital and making a small profit". Encourage financial institutions to provide credit support for rural culture and tourism business entities through door-to-door contracting, flexible guarantee, active concessions and other means, in accordance with local conditions and innovative products. Guide various investment institutions to invest in rural culture and tourism projects. Encourage insurance organizations to carry out insurance business for rural culture and tourism projects.

4. Coordinating the protection of rural cultural resources

As a large traditional agricultural country, China has a rich stock and wide distribution of agricultural cultural resources, which is an important advantageous resource for building a strong agricultural country. However, the monolithic nature of the long-term traditional agricultural economy has rendered a large number of agricultural cultural resources dormant. It is imperative that these rural cultural resources be awakened and that their culture-promoting functions be reasonably utilized to promote rural cultural revitalization.

Comprehensive excavation, systematic organization, and do a good job of the basic work of agricultural cultural resources come to life. From a general point of view, agricultural cultural resources can be summarized into three aspects: First, agricultural production form cultural resources. It mainly includes some composite agro-ecosystems formed in long-term agricultural production, including agricultural breeding system, water conservancy and irrigation system, and production tool system. The second is the cultural heritage of rural life forms. It mainly includes some composite lifestyles formed in the long-term rural life, such as folk customs, local literature and art, ideological concepts and so on. Thirdly, some cultural landscapes and symbol systems of human environment closely related to agricultural production and farmers' life, including some cultural imprints related to agricultural production and rural life, which all belong to the content of agricultural cultural heritage. Progressive and comprehensive development is the focus of making agricultural cultural resources come alive. The industrialization of agricultural cultural heritage to promote economic and cultural development is the path to realize the contemporary value of agricultural cultural heritage. Protecting first, scientific planning and strengthening top-level design are the fundamental guarantee to make agricultural cultural resources come alive. Coordinate the excavation, finishing, protection, development and utilization of agricultural cultural resources, do a good job of top-level design, scientific planning, the establishment of a complete set of comprehensive utilization mechanism of agricultural cultural resources, the formation of government-led, social participation, village-based protection and utilization pattern. Under the guidance of scientific planning, a hierarchical agricultural cultural heritage protection list will be established, and geographic charts of important agricultural and cultural heritage sites at various levels will be compiled, so that they can be protected and utilized in a phased, step-by-step and holistic manner.

5. Strengthening rural cultural and artistic education and training

The use of the arts to change villages and promote rural revitalization in accordance with local conditions requires targeted measures that take into account local culture, resources and the actual situation. Art education and training activities should be carried out to improve the artistic quality and creative ability of local villagers. Local villagers' artistic quality and creative ability can be improved by organizing art training courses, introducing artistic talents and carrying out art exchanges. Create local art brands, combining local cultural and art resources with local characteristics to create distinctive art brands and improve the popularity and influence of local art. Through organizing art festivals, exhibitions, competitions and other activities, the unique charm and vitality of local art is demonstrated. Combine local resources to develop art industries, such as handicraft production, art exhibitions, cultural tourism, etc., to improve the industrialization of local art and promote the development of rural economy. Protecting local traditional culture, the countryside is rich in traditional culture and art resources, and the protection and inheritance of these cultures is an important prerequisite for using art to change the countryside. Local traditional culture can be protected and inherited through the formulation of traditional culture protection plans, the establishment of traditional culture exhibition halls, and the development of traditional culture inheritance activities.

◎ Chapter IV International Rural Ecological Governance

Abstract

Rural ecology is an important part of the whole ecosystem, and the protection and improvement of rural ecological environment is an important prerequisite and guarantee for the realization of rural revitalization and sustainable development. Global poor population is mainly concentrated in the rural areas, poor areas are basically located in regions with relatively good ecological environment quality but weak environmental governance and protection capabilities. An in-depth analysis of the international rural resources and environmental conditions will contribute to better responses to climate change. At the same time, ecological governance and protection in these areas are critical to rural revitalization. There are regional differences in rural resource endowments, and due to the influence of natural and human factors, most countries and regions have suffered from varying degrees of rural ecological problems. Rural ecological governance has received increasing attention worldwide due to its complexity arising from numerous issues, including climate change, biodiversity loss, and pollution. International rural ecological governance is a complex and urgent task, which requires concerted efforts from governments, enterprises and the public worldwide. International policies for rural ecological governance have gradually shifted from localized environmental management to comprehensive ecosystem management, encompassing not just the agricultural environment but the entire rural environment, including forests, wetlands, water bodies, and more. This transformation also entails a shift from sole government management to diversified governance involving multiple forces, including governments, markets, societies, and technologies. Looking forward to the future: International rural ecological governance policies will pay more attention to scientific and technological innovation and green development, promote the upgrading and transformation of rural industries, and promote the harmonization of rural ecological environment and economic development.

I. Current status of rural ecology

1. Rural areas are rich in natural resources

Natural resources are not only the constituent elements of the rural natural geographic system, but also the environmental conditions on which human beings in rural areas depend for their survival and the materiral basis for their socio-economic development. Rural natural resources have various functions and uses, which can be used for agricultural production and industrial production, and for the development of rural tourism and the rural living environment.

(1) Land is an important carrier of rural development

The global share of agricultural land has stabilized. Before 1988, the global share of agricultural land steadily increased, followed by a sudden decline between 1988 and 1991. Since then, the share of agricultural land entered a stable phase, fluctuating slightly around 37% (Figure 4.1). The reasons for its change are closely related to the global agricultural development stage. In the middle of the 19th century, due to the rapid progress of production tools, the world entered the stage of modern agriculture, and the efficiency of agricultural production was greatly improved, and the demand for agricultural land was increasing accordingly. The decline in the proportion of global agricultural land use around 1990 may be related to the three El Nino events, which led to a long drought in Africa and Oceania in the southern Hemisphere, and large-scale floods and typhoons in the northern Hemisphere, which affected and restricted agricultural production. The modern agricultural stage represents a socialized phase of agriculture that leverages contemporary scientific technologies and management methodologies, achieving a high level of comprehensive productivity while emphasizing scientific planning.

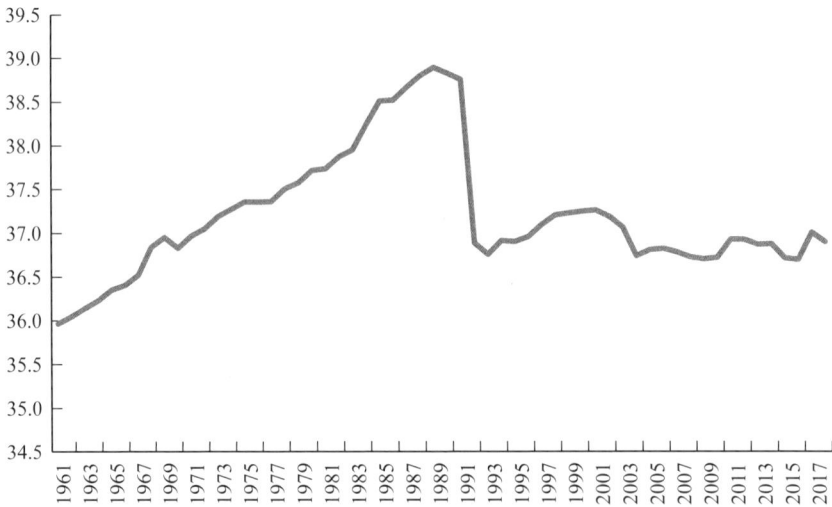

Figure 4.1   Global agricultural land proportion (unit: %)

Data source: the World Bank.

Countries with higher incomes have a lower share of arable land in land area. Since 2001, the proportion of cultivated land area in high-income countries worldwide has exhibited a declining trend, accounting for approximately 35% as of 2018. With the national economic development and technological progress, the proportion of the primary industry in high-income countries has gradually decreased, the allocation of resources is continuously optimized, and the resources invested in rural land gradually turn to the tertiary industry with good benefits. In terms of income group, lower-middle-income countries exhibit the highest proportion of cultivated land to total land area, consistently maintaining approximately 42% in recent years; whereas, this proportion has risen steadily in low-income and middle-income countries

(Figure 4.2). The agricultural production in the vast majority of developing countries remains relatively underdeveloped, necessitating a substantial boost in agricultural development to provide support for other sectors of the national economy.

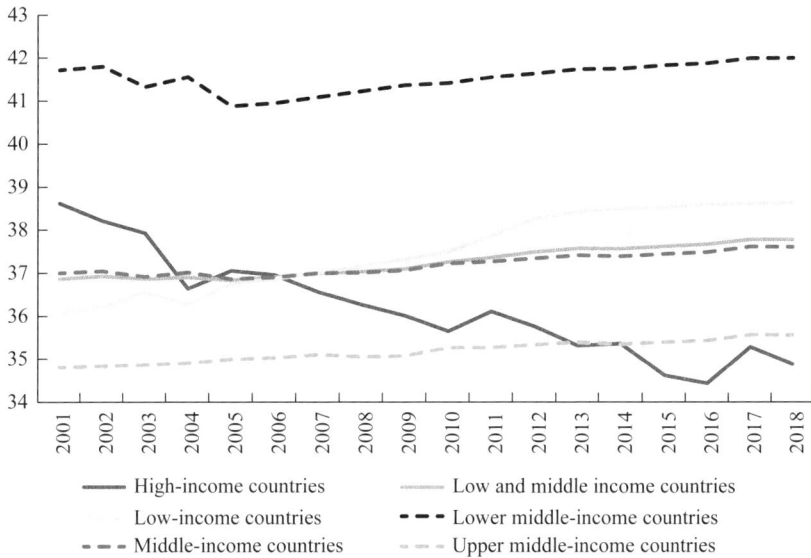

Figure 4.2   The proportion of cultivated land in different income countries (unit:%)

Data source: the World Bank.

The larger the per capita arable land area, the less the pressure on rural resources and the environment. The top 10 countries ranked globally in terms of per capita cultivated land area are distributed across the major population centers of Asia, Europe, Africa, North America, South America and Oceania. A common characteristic among these countries is their relatively smaller population sizes (Figure 4.3). The larger the per capita cultivated land area, the smaller the land pressure, and correspondingly, the pressure on rural resources and environmental carrying capacity is relatively lower. Regions characterized by limited land area and high population density often encounter issues such as insufficient land supply during rapid development, which can subsequently lead to high land prices and related problems. A larger per capita cultivated land area represents a resource advantage that is conducive to a country's future sustainable development. Protecting rural cultivated land resources is conducive to the steady development of agriculture in developing countries. This involves stringent protection measures, including quantitative management, quality enhancement, and purpose control, to rigorously protect and improve the quality of cultivated land. Expediting the construction of high-standard farmland that ensures drought- and flood-resistant, high-yield, and stable production is crucial to ensure that farmland is not merely farmland but also fertile land. Additionally, prioritizing ecological protection of cultivated land and adopting efficient, sustainable farming practices is essential to sustainably maintain high productivity on limited land resources.

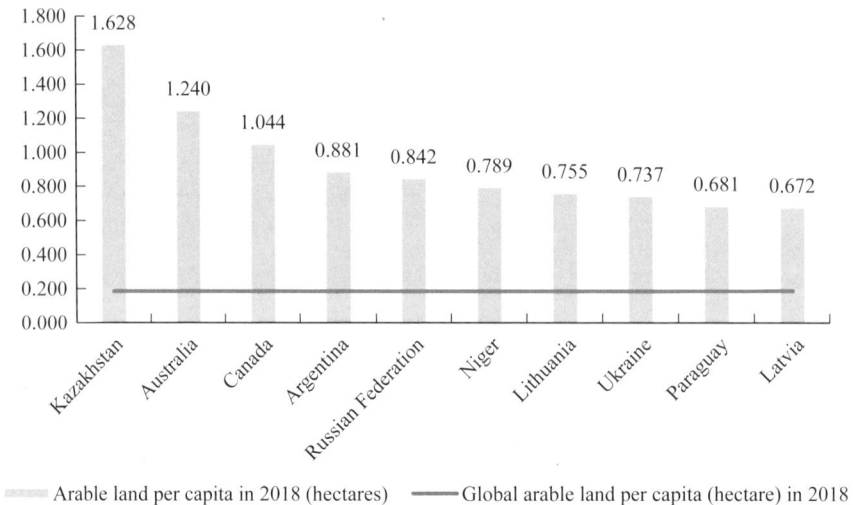

Arable land per capita in 2018 (hectares)   ——Global arable land per capita (hectare) in 2018

Figure 4.3   Top 10 countries in the global per capita arable land area in 2018

Data source: the World Bank.

(2) Water is crucial to agricultural production and farmers' life

Agricultural water accounts for the largest proportion of fresh water extraction in the world. Human and environmental water needs vary spatially and culturally, such as in rural and urban areas. While an average of 70% of water intake is used for agricultural production, it varies widely between regions and countries (Hoekstra and Mekonnen, 2012; Food and Agriculture Organization of the United Nations, 2016; United Nations Water Mechanism, 2017). Due to its large population and large cultivated area, the extraction of fresh water is much higher than that of other continents, and the total annual extraction of fresh water is about 6 times that of other continents (Figure 4.4). Due to the favorable climatic conditions in Eastern and Southern Asia for rice cultivation, significant amounts of water are utilized for agricultural irrigation. Both China and India, being populous countries located in Asia, also exhibit higher domestic water consumption compared to other continents. To date, agriculture remains the most important part of the Asian economy, while the industrial sector accounts for only 10% of freshwater extraction, even slightly less than the industrial sector extraction in North America. More than 80% of available fresh water in Southeast Asia is used in agriculture (Food and Agriculture Organization of the United Nations, 2016). As a region with strong industrial base and huge industrial productivity, the amount of fresh water

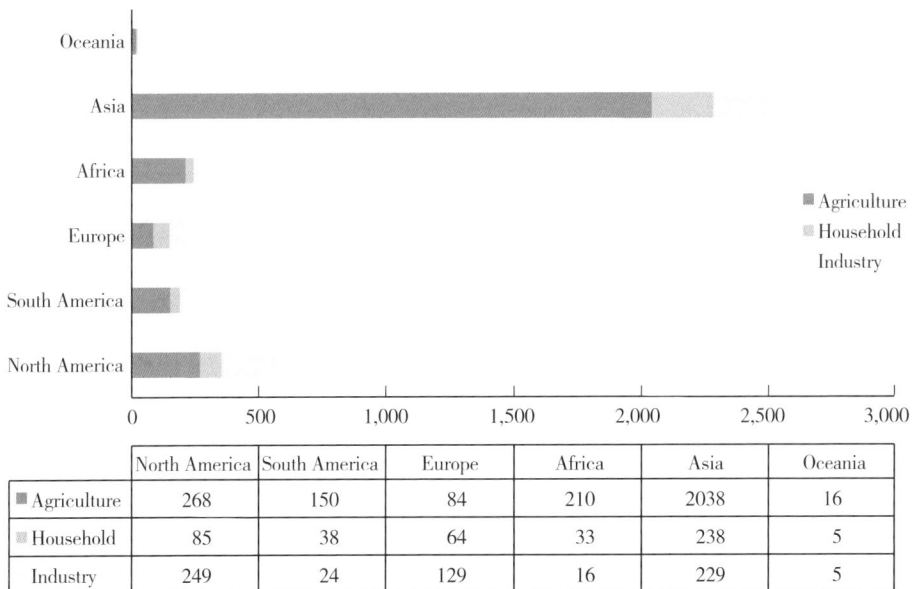

	North America	South America	Europe	Africa	Asia	Oceania
Agriculture	268	150	84	210	2038	16
Household	85	38	64	33	238	5
Industry	249	24	129	16	229	5

Figure 4.4   Fresh water extraction volume and sub-departmental use in 2017 (unit: km³/year)

Data source: the United Nations World Water Development 2022.

extracted from its industrial sector reached about 40%. On the other hand, in terms of freshwater mining from all continents, Asia accounts for more than half of the world's total production (64.5%), followed by North America and Europe with 15.5% and 7.1%, respectively.

The global use of drinking water in rural areas has been improved year by year. Between 2001 and 2020, the proportion of rural population using at least basic drinking water services and the proportion of population using safe managed drinking water services increased year by year (Figure 4.5). As countries around the world vigorously promote the safety of drinking water in rural areas, the penetration rate of safe drinking water in rural areas reached about 60% in 2020, and the problem of drinking water that has plagued many rural residents for generations has been historically alleviated. However, the global drinking water problem for the rural population still needs to be consolidated to ensure that rural residents drink safe and safe water for a long time. The development of rural safe drinking water projects in various countries has ensured the domestic water demand of rural people, and effectively solved the water shortage problem encountered by rural population and agricultural production. At the same time, it can also optimize and adjust the industrial

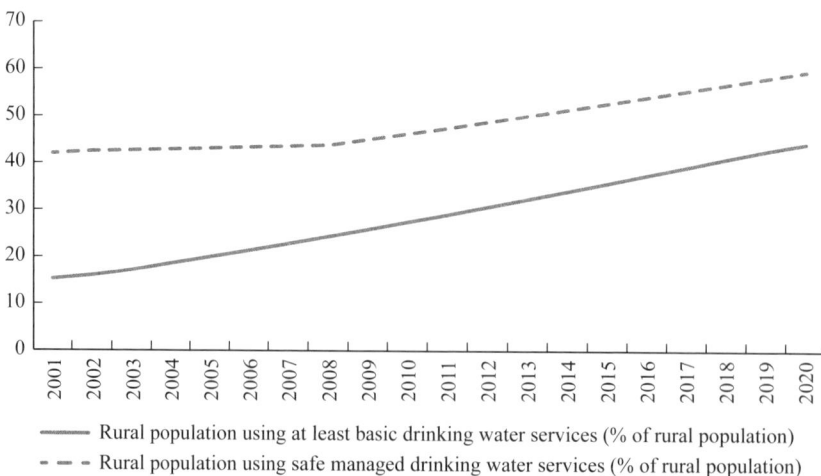

———— Rural population using at least basic drinking water services (% of rural population)
- - - Rural population using safe managed drinking water services (% of rural population)

Figure 4.5   Global population portion of rural drinking water services (unit:%)

Data source: the World Bank.

structure, improve the economic benefits of agricultural production, promote the people's spiritual and cultural construction, and improve the rural ecological environment. However, in the poor areas, whether from the engineering technology or the concept of water use, the traditional concept is still dominant, the development of advanced management technology is slow, and the lack of unified technical standards and norms. Strengthening the promotion and application of the related technologies in the water conservancy industry is the leading force of development, ensuring sufficient capital investment is the foundation, and adhering to the people-oriented publicity and implementation is the means.

(3) Forest is not only an important ecological barrier, but also an important means of production for farmers

Forests constitute a crucial element within ecosystems, capable of conserving water resources, preventing soil erosion and mitigating climate-induced droughts. They also function as windbreaks, diminishing the frequency of dust storms, elevating negative air ion concentrations, enhancing air quality, and regulating local microclimates. Furthermore, forests harbor not only trees but also herbaceous and vine plants, as well as diverse animal species, thereby fostering biodiversity. Given that the majority of forests are situated in rural areas, enhancing forest cover undoubtedly bears significant positive implications for improving rural ecological environments. Concurrently, increasing rural forest cover strongly promotes agricultural production, and rational planning of forest ecosystems coupled with sustainable exploitation of biological resources can positively reshape rural industrial structures. Additionally, leisure, sports, recreation, and tourism activities centered around forests are highly favored by tourists, and the development of related industries fosters rural economic growth, contributing to poverty eradication and prosperity among farmers.

Global forest resources exhibit notable regional disparities in their distribution. According to the 2020 Global Forest Resources Assessment, forests currently account for 30.8% of the global land area, with a total forest area of 4.06 billion hectares and a per capita forest area of about 0.52 hectares. Globally, natural forests account for 93% and plantations account for 7%. Since 1990, the area of natural forests has been decreasing, but the rate of loss has decreased, while the area of plantations has increased by 123 million hectares[67]. In terms of the distribution of forest resources, more than half (54%) are in Russia, Brazil, Canada, USA, and China, more than 60 countries have less than 10% of the land area, some of which are less than 0.5%.

The decline in forest area has slowed down. Forests account for 31% of the earth's land area (4.06 billion hectares), and the area is constantly shrinking (Figure 4.6). Due to human activities, massive deforestation, grassland reclamation, and wetlands dry up, the biodiversity was greatly damaged. Forests are an important part of the earth's biosphere, the largest ecosystem on land, and the basis of human survival. Forest not only provides wood and forest by-products, but more importantly, it has ecological functions such as water conservation, water and soil conservation, windbreak and sand fixation, regulating climate, ensuring agricultural and animal husbandry production, preservation of forest biological species, maintenance of ecological balance and purification of environment, etc. Between 1990 and 2020,420 million hectares of forest were lost by deforestation. While the rate of deforestation is slowing down, it still reaches 10 million hectares per year between 2015 and 2020. Between 2000 and 2020, about 47 million hectares of virgin forest have disappeared. Foreplantation are 294 million hectares (7% of global forest area). Between 2015 and 2020, the plantation area grew by just under 1% per year, and 1.4% between 2010 and 2015. Between 2000 and 2020, other woodland areas declined by nearly 1%; but other tree cover (including urban trees, orchards, palm trees, and agroforestry landscapes) increased by more than a third between 1990 and 2020. The area of land used for agriculture and forestry is at least 45 million hectares and is showing an increasing trend[68].

---

67 The Global Forest Resources Assessment 2020, released by the Food and Agriculture Organization of the United Nations (FAO).

68 The State of World Forests 2022: Forest Approaches to Green Recovery and an Inclusive, Resilient and Sustainable Economy, released by the Food and Agriculture Organization of the United Nations.

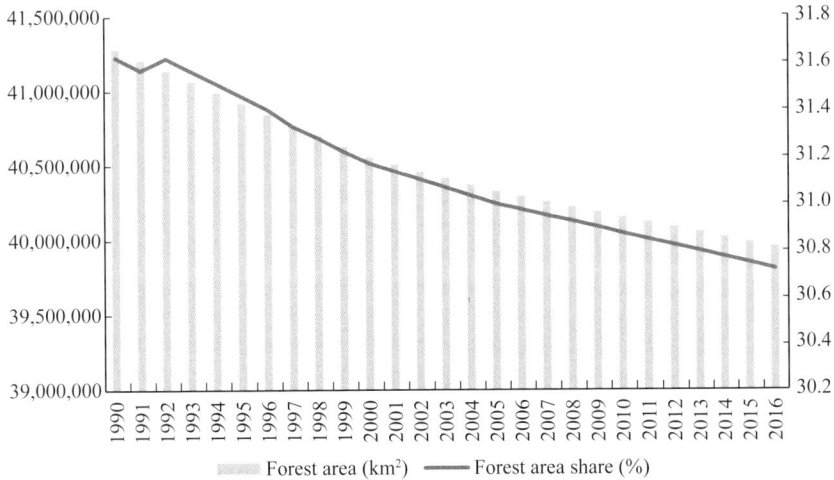

Figure 4.6   World forest area and its proportion in 1990-2016

Data source: drawn from the World Bank's World Development Indicators Database.

2. Rural ecology faces multiple challenges

Influenced by both natural and anthropogenic factors, various degrees of environmental issues have arisen in most countries and regions worldwide. Particularly in the past half-century, with the escalation of global urbanization, the global environment, particularly rural environmental problems, has become increasingly prominent. This has led to a grimmer situation in environmental governance and protection, impacting the normal survival and sustainable development of humans and other organisms.

(1) The risk of climate change increases, and air pollution threatens the global climate and ecosystem security

The Intergovernmental Panel on Climate Change (IPCC) officially released the Working Group II contribution to the Sixth Assessment Report (AR6), titled *Climate Change 2022: Impacts, Adaptation, and Vulnerability*, on February 28, 2022. The report highlights that humanity is confronted with significant climate change risks, which are impacting the productivity of agriculture, forestry, fisheries, and aquaculture. About 3.3 billion to 3.6 billion people worldwide live in highly vulnerable environments for climate change, and although vulnerability varies between regions and within regions, most species show vulnerability to response.

On September 7,2022, the *2022 Air Quality and Climate Bulletin* states that the interaction of air pollution and climate change will face hundreds of millions of people with additional "climate penalties". As defined by the World Health Organization (WHO), air pollution is the pollution of the indoor or outdoor environment by any chemical, physical, or biological agent that alters the natural characteristics of the atmosphere. The main pollutants include particulate matter ($PM_{2.5}$, etc.), carbon monoxide, ozone, nitrogen dioxide, and sulfur dioxide.

The $PM_{2.5}$ standards vary from country to country (Table 4.1). China's implementation standard adopts the maximum width limit set by WHO, which is the same as the WHO transition period target-1. The $PM_{2.5}$-year and 24-hour average concentration limits in the standard are set at $35mg/m^3$ and $75mg/m^3$, respectively. The US and Japanese standards are basically the same as the target-3. The EU standards are slightly loose, in line with target-2, with Australia has the most stringent standards annually lower than the WHO guidelines. The severity of the standards basically reflects the air quality of all countries, and the better the air quality, the more capable countries are to set and implement stricter standards.

Air pollution will cause the respiratory tract and other diseases. In September 2022, the chief scientist of the World Health Organization, the International Union for Conservation of Nature, the World Meteorological Organization and the United Nations Environment Programme jointly issued a statement saying that less than 1 percent of people now breathe air in line with the WHO's most stringent air quality guidelines. According to WHO estimates, 7 million people die prematurely each year due to air pollution, including about 600,000 children under the age of 15, and millions suffer from chronic diseases related with air pollution. According to the statistics of the World Bank's World Development Index on the proportion of people exposed to $PM_{2.5}$ in 243 countries and regions above the WHO guidance, it was below 90% in only 21

Table 4.1   Typical country / organizational PM$_{2.5}$ related criteria

Country / Organization	Annual mean	24 hours average	Release and implementation time
The WHO transition period target is in-1	35	75	
The WHO transition period target is in-2	25	50	Released in 2005
The WHO transition period target is in-3	15	37.5	
WHO criterion value	10	25	
Australia	8	25	Published in 2003, not mandatory standards
the United States	12	35	The latest standard, dated December 13,2012, is stricter than those issued in 2006
Japan	15	35	Posted on September 9,2009
EU	25	not have	Published published on 1 January 2010 The mandatory standard took effect on January 1,2015
China	35	75	The target value was published in February 2012 and implemented in 2016

countries and regions in 1990. By 2017, it had increased to 45, showing initial results in global atmospheric governance.

Air quality is closely related to the global climate and ecosystems. Numerous drivers of air pollution, such as the combustion of fossil fuels, are also sources of greenhouse gas emissions. Consequently, policies aimed at reducing air pollution offer a win-win strategy for both climate and health, mitigating the burden of diseases caused by air pollution and contributing to both short-term and long-term climate change mitigation.

(2) Biodiversity loss is one of the three major environmental crises

Biodiversity is the ecological foundation that maintains the balance of natural ecosystems and supports the survival and development of humanity. It encompasses genetic diversity, species diversity, and ecosystem diversity. Since the emergence of life on the earth, it has been about 3 to 4 billion years of evolution, and there have been six events similar to the extinction of dinosaurs, leaving 52% of marine animal families, 78% of amphibian families and 81% of reptiles disappear. The number of living species on the earth is about 5 million to 30 million, including over 4,300 mammals, 6,000 reptiles, 3,500 amphibians, 9,000 birds and 23,000 fish, and the number of marine and rainforest organisms probably exceeds 30 million.

Biodiversity loss is one of the three major environmental crises. Environmental deterioration reduces the living environment of organisms, and many organisms are on the verge of extinction. Since 2000, some 110 animals and 130 birds have become extinct; about 25,000 plants and 1,000 vertebrates are on the verge of extinction (Figure 4.7). Recently, the disappearance of biological species has accelerated and the ecosystem has been simplified, with about 50-100 species becoming extinct every day, which is the fastest extinction since dinosaurs disappeared. But once the existing wild species on the earth become extinct, there is no chance of recurrence. The World Bank's World Development Indicator Database counts the number of endangered organisms (including plants, mammals, fish and birds) in 2018, and the ecological environment is not optimistic.

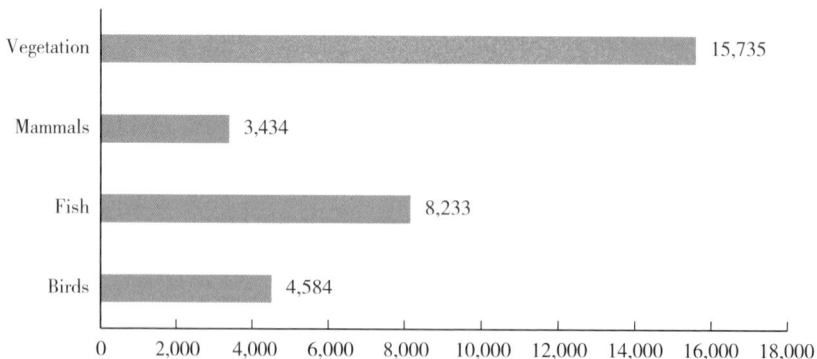

Figure 4.7 Number of world endangered species in 2018 (unit: species)

Data source: data drawn from the World Bank's World Development Indicators Database.

All major biological communities on the earth are experiencing biodiversity loss. The loss of biodiversity reduces the resilience of ecosystems in the face of negative impacts such as climate change, increases their vulnerability, and affects human health and equity. *The Convention on Biological Diversity* is an important global convention on biodiversity in recent decades. It has three core goals: biodiversity conservation, sustainable use of its components, and fair and equitable sharing of the benefits of the use of genetic resources. In 2018, a total of 196 Parties participated in the establishment of international guidelines, providing a platform for countries to cooperate, share information and coordinate policies. According to the fifth edition of the *Global Biodiversity Outlook* (GBO-5) released by the United Nations in 2020, the world "had partially achieved" six of the 20 Aichi Biobiodiversity targets set in 2010 by the deadline of 2020. Positive progress was made in the consultation on the Post-2020 Global Biodiversity Framework at the 15th Conference of the Parties to the United Nations Convention on Biological Diversity (COP 15) in December 2022.

(3) Pollution restricts rural development and affects ecological security

Soil pollution threatens rural development. The use of chemical fertilizer is the main cause of soil pollution. Fertilizer is a chemical or physical fertilizer that contains nutrients for one or more of crops. Fertilizer, which is the "food" of food, contains nitrogen, phosphorus, potassium and other elements that can help crops grow. Since the 1950s, chemical fertilizers have been applied on a large scale. In various agricultural production measures, the role of fertilizer is about 30%.

Global fertilizer consumption has fluctuated higher. Over time, the global fertilizer consumption shows certain change patterns (Figure 4.8). From the 1950s to the 1990s, influenced by the Industrial Revolution, the consumption of fertilizers in various countries experienced exponential growth. Prolonged and excessive use of fertilizers not only reduces crop yields but also adversely affects soil quality. Over-fertilization and blind fertilization practices not only increase agricultural production costs and waste resources but also lead to soil compaction and acidification. Since the 1990s, countries have gradually become aware of the environmental pollution problem caused by the abuse of chemical fertilizer, and the consumption of chemical fertilizer has shown a declining

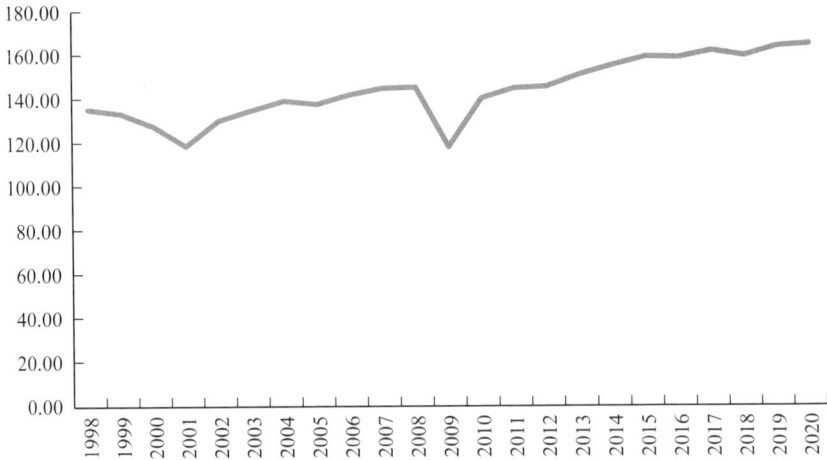

Figure 4.8   Global change in fertilizer consumption from 1998
to 2020 (unit: kg / hm^2 of cultivated land)

Data source: data drawn from the World Bank's World Development Indicators Database.

trend. Since the 1950s, developed countries such as Europe and the United States have been committed to the development of green and efficient chemical fertilizer products. The utilization rate of fertilizer has been continuously improved, and the soil pollution caused by chemical fertilizer has been continuously reduced. With the promotion of new fertilization technologies, new products and new machinery, the level of scientific fertilization has been continuously improved, and the consumption of chemical fertilizer has increased (Table 4.2).

Soil pollution has attracted much attention, and some areas have achieved initial results. Soil health is critical for life, food security, and the ecosystems that the soil provides. Many chemicals coming from industry, cities, and agriculture eventually contaminated the soil. In most developed countries, the main direct causes of land pollution are industrial and commercial activities. In many Asian countries, trace elements pollute agricultural soils and crops (Thangavel and Sridevi, 2017). In many areas of Latin America, the intensive use of agricultural resources is responsible for soil pollution. In Africa, pesticides, mining, spill, and improper waste disposal have already

Table 4.2   Consumption of agricultural land and chemical fertilizer in typical countries in 2020

Country	The proportion of agricultural land (%)	The proportion of agricultural land world ranking	Fertilizer consumption (Kos of cultivated land per hectare)	Fertilizer consumption world ranking
Malaysia	26.09	189	1952.09	1
Ireland	65.50	30	1563.35	3
China	56.08	49	383.32	10
Britain	71.34	16	233.17	23
India	60.22	35	209.41	27
America	44.36	94	126.16	65
South Africa	79.42	4	63.49	93

Data source: data compiled from the World Bank's World Development Indicators Database.

contaminated the soil (Gzik et al., 2003; Kneebone and Short, 2010). In the Middle East and North Africa, soil pollution is mainly caused by oil production and heavy mining activities.

China is a major producer and user of chemical fertilizers[69]. In 2017, in order to promote the reduction of chemical fertilizer and improve the efficiency, reduce the amount of pesticides and control hazards, and actively explore the road of modern agricultural development with output efficiency, product safety, resource conservation and environmental friendliness, the Ministry of Agriculture of China formulated the *Action Plan for Zero Growth of Fertilizer Use by 2020*, focusing on soil pollution control. Currently, China's soil pollution control work has achieved initial results, but there is still much room for improvement. According to the *2019 National Bulletin on Cultivated Land Quality Grade* issued by the Ministry of Agriculture and Rural Affairs on May 6,2020, China's cultivated land, totaling 2.023 billion acres, is classified into ten grades. Among them, Grade 1 to 3 cultivated land amounts to 632 million acres, accounting for 31.24% of the total cultivated land area, an increase of 3.94

---

69   http://www.moa.gov.cn/nybgb/2015/san/201711/t20171129_5923401.htm.

percentage points compared to the first grading in 2014. Grade 4 to 6 cultivated land comprises 947 million acres, accounting for 46.81% of the total cultivated land area, representing an increase of 2.02 percentage points from 2014. Meanwhile, Grade 7 to 10 cultivated land totals 444 million acres, occupying 21.95% of the total cultivated land area, a decrease of 5.95 percentage points from 2014.

Water pollution threatens the earth's ecology, and freshwater pollution aggravates the water resource crisis. Surface water refers to the general term of dynamic water and static water on the land surface, also known as land water, including a kinds of liquid and solid water, mainly rivers, lakes, swamps, glaciers, ice sheets, etc. It is one of the important sources of human living water, but also the main component of water resources in various countries. Surface water accumulates from natural precipitation over the years, and eventually flows naturally into the ocean, evaporated or infiltrated underground. Although the natural water source of any surface water system comes only from the precipitation in this catchment area, there are still many other factors affecting the total amount of water in this system. These factors include the storage capacity of lakes, wetlands and reservoirs, and the soil permeability, and the characteristics of surface runoff in this catchment area. Human activities have a significant impact on these properties. Humans build reservoirs to increase the amount of water and release water to reduce the amount of wetlands. Human reclamation activities and the construction of ditches increase the amount of water and intensity of runoff. Safe fresh water is an essential element of maintaining life on earth. The global freshwater reserves are about 3.5×10^7 billion cubic meters, accounting for 2.53% of the earth's water reserves. Rivers, lakes and shallow groundwater, which are closely related to human life, are only 104.6×10^4 trillion cubic meters, accounting for 0.34% of the total fresh water reserves. Approximately 70%-80% of the freshwater resources are used for irrigation, less than 20% for industry and 6% for households.

Due to the uneven distribution of fresh water resources, water shortage has become a worldwide problem with the surge of population and the development of industrial and agricultural production. More than 10 countries in the world are short of water, and more than 40 are in serious water shortage, accounting for 60% of the global land area. At least three-quarters of the rural population and a fifth of the urban population do not have access to safe and hygienic drinking water; 80% of diseases and a third of mortality are associated with contaminated water.

According to the classification of the World Bank's world development indicators database, it is divided into seven regions, such as Latin America, Europe and Central Asia, Middle East and North Africa, East Asia and the Pacific, South Asia, sub-Saharan Africa and North America. From 1962 to 2018, the regional per capita renewable internal fresh water resources were significant obvious downward trend, and the surface water situation was grim (Figure 4.9).

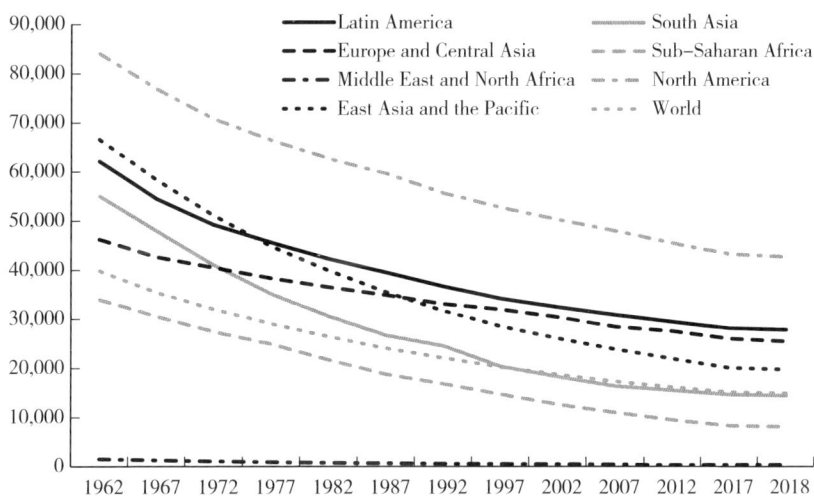

Figure 4.9   Global renewable internal freshwater resources per capita in 1962-2018 (unit: cubic meters)

Data source: data drawn from the World Bank's World Development Indicators Database.

Water pollution has exacerbated the water crisis. Water pollution not only affects the use of fresh water, but also seriously affects the natural ecosystem, and causes harm to living organisms. About 426 billion tons of sewage is discharged into rivers and lakes, causing 5.5 trillion cubic meters of water to be polluted, accounting for more than 14% of the total runoff and 40% of the stable flow of rivers is polluted and deteriorating.

Marine pollution impedes the development of rural fisheries. The ocean area of the earth is 362 million km^2, 70.9% of the earth surface; seawater volume is 1.37 million km^3, accounting for more than 97% of the total water supply on the earth's surface. Sixty percent of the world live at 60km^2 on the wide coastal line. The ocean has the most abundant biological resources, mineral resources, chemical resources and power resources on the earth. With the growth of global population and industrialization, more and more waste and harmful substances flow directly or indirectly into the sea. Marine health is closely related to the development of rural fisheries, which cannot be ignored.

The global marine environment is not optimistic. Historically, the vast oceans have been regarded as natural treatment plants for pollutants. Due to the continuous flow of seawater and the interplay of marine biological, chemical, and physical processes, pollutants entering the ocean can be decomposed into harmless substances through a combination of dilution, oxidation, reduction, biodegradation, and other mechanisms within the marine environment. Consequently, the ocean, on the whole, has the capacity to maintain its cleanliness. But the ocean's self-purification ability is not unlimited, and the process takes some time to realize. If the amount and rate of pollutants entering the ocean exceeds the ocean's self-purification ability, it will cause pollution of the marine environment. According to the provisions of *the United Nations Convention on the Law of Ocean*, marine environmental pollution refers to the material or energy into the marine environment, including estuary bay, or may damage biological resources and marine life, harm human health, obstruction, including fishing and other Marine Marine activities, damage seawater use quality and damage beautiful environment. The Sustainable Development Report Database quantifies the marine health of various countries using an index ranging from 0 to 100, with higher scores indicating better marine health. From the regional averages, the global marine health is not optimistic, with Oceania boasting the highest marine health index and Southeast Asia recording the lowest. Marine environment needs to be improved (Figure 4.10).

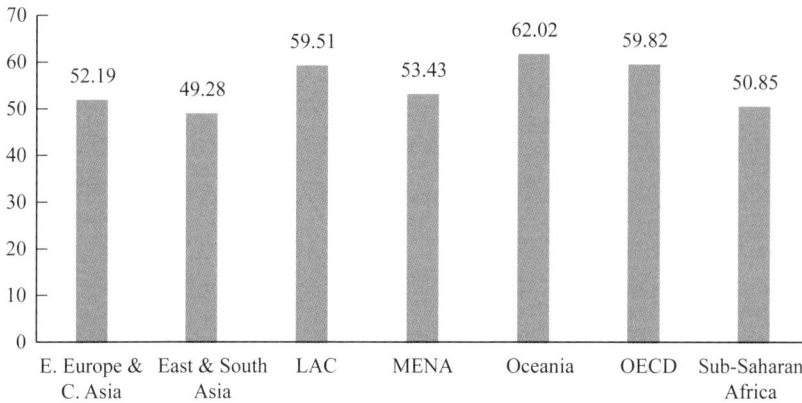

Figure 4.10   Global regional marine health index in 2020 (minimum 0-maximum 100)

Data source: plotted from SDR.

Marine pollution cannot be ignored. The ocean is crucial to global economic development and prosperity. Marine pollution, especially that in coastal waters, has directly affected marine ecology and human life. The destruction of marine ecological environment comes from various pressures exerted by human beings on marine ecology, and marine garbage dumping is the primary cause of the destruction of marine ecological environment. The contribution of the oceans to the global economy is estimated at $3 billion to $6 billion per year. In 2010, the global marine fishery provided 128 million tons of fish, with fisheries-related industries including packaging, shipbuilding and maintenance, estimated to absorb 660 million to 820 million workers. Fisheries feed 4.3 billion people worldwide, representing 15% of human animal protein consumption; 90% of goods in global trade are transported by sea; coastal areas of the world are important in regional economic development. Human society has increasingly realized that the ocean is of great significance to the development of human society.

In 1992, the United Nations, 21st Agenda emphasizes the sustainable development of marine and the environmental problems, however, the marine environmental problems in the world has not been the same attention as the land, the international union for nature conservation (International Union for

Conservation of Nature, IUCN) comprehensive statistical data, concluded that "marine ecological environment protection lags behind the land protection" conclusion. In response to the challenge of marine environment deterioration, an important and effective way is to establish marine reserves (Marine Protected Areas, MPAs), IUCN defined as: any by law or other effective way, clearly defined on geographical space, for part or all of the closed environment protection intertidal or tidal shelf area, including the covered water and related plant community, historical and cultural properties. The FAO simply defines it as: any marine geographic area that provides more powerful protection than its surrounding area for biodiversity and fisheries management purposes can be called a "marine reserve". According to the statistics of the World Bank's World Development Indicators Database, the proportion of the sea area occupied by the global marine reserves increased from 7.42% to 9.50% from 2016 to 2021. The marine environment has improved, but the overall situation is still not optimistic (Table 4.3).

Table 4.3　Proportion of typical sea area from 2016 to 2021 (unit:%)

Country	2016	2017	2018	2019	2020	2021
China	3.77	5.41	5.41	5.41	5.48	5.48
America	41.08	41.06	41.06	41.06	37.37	19.05
Canada	0.87	0.87	0.87	2.91	8.78	8.86
Australia	40.65	40.56	40.56	40.56	40.84	44.34
Britain	20.24	28.87	28.87	29.16	44.20	44.20

Data source: data created from the World Bank's World Development Indicators Database.

In addition, rural ecological environment governance often requires a large amount of capital investment, but many areas cannot bear the cost of governance due to their poor economic foundation and limited financial resources. At present, the financing channels of ecological environmental protection and restoration are relatively single, and the scale is relatively small, mainly relying on the government's financial expenditure. At the same time, the ecological protection and restoration project cycle is very long and on a large scale. Large investment and slow income make it difficult to attract social capital.

According to the Report on the State of Finance for Nature jointly released by the United Nations Environment Programme (UNEP) and the World Economic Forum (WEF), in order to effectively respond to the natural world, the total global investment will reach $8.4 trillion by 2050 to effectively respond to the global environmental crisis. That means an annual investment of $536 billion a year. However, the current investment level is far lower than this demand, showing the serious shortage of total funds for global rural ecological environment governance. According to the OECD data, developed countries raised only $79.6 billion in climate funds in 2019, a far cry from their $100 billion a year commitment. In addition, 71% of all funding was provided by the multilateral development bank, compared with only 27% of direct funding, adding to the debt burden of developing countries.

Financing indeed plays a vital role in the international rural ecological environment governance. Rural ecological environment governance involves many aspects, such as sewage treatment, garbage treatment, soil remediation, vegetation restoration, etc., all of which require a large amount of capital investment. Financing can provide the necessary financial support for these projects, and promote the smooth progress of the rural ecological and environmental governance work.

II. Rural ecological governance policy

"*Peace with Nature*" points out that the earth is facing three major crises: climate change, biodiversity destruction and pollution problems, and human beings must change the relationship with nature. Natural resources are not only the elements of rural natural geographical system, but also the environmental conditions for human survival in rural areas and the material basis of social and economic development. The global policies formulated to deal with rural ecological governance are shown in Figure 4.11.

The United Nations' Declaration on the Human Environment defines the importance of protecting and improving the quality of the global environment and calls on states to take action.

Johannesburg Declaration: It calls on countries to strengthen cooperation to address global challenges, including poverty reduction, the eradication of hunger, and the protection of the environment.

The United Nations established the Joint Action Group on Sustainable Rural Development, which aims to strengthen cooperation among UN agencies on rural development and ecological governance.

World Social Report 2020: climate change, and national policies to address it, have the potential to exacerbate inequalities, and the interests of low-income groups should be safeguarded.

1972 1992 2002 2015 2016 2017 2020 2021

The United Nations' Framework Convention on Climate Change: Aims to address the issue of climate change by encouraging counties to take measures to reduce greenhouse gas emissions and protect the Earth's ecosystems through adaptation and mitigation.

Sustainable Development Agenda 2030: Rural development and ecological governance are included as one of the core objectives of sustainable development.

Fao and UNDP have jointly launched Our Common Agenda: the "Rural Renaissance and Ecological Governance Initiative," aimed at fostering enhanced sustainable development and ecological conservation in rural areas across nations.

Our Common Agenda: Supporting Member States in advancing new skills, strategies, and solutions across all regions to chart a path towards resilience and sustainability for the world.

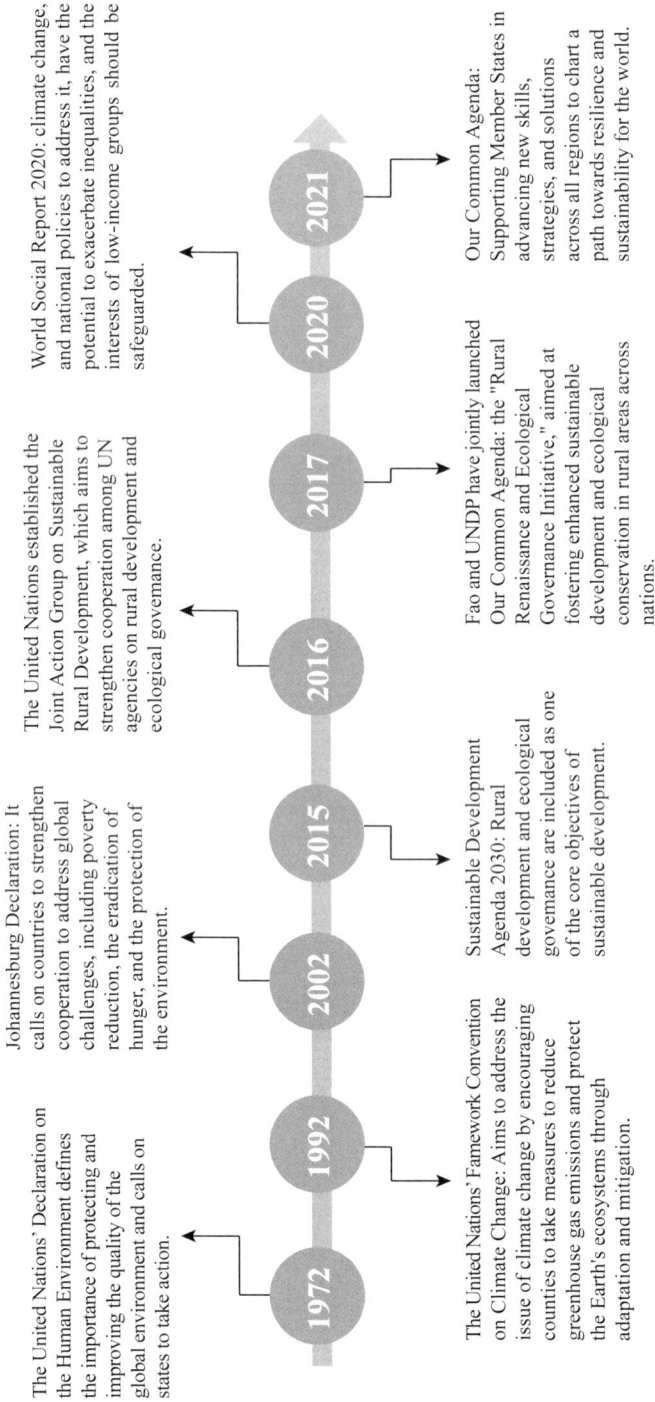

Figure 4.11   Map of global response to ecological governance policies

Data source: compiled and illustrated based on the relevant data of the global response to rural ecological governance.

1. Climate change response policies

Climate change is a common challenge facing all mankind and concerns the sustainable development of mankind. According to the Global Risk Report 2022, climate risk is one of the major global risks in 2022. The global average temperature increases year by year (Figure 4.12). The United Nations and other international organizations, regional organizations such as ASEAN, the European Union and the African Union, as well as China, the United States, Japan, India and other countries have all attached great importance to climate change and actively responded to climate change. According to the IPCC sixth assessment report Climate Change 2022: Impact, Adaptation and Vulnerability (IPCC, 2022), since the fifth comprehensive impact assessment in 2014, climate risks have emerged faster and become more severe, with about 3.3 to 3.6 billion people living in highly vulnerable areas, especially in West Africa, Central Africa and East Africa, South Asia, Central America and South America, small island developing countries and the Arctic.

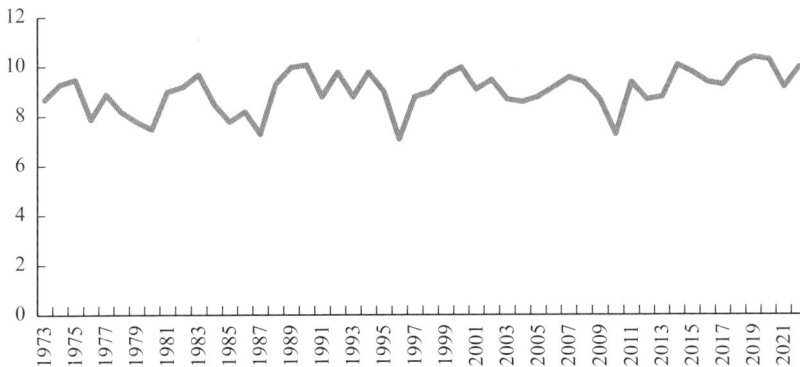

Figure 4.12   Global annual average air temperature (unit: °C)

Data source: compiled based on the data from the National Oceanic and Atmospheric Administration (NOAA) of the United States.

Climate change mitigation and adaptation to climate change are two aspects of addressing the challenge of climate change. Climate change mitigation refers to the reduction of greenhouse gas emissions and the increase of carbon sink through the prolonged adjustment of energy, industrial and other economic systems and natural ecosystems, so as to stabilize and reduce the concentration of atmospheric greenhouse gases and mitigate the rate of climate change. Adaptation to climate change means to strengthening the risk identification and management of natural ecosystems and economic and social systems, taking adjustment measures, making full use of favorable factors and preventing adverse factors, so as to reduce the adverse effects and potential risks of climate change. Climate change mitigation and adaptation to climate change are interrelated and complementary. Climate change mitigation is the basis of coping with climate change, and adaptation to climate change is an important means to deal with climate change. Major history of global action on climate change (Figure 4.13).

(1) Mitigating climate change

To address climate change, international agencies, regional organizations and many countries around the world have introduced a number of climate change mitigation policies. It mainly focuses on five aspects: First, carbon emissions are reduced. Many countries have already implemented plans to reduce greenhouse gas emissions, and issued stricter emissions restrictions, to curb the global temperature rise, and to prevent further threats from the earth to human life and their habitats. Second, improving energy efficiency, promoting the energy transition, designed to improve energy efficiency, it is to reduce its dependence on fossil fuels, and move on to cleaner energy sources, such as solar energy, wind energy and water energy. Third, promoting renewable energy sources, many countries are promoting renewable energy sources, such as solar, wind and water energy, as an alternative to conventional fossil fuels, thus reducing greenhouse gas emissions. Fourth, forest carbon sinks, forests can absorb and store carbon dioxide, protection of the existing forests, afforestation and the restoration of degraded land are important measures to reduce greenhouse gas emissions. Fifth, promoting a green and low-carbon life, for example, energy conservation and emission reduction, green travel, green consumption, reduce greenhouse gas emissions.

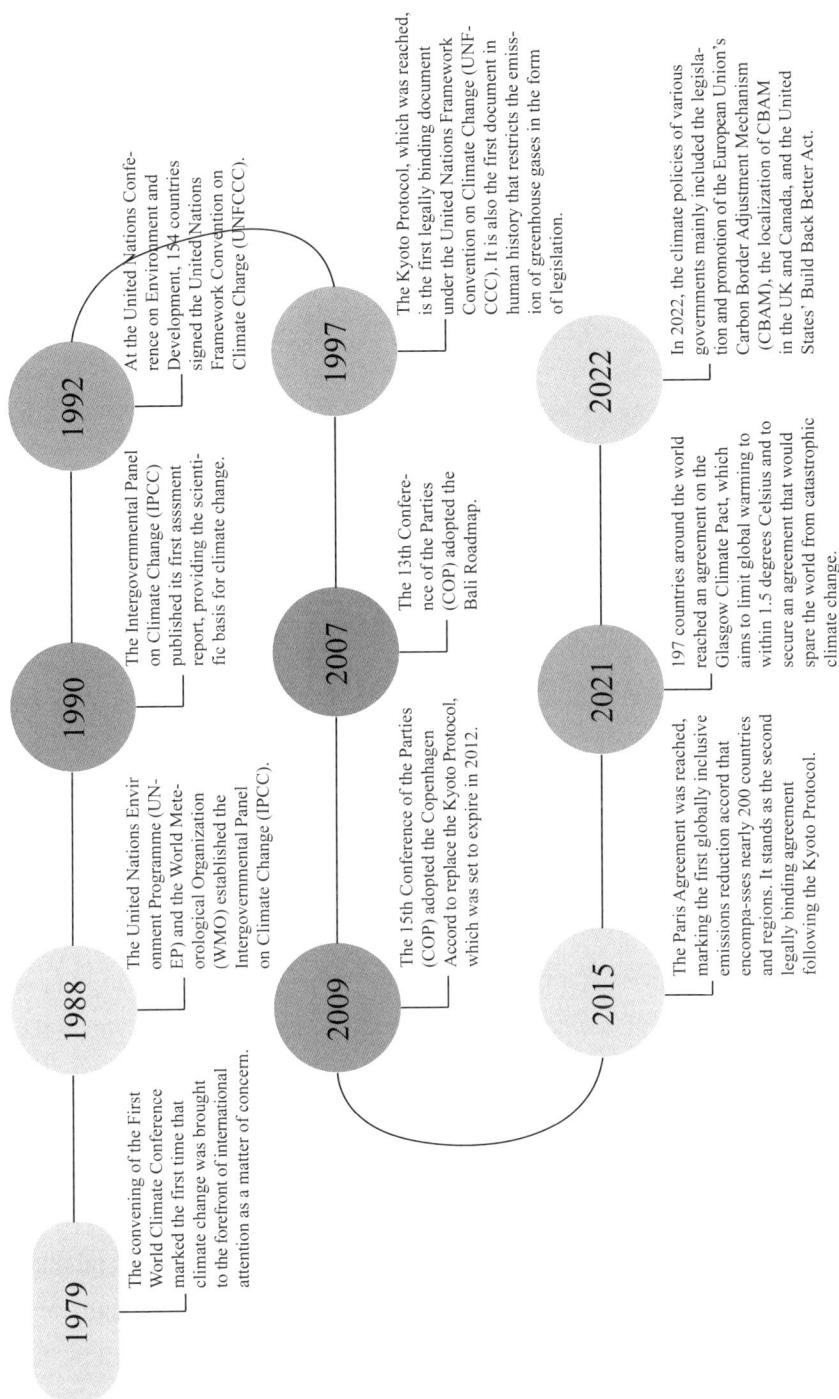

1979
The convening of the First World Climate Conference marked the first time that climate change was brought to the forefront of international attention as a matter of concern.

1988

1990
The United Nations Environment Programme (UNEP) and the World Meteorological Organization (WMO) established the Intergovernmental Panel on Climate Change (IPCC).

1992
The Intergovernmental Panel on Climate Change (IPCC) published its first assessment report, providing the scientific basis for climate change.

At the United Nations Conference on Environment and Development, 154 countries signed the United Nations Framework Convention on Climate Charge (UNFCCC).

1997
The Kyoto Protocol, which was reached, is the first legally binding document under the United Nations Framework Convention on Climate Change (UNFCCC). It is also the first document in human history that restricts the emission of greenhouse gases in the form of legislation.

2007
The 13th Conference of the Parties (COP) adopted the Bali Roadmap.

2009
The 15th Conference of the Parties (COP) adopted the Copenhagen Accord to replace the Kyoto Protocol, which was set to expire in 2012.

2015
The Paris Agreement was reached, marking the first globally inclusive emissions reduction accord that encompasses nearly 200 countries and regions. It stands as the second legally binding agreement following the Kyoto Protocol.

2021
197 countries around the world reached an agreement on the Glasgow Climate Pact, which aims to limit global warming to within 1.5 degrees Celsius and to secure an agreement that would spare the world from catastrophic climate change.

2022
In 2022, the climate policies of various governments mainly included the legislation and promotion of the European Union's Carbon Border Adjustment Mechanism (CBAM), the localization of CBAM in the UK and Canada, and the United States' Build Back Better Act.

Figure 4.13   Global actions to combat climate change

Data source: compiled and illustrated based on global materials related to climate change mitigation.

Since the 1980s, mankind has gradually recognized and increasingly attached great importance to the issue of climate change. International agencies such as the United Nations Environment and Development Programme (UNEP), the Intergovernmental Panel on Climate Change (IPCC), the International Energy Agency (IEA) and the International Renewable Energy Agency (IRENA) are committed to slowing climate change and responding to climate change. International agencies, represented by the United Nations Environment Programme (UNEP), have introduced a number of climate change mitigation policies. First, the *United Nations Framework Convention on Climate Change* (hereinafter referred to as the Convention), is the first international agreement on climate change, on May 9,1992 in Rio de Janeiro, Brazil, by the United Nations conference on environment and development, took effect on March 21,1994, as of July 2023, a total of 198 parties, is the world's first for comprehensive control of carbon dioxide and other greenhouse gas emissions, in order to address the global climate change problem of international legal text, but it does not set mandatory targets. Second, the *Kyoto Protocol*, in order to strengthen the implementation of the convention, the convention in 1997 the third meeting of the parties through the *Kyoto Protocol* (hereinafter referred to as the protocol), the protocol took effect on February 16,2005, as of July 2023, a total of 192 parties, established three flexible cooperation mechanism-emissions international emissions trade mechanism, joint performance mechanism and clean development mechanism, this is the first time in human history in the form of regulations limit greenhouse gas emissions. Third, the *Paris Agreement*, is adopted in 2015 in the 21st conference of the parties to convention and the 11th conference of the parties to the protocol (climate change parties conference) by a global climate agreement, after 2020, marks the global response to climate change into a new stage, as of July 2023, the *Paris Agreement* signed 195,195 parties. UNEP helps countries reduce greenhouse gas emissions and enhance resilience, and provides technical support and financial assistance by implementing various programs and programs for climate change mitigation and adaptation. UNEP also makes extensive efforts in climate change mitigation through educational and advocacy campaigns to increase public awareness and understanding of climate change and promote participation and action in all sectors of society.

The United Nations has also addressed climate change by introducing programs and plans, education and advocacy activities. In 2010 in Cancun, Mexico, the *United Nations Framework Convention on Climate Change*, the 16th conference of the parties (COP 16) established the green climate fund, is the global climate framework in developing countries special financing tools, aims to support developing countries to meet the challenge of climate change, limit or reduce greenhouse gas emissions of developing countries, promote climate flows to low carbon and climate adaptive development project, in help developing countries to meet the challenge of climate change has significant influence. The United Nations hosted the Global Climate Action Summit in 2019, which aims to promote awareness and action among global leaders and the public about climate change.

In addition, there are some regional organizations and civil institutions, such as the European environment ministers meeting, the African union committee, the organization of oil exporting countries and green and equality, sovereign countries such as China, the United States, Britain, Japan and the Republic of Korea also set up the relevant state institutions, to promote policy research and implementation of climate change mitigation.

Since 1992, the European Union has been committed to promoting its progress on tackling global climate change through joint solutions, with several policies on climate change mitigation. First, the *European Green Agreement*: on December 11,2019, the European Commission issued the *European Green Agreement*, put forward the EU towards climate neutral roadmap, through to clean energy and circular economy transformation, prevent climate change, protect biodiversity and reduce pollution, and improve the efficiency of resource utilization, in order to make Europe before 2050 to achieve the world's first "climate neutral". Second, the *European Climate Law*: On June 28,2021, EU countries passed the *European Climate Law*, the first European climate law that has set a medium-term goal of reducing net greenhouse gas emissions by at least 55 percent by 2030 from 1990 levels. Third, Fit for 55 ("adapt to 55") package, is a supplement to the *European Climate Act*, the *European Climate Act*, by 2030 to achieve EU emissions by at least 55% is a legal obligation, and "Fit for 55" is to make the EU legislation consistent with 2030 target, mainly including strengthening carbon trading, carbon border regulation mechanism, 2035 to stop diesel locomotive sales, alternative fuel infrastructure, shipping, green fuel, social climate fund 12 specific content. Fourth, REPowerEU plan: in order to get rid of the dependence on fossil fuels in Russia and accelerate the green energy transformation, the European commission on May 18,2022 officially announced the "REPowerEU" energy transformation action, which plans to invest 300 billion euros in 2030 years ago, by speeding up the deployment of renewable energy capacity, energy supply diversification, improve the three pillar measures to achieve European energy independence and green transformation.

Climate change has increasingly become one of the most important threats to seriously restrict the sustainable and inclusive development of Africa's economy and society. In order to enhance its ability to manage climate risks, Africa has explored and proposed a systematic governance vision to promote climate adaptation. Guided by the concept of pan-Africanism and African rejuvenation, African countries will strengthen cooperation and consolidate consensus on climate change, and gradually promote the realization of "climate intelligence" (climate smart) social and economic development in Africa from 2015 to 2035. In 2010, the East African Community issued the Eastern Community Climate Change Policy (EAC Climate Change Policy), which provides guidelines on how to respond to environmental challenges such as drought, flood, famine and pollution, and provides mechanisms and timetable for regular assessments of the results of promoting climate adaptation in the East African sub-region. In 2011, the Common Market and the Southern African Development Community jointly launched the *Programme on Climate Change Adaptation and Mitigation in COMESA-EAC-SADC Region*, which developed an action plan for a five-year cycle on how to support the African Union's climate adaptation vision and coordinate regional countries to develop a "climate resilient" economy. In November 2021, China, 53 African countries and the African Union Committee adopted the *Declaration on China-Africa Cooperation on Climate Change*, established the China-Africa strategic partnership on climate change in the new era, implemented South-South and trilateral cooperation projects on climate change, and set an example of South-South cooperation on climate change. In 2022, the African Union issued the *African Union's Strategy and Action Plan for Climate Change and Elastic Development (2022-2032)*, establishing an action program for climate governance and sustainable development in Africa.

The intensification of climate change has had a significant impact on the natural environment, human health and economic development in Southeast Asia. In 1978, Southeast Asian countries established the ASEAN Environmental Expert Group and upgraded it to the ASEAN Environmental Senior Officials' Conference in 1989. The ASEAN Senior Environmental Officials' Conference has several working groups, among which the ASEAN Working Group on Climate Change established in 2008 is a specialized agency for addressing climate change. ASEAN environmental ministerial meeting in 1992 first proposed to take emergency measures to deal with climate change, in 2006 the *Sustainable Development Cebu Resolution* took climate change issues as part of the environmental declaration. The *ASEAN Environment Bangkok Declaration* and *ASEAN Action Plan on Climate Change* were proposed in 2012. The 2019 conference considered climate change and marine waste pollution as emerging core problems such as regional collective action need to solve the huge challenges and adopted the ASEAN joint statement on climate change. Among them, the *ASEAN Joint Action Plan on Climate Change* is the action guide for climate governance in Southeast Asia. ASEAN countries jointly take comprehensive measures such as adaptation action, emission reduction action, fund investment and technology transfer to address climate change.

(2) Adapt to climate change

To improve our capacity to address climate change, promote the sustainable development of nature and society, and reduce the negative ecological and social impacts of climate change, the global policy to adapt to climate change mainly includes the following aspects: First, setting a net zero emission target. Global response to climate change has become one of the core issues of national governments, setting a net zero emissions target is one of the most important initiatives. Second, carbon-neutral action plan. An action plan on carbon neutrality is also an important step to combat climate change, like china's targets for carbon peak and carbon neutrality, plans to peak greenhouse gas emissions by 2030, and become carbon neutral by 2060. Third, to curb methane emissions. Methane is a potent greenhouse gas, can lead to climate warming, many countries around the world are trying to curb methane emissions. Fourth, carbon-pricing policy, including carbon taxes and carbon emissions trading, promote the development of low-carbon economy through the market mechanism. Fifth, fnergy-saving transformation. Implement energy conservation renovation in construction, transportation, industry and other fields, improve energy efficiency, and reduce carbon emissions. International agencies such as the United Nations Environment Programme, regional organizations such as the European Union, ASEAN and the African Union, as well as countries around the world are gradually strengthening efforts to adapt to climate change.

The United Nations and its branches are committed to promoting global policy and action to climate change. UNEP's policies and measures to adapt to climate change mainly include: First, the *National Adaptation Plans* (NAPs). are designed to strengthen the global ability to adapt to climate change, reduce the vulnerability to the impacts of climate change, by providing policy guidance, technical support, and financial assistance, to help countries formulate and implement adaptation strategies and plans. Second, the *Guidelines for National Adaptation Plans* provide a set of guiding principles and methods, and help countries adapt their policies and plans to climate change, including recommendations on policy making, planning, implementation and monitoring. Third, *Guidelines for Integrating Ecosystem-based Adaptation into National Adaptation Plans*. The guideline provides principles and approaches to ecosystem management for adaptation to climate change, to protect and restore the resilience and adaptability to ecosystems. These policies and guidelines are designed to provide guidance and support to help countries and industries develop and implement them. In August 2023, the United Nations Environment Programme issued the *Strategy for Humanity and the Earth: The United Nations Environment Programme on Climate Change 2022-2025*, which is a strategy proposed by the United Nations Environment Programme in response to the current environmental problems such as climate change, natural loss and pollution. This strategy aims to support countries in building capacities to achieve environmental goals and commitments under international agreements by strengthening the environmental dimensions of the *2030 Agenda for Sustainable Development* and adopting a forward-looking perspective towards earth's sustainability in 2050. It places the three environmental crises of climate change, biodiversity loss, and pollution at the core of its work, charting a path forward for the first five years of the "Decade of Action".

The EU has been actively responding to climate change, and its policies and measures to adapt to climate change are as follows: First, on June 29, 2007, the European Commission released the Green Paper on climate change adaptation, *Europe Adapt to Climate Change-EU Action Choice*, which established the four pillars of the EU's adaptation action. Second, on April 1, 2009, the European Commission issued a *White Paper on Adaptation to Climate Change: A Framework of Action for Looking Forward to a Europe* to improve the EU's resilience to address the impacts of climate change. Third, the core of the EU's climate policy is its carbon emission trading system (EU Emissions Trading System, ETS), from focusing on CO_2 to include all greenhouse gas emissions sectors, such as aviation, marine transport and forestry, into ETS.

ASEAN has adopted a series of policies, strategies, and plans in adapting to climate change. Since 2009, China and ASEAN countries have collaborated through the joint formulation and implementation of the *China-ASEAN Environmental Cooperation Strategy 2009-2015*, the *China-ASEAN Environmental Cooperation Strategy 2016-2020*, and their respective action plans. These endeavors have fostered multi-stakeholder dialogues and cooperation in priority areas such as policy dialogue, environmental impact assessment, climate change, biodiversity conservation, and environmentally sustainable cities. In 2021, both sides jointly approved the *China-ASEAN Environmental Cooperation Strategy and Action Framework 2021-2025*.

Africa is the continent most affected by climate change. Temperatures in Africa have risen faster in recent decades, and natural disasters related to weather and climate have become increasingly serious. According to the report of the World Meteorological Organization, more than 110 million people were directly affected by climate disasters on the African continent in 2022, killing more than 5,000 people and resulting in economic losses of more than 8.5 billion US dollars. The indirect impact of climate change on Africa's economy and society is also increasing. In 2006, the United Nations Economic Commission for Africa (UNECA) launched the process of establishing the African Climate Policy Center, aiming to provide climate policy guidance to member states, aiming to ultimately promote poverty reduction through successful mitigation and adaptation to climate change in Africa, and improving the ability of African countries to effectively participate in multilateral climate negotiations. The AU Agenda 2063 makes improving the capacity to address climate change and achieve sustainable development one of its important goals. *African Adaptation to Climate Change Strategy* (AACS) formally adopted by the African Union Summit, and in 2015 at the United Nations climate change conference, is a strategic plan of African Union, aims to help African countries and communities cope with the challenge of climate change, and improve its ability to adapt. These policies, strategies and programs aim to strengthen cooperation and action among African countries in adapting to climate change, improve resilience and reduce vulnerability. At the same time, the AU also works with other international organizations and partners to jointly address the challenges of global climate change.

By 2023, dozens of countries and regions have put forward the "zero carbon" or "carbon neutral" climate target, and Energy & Climate Intelligence Unit net zero emissions tracking table have counted the progress of various countries, including: two countries realized, six countries legislated, in the legislation of the European Union (as a whole) and other three countries. In addition, 15 countries (including EU countries) have issued policy statements (Table 4.4).

Table 4.4 Progress in climate targets

Progress	Country and region (commitment year)
Realized	The Republic of Suriname, Bhutan
Legislation has been enacted	Sweden (2045), the United Kingdom (2050), France (2050, Denmark (2050), New Zealand (2050), Hungary (2050)
In legislation	European Union (2050), Spain (2050), Chile (2050), Fiji (2050)
Policy declaration	Finland (2035), Austria (2040), Iceland (2040), Germany (2050), Switzerland (2050), Norway (2050), Ireland (2050), Portugal (2050), Costa Rica (2050), Slovenia (2050), Marshall Islands (2050), South Africa (2050), South Korea (2050), China (2060), Japan (as soon as possible in the second half of the century)

Data source: compiled from the net zero emission tracking table of Energy & Climate Intelligence Unit.

2. Policies on biodiversity conservation and restoration

Biodiversity is an important basis for human survival and development, however, the global loss of biodiversity is facing severe challenges. According to the *WWF's Earth Life Report 2022*, released in October 2022, the global wildlife population fell by an average of 69 percent between 1970 and 2018. The widespread threat to global biodiversity continues to deteriorate. To this end, all regions and countries in the world have adopted active policies on biodiversity conservation and restoration. Major global initiatives on biodiversity are shown in Figure 4.14.

International Organizations	Regional Organizations	Countries /Regions
(1) In 1992, the United Nations Convention on Biological Diversity was signed.	(1) ASEAN: "China-ASEAN Environmental Cooperation Strategy and Action Framework", and the "China-ASEAN Investment and Trade Cooper-ation Biodiversity Conservation Guidel-ines" in 2022.	(1) China: "Wildlife Protection Law", "Biodiversity Strategy and Action Plan for 2011-2020", "China Biodiversity Conserv ation Strategy and Action Plan (2011-2030)", etc.
(2) In 2000, the Cartagena Protocol on Biosafety to the Convention on Biological Diversity was adopted.		
(3) In 2010, the Nagoya Protocol on Access and Benefit-sharing was adopted.	(2) European Union: "EU Biodiversity Strategy 2030", "Nature Restoration Law", "European Green Deal", and "Natura 2000" in the EU.	(2) Brazil: "National Biodiversity Action Plan", "National System of Conservation Units", "Biosecurity Law", "Provisional Measure for the Protection of Biodiversity and Genetic Resources", etc.
(4) In 2010, the Strategic Plan for Biodivers ity 2011-2020 was confirmed for implementation, and the Aichi Targets were established.	(3) African Union: "Convention for the Protection of Wildlife, Birds, and Fish in Africa", "China-Africa Cooperation Forum-Dakar Action Plan 2022-2024".	(3) Australia: "Environment and Biodiversity Conservation Act", "Important Habitats Register" system, "Australian National Biodiversity Conservation Strategy", etc.
(5) In 2022, the "Post-2020 Global Biodiversity Framework" was reached.		

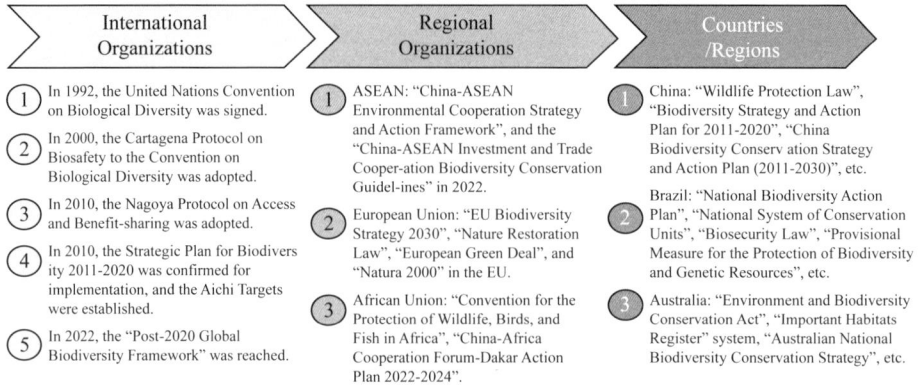

Figure 4.14 Global response to biodiversity

Data source: drawn according to the relevant policies on biodiversity conservation and recovery.

The United Nations Convention on Biological Diversity is a legally binding international convention. According to the *United Nations Convention on Biological Diversity*, there are three main objectives: biodiversity conservation, a sustainable use of biodiversity, and a fair and equitable sharing of the benefits arising from the use of genetic resources. The 15th Conference of the Parties to the *United Nations Convention on Biological Diversity* has adopted the *Kunming-Montreal Global Biodiversity Framework. The Kunming-Montreal Global Biodiversity Framework* aims to prevent and reverse the loss of the natural environment. The framework contains the global goals to be achieved within 2030 and beyond for the conservation and sustainable use of biodiversity. Under the framework, the four overall goals to be achieved by 2050 focus on ecosystem and species health, including: end ing human-induced extinctions, sustainable use of biodiversity, fair sharing of benefits, and implementation and financing, including filling the $700 billion a year in biodiversity financing gaps. The 23 specific goals to be achieved by 2030 include protecting 30 percent of land and sea, restoring 30 percent of degraded ecosystems, halving the introduction of invasive species, and reducing subsidies to damage biodiversity by $500 billion a year.

According to the second edition of *State of Finance for Nature* issued by the United Nations Environment Programme, funding for the natural environment remains insufficient for the *Post-2020 Global Biodiversity Framework*; funding for nature-based solutions needs to double by 2025. Preventing biodiversity loss requires significant and urgent action in the conservation of nature, and nature-based solutions face many challenges. The *State of Finance of Nature* says that preventing biodiversity loss will require an additional $230 billion a year until 2025. According to the *State of Finance for Nature*, to meet future climate, biodiversity and land degradation targets, both public and private actors will need to increase their annual investment by at least quadruple in the next 30 years. By 2050, the total investment demand will reach $8.4 trillion, or more than $536 billion a year, four times the current investment, to control climate change, reverse losses and stabilize biodiversity.

The *European Commission's Global Biodiversity Strategy 2030* and the *Farm to Table Strategy* work together to restore biodiversity in the EU by 2030, strengthen conservation of land and sea, restore degraded ecosystems, and build a sustainable food chain. The *Global Biodiversity Strategy 2030* focuses on biodiversity factors such as the unsustainable use of land and oceans, invasion of alien species, and overexploitation of natural resources, aiming to make conservation and restoration of biodiversity part of the EU's overall economic growth strategy. The strategy proposes to establish at least 30% of Europe's land and oceans as ecological reserves, strictly protect areas with high biodiversity and high climate value, allow at least 25,000 kilometers of rivers to resume free flow, and improve the health of European forests. The EU plans to spend at least 20 billion euros a year on the strategy, coming from public and private funds from the EU and member states, as well as the EU's budget for climate change. The *Farm to Table Strategy* aims to create a fair, healthy and environmentally friendly food system. The strategy proposes to promote the sustainable use of pesticides, eliminate soil pollution, develop organic agriculture, establish a sustainable food system, and support farmers, fishermen, and farmers in the transition to sustainable production. The European Commission will set a legally binding target to reduce food waste by 2023, investing 10 billion euros on research and development innovation in food, agriculture, fisheries, aquaculture, bioeconomy and other sectors to accelerate the green and digital transformation of agriculture.

As a biodiversity resort, Southeast Asia is rich in wildlife and plant resources. The destruction and pollution of natural habitats, climate change, and invasive species have all brought biodiversity in Southeast Asia into crisis. In order to protect and restore biodiversity, ASEAN countries have adopted policies to protect and restore biodiversity: First, Biodiversity Reserve Network: ASEAN member states have set up a series of nature reserves and wildlife reserves to protect rare and endangered species and ecosystems. These protected areas form a networked system that facilitates species migration and gene flow. Second, Sustainable forestry management: ASEAN countries are committed to promoting sustainable forestry management, reducing deforestation and illegal timber trade. They achieve this by establishing forestry certification systems, strengthening law enforcement and regulation, and promoting community engagement. Third, Protection of endangered species: ASEAN member states have formulated laws and policies to protect endangered species, including stopping illegal wildlife trade and smuggling activities. They have also strengthened their capacity to monitor wildlife and fight wildlife crime. Fourth, Biodiversity conservation and climate change adaptation: ASEAN countries combine biodiversity conservation and climate change adaptation to mitigate the impact of climate change and improve the adaptability of ecosystems by protecting and restoring the wetland, forest and Marine ecosystems. Fifth, Community participation and sustainable development: ASEAN countries paid attention to the principles of community participation and sustainable development, and encourage local communities to play an active role in biodiversity conservation and management. They support community natural resource management programs to ensure that local residents reap economic and social benefits from biodiversity conservation.

According to the *National Biodiversity Strategy 2023-2030* approved by the Japanese Cabinet, Japan's main strategies in biodiversity conservation and restoration are as follows: First, restoring ecosystem health. Second, Using nature to solve social questions. Third, Realize natural economy. Fourth, Recognize the value of biodiversity in daily life and consumption activities and actions. Fifth, Develop infrastructure to support biodiversity initiatives and promote international cooperation. The National Biodefense Strategy issued by the US government is the most comprehensive and systematic strategic document to respond to all kinds of biosafety threats, representing the new direction of the US to build domestic and international biosafety capacity. The main measures include: First, enhancing situation awareness, accident characterization and consequence assessment of the global biological monitoring system. Second, Strengthening the monitoring and operation capabilities of domestic and foreign biological monitoring laboratories. Third, Strengthening the ability to assess the biological defense capabilities of domestic and other countries. Fourth, Strengthening the identification, investigation, attribution and destruction of domestic and foreign biological weapons. Fifth, Strengthening the ability to intercept, prohibit, destroy and accountability of biological weapons materials; strengthening the sharing of international specimens, reagents and intelligence. Sisth, strengthening the capacity of international investigation, accountability and sanctions. In order to protect Australia's biodiversity, Australian governments at all levels strictly implement the convention on biological diversity, at the federal level formulated the Australian national ecological and sustainable utilization development strategy and the Australian national biodiversity conservation strategy two special strategic measures to guide the national biodiversity conservation work. According to the report, Australia's main measures for biodiversity conservation and recovery include: First, Improving relevant laws and regulations. Second, Building national parks to protect biodiversity. Third, Conducting innovation in biodiversity management. Fourth, Promoting research on biodiversity conservation technologies. Many countries in the world have mode a lot of measures to protect and restore biodiversity, including formulating laws and regulations, building national parks and so on.

    Policies on biodiversity conservation and restoration have been continuously improved. The National Biodiversity Strategy and Action Plan (NBSAP) is the primary policy tool for the implementation of the CBD at the national level. To date, 193 of the 196 States Parties have developed at least one national biodiversity strategy and action plan. The effect of biodiversity conservation and recovery needs to be improved. According to the *Global Biodiversity Outlook* (GBO-5), none of the 20 Biodiversity Action targets were fully achieved, but six were partially met (targets 9,11,16,17,19,20) (Figure 4.15). Of these, only 12% of the 60 specific elements of the biodiversity action target were achieved. The theme of the International Day on Biodiversity 2022 is "Building a Community of Life on Earth". The theme conveys the message: biodiversity is the basis of we can rebuild a better home, involving ecosystem climate and for climate, health, food security, water security and sustainable livelihood based on natural solutions, countries need to join hands to protect and restore biodiversity.

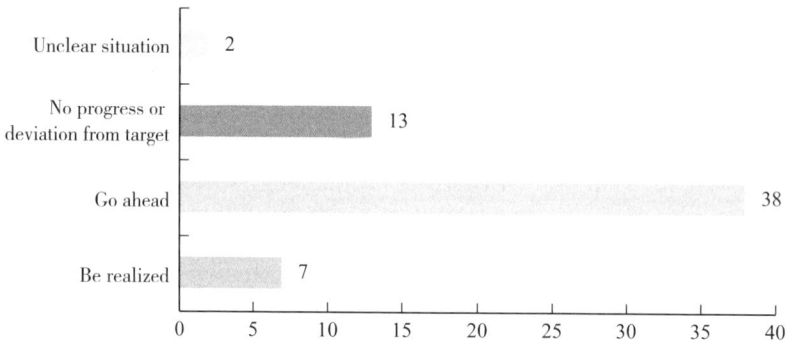

Figure 4.15 Progress in the implementation of 60 specific elements of the 20 action targets in the Strategic Plan for Biodiversity 2011-2020 (units: one)

Data source: drawn based on the Global Biodiversity Outlook.

3. Pollution control policies

More and more serious environmental pollution has seriously affected people's food, clothing, housing and transportation, and it is urgent for all organizations and countries around the world to take active actions to control environmental pollution to protect the ecological environment. Global pollution control is a broad and complex problem, mainly including: air pollution control, water pollution control and soil pollution control.

(1) Air pollution

Air pollution not only poses a serious threat to human health, but also has a profound impact on the ecological environment. Industrial emissions, traffic exhaust, agricultural activities and household garbage are the main causes of air pollution. These pollutants can destroy the ozone layer in the atmosphere, leading to global warming and environmental pollution, and have a serious impact on the future of humanity and the earth. The average annual exposure to $PM_{2.5}$ air pollution is shown in Figure 4.16. Over the past five years, a growing number of countries have introduced policies on key sectors that cause air pollution, according to the UN Environment Programme's Global Air Quality Action: A Summary of Global Policies and Plans for Air pollution Reduction. National statistics of global policies that motivate or promote industrial cleaner production, energy efficiency and pollution reduction are shown in Figure 4.17.However, there are large gaps in implementation, funding, capacity, and monitoring. The United Nations Environment Programme has called on countries to invest in air pollution control and include it in their respective post-COVID-19 recovery plans. UNEP also called for benchmarks to assess current and future clean air actions to remove barriers in policy and program

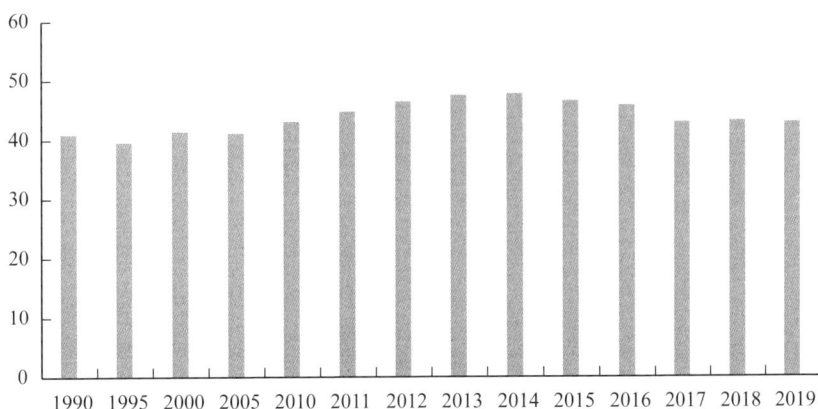

Figure 4.16   Average annual exposure of $PM_{2.5}$ air pollution (unit: mg / m^3)

Data source: collated and drawn according to the relevant data of the World Bank.

implementation, including funding and capacity gaps, affordability of air quality monitoring equipment and maintenance challenges. The European Union issued EU Action Plan: achieve zero pollution of air, water and soil, the ultimate goal is to 2050 air, water and soil pollution to human health and no longer harmful to the natural ecosystem, the action plan is a key achievement of the European green agreement, around the zero pollution in 2050 vision, the action plan set the key to achieve the target by 2030, and put forward a series of measures (Figure 4.17).

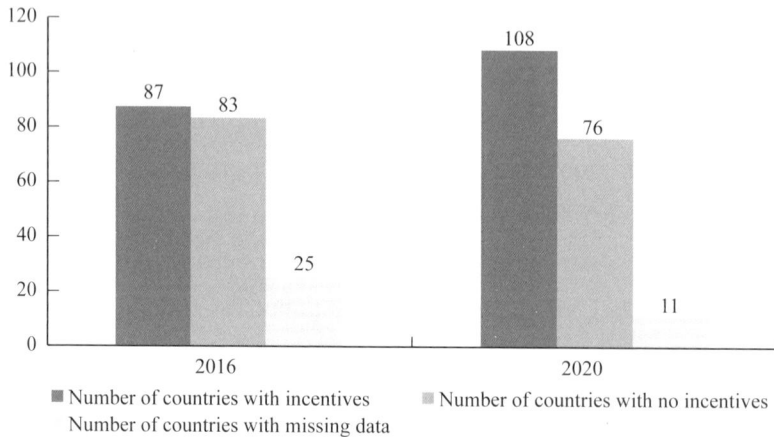

Figure 4.17　Global national statistics on policies that incentivize or promote cleaner industrial production, energy efficiency and pollution reduction

Data source: drawn based on Air Quality Action: Summary of Policies and Projects for Global Air Pollution Reduction.

The root of air pollution control in the United States originated from the photochemical smog event in Los Angeles in the 1950s, with the *Air Pollution Control Act, the Clean Air Act* and the *Clean Air Interstate Regulations* issued to solve the problems of O_3 and $PM_{2.5}$ pollution near the ground. The US Plastics Convention sets five targets, including a list of plastic packaging to be designated as problematic or unnecessary in 2021, and measures to eliminate these packages by 2025; ensuring 100% reusable, recyclable or composted by 2025, 30% of recycled or responsible biobased components in plastic packaging by 2025, and annual public reports on progress against these targets. Japan's air pollution control stems from a surge in the number of patients with asthma diseases near petrochemical plants in 1960. Since the government promulgated the Air Pollution Control Law in 1968, Japan's air quality has been significantly improved after more than 30 years of efforts. However, in the central urban areas of big cities, $PM_{2.5}$ concentration to reach the standard is very difficult. According to the White Paper on water policy released by the UK, various measures should be taken to address the problems of excessive water intake and water pollution. Main measures are: the white paper emphasizes from the source of pollution control, the core is based on the river basin, and local polluters, beneficiaries and related parties discuss goals and action plan, on the basis of considering the suggestion, including incentives, ecological services and strengthen tracking monitoring, action, including agricultural non-point source pollution, private wastewater treatment facilities, waste metal mines and urban non-point source pollution, pollution problems. Countries in the world have taken a lot of measures against their own pollution and made good progress. On the whole, the main evolution trends of global air pollution prevention policies and measures are as follows:

From regional to global: early air pollution policies were often confined to national or regional scopes, exemplified by Belgium's enactment of the *Law Against Atmospheric Pollution* following the Meuse Valley Fog Incident, the successive promulgation of the *Air Pollution Control Act 1955*, *Clean Air Act 1963*, and *Air Quality Act 1967* by the United States federal government, and the United Kingdom's *Clean Air Act 1956*. However, with the escalating prominence of global environmental issues, there has been a proliferation of air pollution policies on a global scale, such as the World Health Organization's *Global Air Quality Guidelines 2021*. Remarkable progress has been made in air pollution control efforts. According to the UNEP's *Air Pollution Series: Air Quality Action*, as of 2020, over a quarter of countries have formulated national air quality management strategies, and 124 countries (approximately two-thirds) have enacted legal instruments for ambient air quality standards.

Nations are expanding their air quality monitoring networks through various means, yet many still lack reliable and routine monitoring systems (Figure 4.18, Figure 4.19).

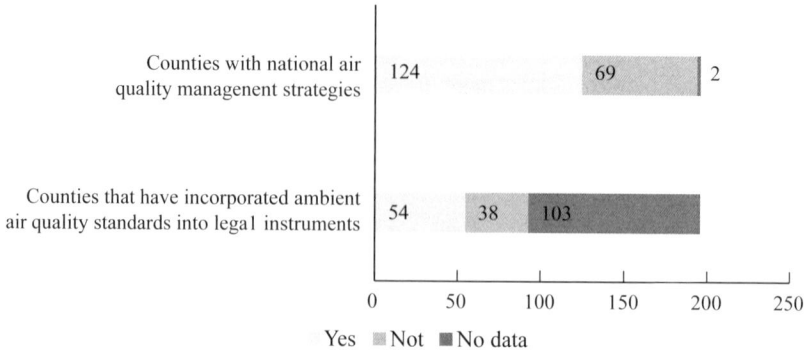

Figure 4.18   National statistics of Global Air Pollution Control Action

Data source: drawn based on *Air Quality Action: Summary of Policies and Projects for Global Air Pollution Reduction.*

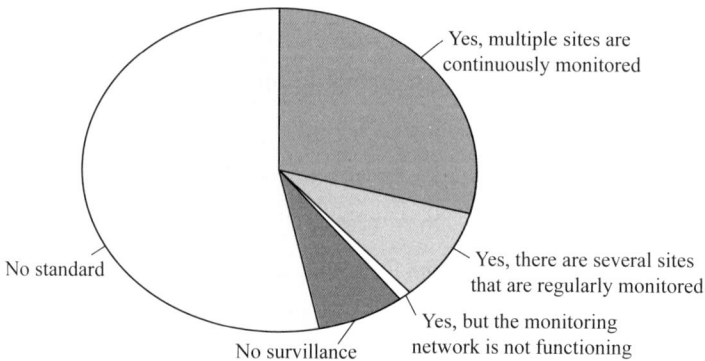

Figure 4.19   Percentage of countries with a National Ambient Air Quality Monitoring Network

Data source: drawn based on *Air Quality Action: Summary of Policies and Projects for Global Air Pollution Reduction.*

From single to multiple: the early air pollution policies were mainly aimed at certain or several specific air pollutants, such as Belgium's *Anti-Air Pollution Act*, mainly aimed at sulfur oxides and nitrogen oxides. Now, air pollution policies are more diverse, focusing on multiple air pollutants, such as the

WHO's *2021 Global Air Quality Guidelines*, providing medium-term targets for six major air pollutants.

From end-treatment to whole-process control: early air pollution policies often focused on end-treatment of pollutant emissions, such as installing filters in factory chimneys. The current air pollution policy focuses more on controlling the whole process starting from the source, including optimizing the energy structure, encouraging green transportation, and improving energy efficiency.

From empirical to scientific: while early air pollution policies were usually based on experience and intuition, air pollution policies now rely more on scientific data and scientific research. For example, *the Clean Air Act* in the United States relies on major air pollutants found by scientific research and their effects on human health.

From unilateral to multilateral: the early air pollution policies were usually formulated and implemented by a single country or organization, while the current air pollution policy is more focused on multilateral cooperation. For example, *the Outline of the United Nations Convention to Combat Desertification and Sandstorms* (SDS) provides information and guidance on how to assess and respond to the risks of desertification and sandstorms and to take action, which requires the cooperation of multiple countries and organizations to be effectively implemented.

(2) Water pollution

The current situation of water pollution is very serious, and the global fresh water resources are under serious threat. Waste water discharge in industry and daily life, the use of chemical fertilizers and pesticides in agriculture, and garbage disposal in the process of urbanization are all the main causes of water pollution. These pollutants will not only destroy the living environment of aquatic organisms, but also lead to the deterioration of water quality, and even affect human health. Global water pollution prevention and control policies and their evolution trends are as follows:

First, from local to global: early water pollution policies were usually limited to one region or country, such as the UK's *Rivers Act* focused on pollution in the Thames. However, with the acceleration of industrialization and urbanization, the water pollution problem gradually shows a trend of globalization, and the national governments and international organizations gradually begin to strengthen cooperation to jointly deal with the global water pollution problem. For example, international organizations such as the United Nations Environment Programme (UNEP) and the World Health Organization (WHO) are actively involved in the formulation of policies and standards for global water pollution control. *The Overview of UN-related Activities and Initiatives on Marine Litter and Microplastics* issued by the United Nations underscores the pivotal role played by various UN agencies in facilitating national-level interventions aimed at mitigating marine litter and plastic pollution, and in driving forward the formulation of a novel global agreement on plastic pollution management, anticipated to be unveiled at the resumed Fifth Session of the United Nations Environment Assembly (UNEA-5.2). According to the APEC report, *Global Plastics Outlook: Economic Drive, Environmental Impact and Policy Choice*, the main purpose of the report is to help policymakers understand the direction and make scientific decisions to achieve "river-sea zero plastics" for future generations.

Second, from single to comprehensive: the early water pollution policy mainly targeted a single source of pollution or pollutants, such as the British *Rivers Act* mainly targeted industrial wastewater discharged into rivers. However, with the complexity of water pollution, water pollution policy gradually changes from single pollution source control to comprehensive pollution control. For example, the implementation of the European Commission *Water Framework Directive* aims to achieve an integrated management of water resources across Europe.

Third, from voluntary to compulsory: Early water pollution policies were mainly based on voluntary principles, such as corporate emissions reduction and voluntary water quality agreements. However, with the increasing problem of water pollution, many countries began to adopt stricter legal and policy measures, forcing enterprises and governments to fulfill their water pollution prevention and control obligations. For example, the EU's *Water Framework Directive* clearly defines the water quality targets and drainage standards of the Member States, and implements strict penalties.

Fourth, from domestic to international: Policies and standards for global water pollution control are not limited to the domestic level, but also involve international cooperation. For example, international organizations such as the World Trade Organization (WTO) and the United Nations Conference on Trade and Development (UNCTAD) have actively participated in the formulation of policies and standards for global water pollution control and promoted international cooperation on global water pollution control.

Water pollution control needs to start from many aspects, including improving laws and regulations, raising environmental standards, strengthening supervision and law enforcement, and promoting cleaner production and circular economy. At the same time, it is also necessary to strengthen publicity and education to raise the public awareness of environmental protection and water resources protection. Only in this way can we effectively control water pollution, protect water resources, maintain the ecological environment, and promote the sustainable development of mankind and society.

(3) Soil pollution

Soil pollution prevention and control is an important link of global environmental protection. Soil pollution sources are complex, including industrial and urban waste, agricultural chemicals, heavy metals, etc. These pollutants are not only harmful to soil organisms and plants, but also enter the human body through the food chain, affecting human health.

According to the United Nations *Global Soil Pollution Assessment*, increasing soil pollution and the spread of waste are threatening future global food production and human and environmental health, and immediate global action is needed to meet this challenge. The growing demand for agricultural food and industrial systems and the growing global population have led to severe soil pollution and widespread environmental degradation, which has become one of the biggest challenges in the global ecological restoration process. Soil health is fundamental to the planet's health, with the use of pesticides increasing by 75% between 2000 and 2017. In 2018, the use of synthetic nitrogen fertilizer reached 109 million tons worldwide. The use of plastics in agriculture has increased dramatically in recent decades. In 2019,708,000 tons of non-packaging plastics were consumed in the EU alone. Since the start of the 21st century, global annual production of industrial chemicals has doubled to 2.3 billion tons; it is expected to grow by another 85% by 2030. The waste generated increases year by year. Currently, global waste production is about 2 billion tons per year; this number is expected to grow to 3.4 billion tons by 2050 as the population grows and urbanizes. Global soil pollution control policies mainly include the following categories:

First, comprehensive policies: Such policies are usually based on the "polluter pays" principle, requiring companies that produce soil pollution to take responsibility for remediation. At the same time, the government will give certain financial and policy support, strengthen technology research and development and application, and promote the development of environmental protection industry. For example, the *European Union's Pan-European Soil Protection Program* and the *United States' Soil Pollution Prevention Act*.

Second, policies for the prevention and control of agricultural non-point source pollution: such policies mainly target chemical fertilizers, pesticides and other chemical substances used in agricultural activities, and reduce soil pollution caused by chemical substances by limiting the use and regulating the amount of use. For example, the *European Union's Fertilizer Use Directive* and the *Pesticide Use Directive*, etc.

Third, industrial pollution prevention and control policies: such policies mainly focus on the discharge of pollutants in industrial activities, through strict emission standards and control measures to reduce soil pollution. For example, the *Clean Water Act* and the *Clean Air Act* in the United States.

Fourth, land use planning policy: this kind of policy is mainly through the formulation of land use planning, reasonable arrangement of urban and industrial development layout, to avoid the soil pollution problem caused by excessive development. For example, the *British Land Use Planning Act* and so on.

Fifth, environmental monitoring policies: such policies require regular monitoring of the soil environment, grasp the status and change trend of soil pollution, and provide scientific basis for taking corresponding prevention and control measures. For example, the *National Soil Pollution Monitoring Program* in the United States.

Sixth, the remediation policy of contaminated sites: such policies require the remediation and treatment of contaminated sites, including cleaning up pollutants, improving soil quality and other measures. For example, the *UK's Contaminated Site Restoration Act*, etc.

Global soil pollution policies are characterized by diversified, comprehensive, interconnected and innovative policies. Global soil pollution control is a work of great significance, which requires the concerted efforts of governments, enterprises and the public around the world.

III. Typical cases of rural ecological governance

1. Tackling climate change

(1) The Noor Solar Power Station

The Noor Solar Power Station is a huge solar power plant located in Morocco, also known as the Noor thermal power plant. Located in Quarzazate in the Sahara Desert, it is one of the largest concentrated solar power plants in the world.

The Noor Solar Power Station uses centralized solar power generation technology, using a large number of flat-panel solar collectors (CSPs) to collect and focus solar energy and convert it into heat. These focused solar energy is used to heat the working fluid (usually oil or salt), which then generates steam to drive the turbines to generate electricity. Construction of the plant began in 2013 and went into operation in 2018. With a total installed capacity of 580 megawatts (MW), the plant is expected to generate about 450 million kilowatt-hours (kWh) per year, enough to power about a million homes.

The goal of the Noor solar power plant is to reduce Morocco's dependence on fossil fuels, improve energy security, and reduce greenhouse gas emissions. The operation of the plant will reduce emissions by about 760,000 tonnes of carbon dioxide, equivalent to planting about 37,000 trees a year. The plant is designed to take advantage of the abundant solar energy resources of the Sahara desert to meet domestic electricity demand and export electricity to Europe. The construction of the Noor solar power plant marks significant progress in the field of renewable energy, and provides a viable model for other countries to use solar energy resources to achieve clean energy development goals. The construction of the plant has also brought economic benefits, creating many jobs in Morocco and reducing its dependence on imported energy sources.

The Noor solar power plant in Morocco is of great significance for tackling climate change and promoting sustainable development. The successful construction and operation of the Noible solar power plant has set an example for Morocco to grow in the renewable energy sector. It not only laid a solid foundation for Morocco to achieve the Sustainable Development Goals, but also provided reference and inspiration for other countries to promote the development and application of global renewable energy. By reducing greenhouse gas emissions, reducing energy dependence, creating jobs and promoting sustainable development, the plant has made a positive contribution to protecting the environment, promoting economic development and improving people's living standards.

(2) China's new energy vehicle industry

China's new energy vehicle industry has developed into one of the world's leading industries. Since 2009, the Chinese government has launched a large-scale promotion plan for new energy vehicles, and has given strong support in policy and funding. By 2023, the number of new energy vehicles in China has exceeded more than half of the world's total, reaching more than 18.21 million.

The rapid development of China's new energy vehicle industry, on the one hand, thanks to the government's support policies, on the other hand, also thanks to the continuous innovation and progress of enterprises. China's new energy vehicle enterprises, such as BYD, Geely, Nio, Xiaopeng, etc., have made a lot of investment and research and development in new energy vehicle technology, intelligent driving, charging facilities and other fields, and constantly launched competitive new energy vehicle products.

At the same time, China's new energy vehicle industry chain has also been continuously improved, including batteries, motors, electric control and other key components have a number of competitive enterprises. In addition, China's new energy vehicle charging facilities are also under continuous construction and improvement, and the coverage of the charging network has become more and more extensive, providing convenience for the use of new energy vehicles.

China's new energy vehicle industry has shifted from policy-driven to market-driven, and continues to maintain rapid development. It is estimated that by 2030, the number of new energy vehicles in China will reach about 20 million, and the market scale will continue to expand. At the same time, China will continue to increase investment and research and development efforts in new energy vehicle technology, intelligent driving, charging facilities and other fields, and constantly improve the technical level and market competitiveness of new energy vehicles.

The new energy vehicle industry is extremely important to cope with climate change. On the one hand, to reduce greenhouse gas emissions, new energy vehicles, such as electric vehicles and hydrogen fuel cell vehicles, use electricity or hydrogen as energy, and do not produce exhaust emissions. Compared with conventional gas-fired vehicles, they can significantly reduce emissions of greenhouse gases such as carbon dioxide, carbon monoxide and nitrogen oxides, helping to mitigate global climate change problems. This is of profound significance for tackling global climate change, slowing down the rise of the earth's temperature and protecting the environment. On the other hand, to improve air quality, the exhaust emissions from traditional fuel vehicles are one of the main sources of urban air pollution, including harmful particulate matter and air pollutants. The zero-emission characteristics of new energy vehicles can significantly reduce harmful substances in the air, improve urban air quality, and reduce the impact on human health. This will not only improve the quality of life of urban residents, but also help to promote global public health levels.

(3) The Great Green Wall for Restoration and Peace

The Great Green Wall for Restoration and Peace , also known as the Great Green Wall of Sub-Saharan Africa, is an initiative designed to combat desertification, restore ecosystems, and mitigate the impacts of climate change. Developed by the African Union in 2007 and supported by the United Nations Environment Programme, the World Bank and others, it has a vision to transform the lives of millions of people by creating a green and productive landscape in 11 countries. The plan has evolved from a tree-planting campaign to a comprehensive rural development initiative, and the goal has shifted to build an 8,000-kilometer ecological shelterbelt along the southern edge of the Sahara desert and control 100 million hectares of desertification land. The plan not only involves ecological projects, but also concerns food security and regional stability. It is an important part of Africa's building of a community of life together for man and nature. The goal is to restore 100 million hectares of land, seal 250 million tons of carbon and create 10 million jobs by 2030.

By restoring degraded land and mass afforestation, the Great Green Wall of Africa will provide food and water security, create habitat for wildlife, and provide reasons for residents to stay in arid and poverty-stricken areas. The plan will also create jobs, promote economic development, and improve the living conditions of the local people. The main goal of the plan is to reverse the trend of the desert advancing southward and establish ecological barriers at the edge of the desert by planting trees, grassland restoration and land management. The main measures are as follows: (a) Combating desertification: take measures to reduce land degradation and desertification, and improve local soil quality and water resources management. Including afforestation, soil and water conservation, windbreak and sand fixation and other technical means. (b) Construction of green belt: Build a green belt about 15 kilometers wide in the southern edge of the Sahara Desert to resist the expansion of the desert and increase the local vegetation coverage. This helps to improve climate conditions and promote rainfall and soil retention. (c) Promoting agricultural development: Provide training and support to local farmers by introducing sustainable agricultural practices and technologies to increase food production, improve food safety and increase farmers' income. (d) Promoting employment and social development: It is planned to create jobs for local residents through greening projects and related economic activities, and to provide education, medical care and other social services to improve people's living standards. (e) Regional cooperation and peaceful promotion: The plan encourages transnational cooperation, strengthens cooperation and communication among African countries, jointly responds to environmental challenges, and promotes peace and stability. These measures can not only mitigate the impact of climate change, but also provide local residents with employment opportunities and ways to improve their living conditions.

By 2023, the plan has involved more than 20 countries, covering more than 11 million hectares of land, and has already implemented numerous afforestation, grassland restoration and land management projects. The Green Great Wall for Restoration and Peace is an important initiative to help African people tackle climate change and ecosystem degradation. It will help to achieve the Sustainable Development Goals, improve the living conditions of local people and make a positive contribution to the global response to climate change.

2. Biodiversity conservation and restoration

(1) Biodiversity conservation and restoration in developing countries-a case study of Peru

Peru is one of the most biodiversity countries in the world, with rich ecosystems and species resources. The Peruvian government has taken various measures to protect and restore biodiversity in and around Manu National Park. Main measures include: (a) Establishment of protected areas: The Peruvian government established the Manu National Park in the early 1980s, dividing the area into areas protected by law. This initiative restricted unregulated development activities and ensured the ecological integrity of the region. (b) Restrictions on illegal hunting and logging: The Peruvian Government has strengthened law enforcement on illegal hunting, illegal logging and mining activities. To reduce the killing of wildlife and habitat destruction by creating patrols, enhanced surveillance and operations against illegal activities. (c) Community participation and sustainable utilization: The Peruvian government works with local communities to promote community participation and benefit from conservation measures. By promoting sustainable land management and resource utilization practices, such as sustainable agriculture, forestry, and tourism, providing economic opportunities for local residents and encouraging them to become key partners in protected areas. (d) Scientific research and monitoring: The Peruvian government supports scientific research and monitoring to understand the status of biodiversity, species distribution and ecosystem function in the region. These data are essential for developing conservation strategies and management plans. Through these measures, the Peruvian government is committed to protecting the biodiversity of people in Manu National Park and working with communities, the scientific community and NGOs to ensure sustainable development and ecological balance in the region.

This project is a typical case study of biodiversity and ecosystem conservation in Peru. Through such projects, Peru strives to protect and restore its biodiversity and ecosystems, further curbing environmental deterioration and the loss of biodiversity.

(2) Biodiversity conservation and recovery in developed countries- a case study of the United States

Yellowstone National Park is the world's first national park and one of the most famous in the United States. Yellowstone is known for its rich biodiversity, with diverse ecosystems and large numbers of wild animal and plant species. The following are the measures and achievements of Yellowstone National Park in biodiversity conservation:

First, species conservation: Yellowstone Park is one of the most important bases for species conservation in the United States. There are a large number of protected animals in the park, including American bison, grey Wolf, bighorn sheep, American black bear and so on. Parks take measures to protect these species, such as restricting human activities, establishing conservation areas, monitoring and research.

Second, ecological restoration: Yellowstone is also working to restore the damaged ecosystem. In the 1990s, for example, the park conducted a massive grey wolf reintroduction program designed to restore the grey wolf population and rebuild the food chain. The program was a huge success, restoring not only grey wolf populations, but also having positive effects on other species and ecosystems. Mainly include: Firstly, promote the recovery of food chain balance: the return of wolves leads to the recovery of food chain balance. Wolves feed on large herbivores such as elk and moose and play an important role in controlling the populations of these species. The reduction in overgrazing and overpredation has allowed for vegetation restoration and improved river environment and soil stability. Secondly, improving species diversity: The return of wolves has had a positive impact on the biodiversity in Yellowstone National Park. By controlling herbivore populations such as elk, wolves indirectly drive the recovery of other species. For example, forest-dwelling birds increase and predators such as eagles and are balanced. Thirdly, it contributes to ecosystem health: the reintroduction of wolves promotes the health of the Yellowstone National Park ecosystem. It changes animal behavior, makes animals afraid of wolves to choose habitats more carefully and reduces overgrazing and feeding, which has positive effects on the restoration of river and vegetation, thus improving the stability of the whole ecosystem.

Third, biological monitoring and research: Yellowstone Park has conducted extensive biological monitoring and scientific research to understand and protect the biodiversity in the park. These studies include monitoring of animal migration, species distribution and abundance, as well as studies of ecosystem function and ecological processes. These data and information provide a scientific basis for the development and implementation of protection measures.

Fourth, education and public participation: Yellowstone Park raises public awareness and understanding of biodiversity conservation through education and public participation activities. The park organizes various activities such as tour guides, lectures, workshops, to introduce visitors to the park's biodiversity and conservation efforts and encourage them to take action to protect the environment.

Yellowstone National Park has made remarkable achievements in biodiversity conservation. The park preserves and maintains a rich biodiversity through species conservation, ecological restoration, biological monitoring and research, and education and public participation. The successful experience of Yellowstone Park provides important reference and inspiration for biodiversity conservation in other countries and regions.

(3) Biodiversity conservation and restoration through multilateral cooperation

The Amazon Basin Conservation Program is a comprehensive program designed to protect the Amazon rainforest ecosystem. As one of the largest tropical rainforests on Earth, the Amazon rainforest is essential for the global climate and biodiversity. The following are some of the main objectives and measures that may be included in the plan:

First, increase reserves: expand existing nature reserves and national parks, and create new reserves to ensure that larger areas of rainforest are protected.

Second, anti-deforestation action: take severe measures to combat illegal logging and deforestation, strengthen law enforcement, and conduct real-time monitoring of forest cover changes through technical means (such as satellite monitoring).

Third, sustainable economic development: Promote and support Amazon residents to turn to sustainable economic activities, encourage them to adopt environmentally friendly agriculture, forestry and tourism, and reduce their dependence on rainforest resources.

Fourth, strengthen land rights to protect the land rights of indigenous people and local communities, respect their traditional knowledge and culture, and involve them in the formulation and implementation of protection plans.

Fifth, international cooperation and financial support: to promote cooperation among the international community, providing financial and technical support for the Amazon Basin Conservation Program, including resources from governments, non-governmental organizations and the private sector. The goals of these measures are to protect the ecological integrity of the Amazon rainforest, mitigate climate change, preserve species diversity, and support the sustainable development of local communities. "Biodiversity Conservation and Restoration in the Amazon Basin Conservation Program" is a comprehensive and ambitious program designed to conserve and restore biodiversity in the Amazon Basin while promoting sustainable development in the region.

The biodiversity conservation and restoration work of the Railway in Kenya is one of the typical cases of biodiversity conservation in the Belt and Road Initiative. Mombasa-Nairobi Railway is a standard gauge railway line in Kenya. The railway was officially opened on 31 May 2017, connecting Nairobi, the capital of Kenyan and the port city of Mombasa, with a total length of about 480 kilometers. The design, construction and operation of the modern railway strictly follow all environmental indicators to ensure harmony between the railway and wildlife. At the design stage of the project, China will consider how to minimize the environmental impact, especially by protecting the wildlife migration routes. In order to ensure the free passage of wild animals, especially large animals such as giraffes and elephants after the completion of the railway, the first phase of the railway adopted the scheme of crossing the park, with the lowest pier of more than 6 meters. In addition, to reduce the impact on wildlife, dozens of bridges and hundreds of culverts have been built. During the construction, the Chinese builders also took a series of measures to protect animals, such as installing sound barriers on both sides of the guardrail of the bridge across the Nairobi National Park to greatly reduce the noise when trains pass through the national park and minimize the impact on wildlife. The biodiversity conservation and restoration work of the Mambasa-Nairobi

Railway in Kenya fully reflects the importance China attaches to biodiversity conservation in the Belt and Road Initiative. The Mombasa-Nairobi in kenya Railway project has successfully demonstrated a multilateral cooperation model in biodiversity conservation and restoration, providing useful experience for ecological protection and sustainable development in the "Belt and Road" construction.

3. Pollution prevention and control

(1) Air pollution prevention and control

Beijing in China and the Ruhr Industrial Zone in Germany are both world-famous typical cases of air pollution control. The following are introduced separately.

In 2013, a sustained, large and high concentration of heavy air pollution occurred in Beijing, and the average mass concentration of $PM_{2.5}$ was close to 160 micrograms per cubic meter, which attracted high attention at home and abroad. The number of days of heavy pollution reached 58, accounting for 15.9% of the whole year, equivalent to an average day of heavy pollution per week. The experience of air pollution prevention and control in Beijing mainly includes:

First, the five-year action plan and the three-year action plan to protect the blue sky: Through a series of policies and measures, Beijing has strengthened the monitoring and prediction of air quality, and promoted the continuous improvement of air quality.

Second, use scientific and technological means to accurately identify the sources of pollution: with satellite remote sensing, navigation, video surveillance and other scientific and technological means, accurately identify the pollution sources and take targeted measures.

Third, adopt multi-pronged measures: in the face of the characteristics of compound pollution, Beijing has taken comprehensive measures from industry, energy, transportation, dust and other aspects, and achieved obvious results.

Fourth, continuously strengthen regional joint prevention and control:

Beijing has strengthened joint prevention and control with surrounding areas to jointly deal with regional air pollution problems, and promoted the overall improvement of regional air quality.

Through the implementation of the above measures, Beijing has achieved remarkable achievements in the prevention and control of air pollution. According to the average annual concentrations of PM_{10}, sulfur dioxide, nitrogen dioxide and carbon monoxide in Beijing dropped by 70 percent, 98 percent, 65 percent and 82 percent, respectively, between 1998 and 2021. At the same time, the number of days with excellent standards in Beijing increased, the number of days with pollution days in winter decreased significantly, and the frequency, peak concentration and duration of heavy pollution weather all decreased significantly. Among them, the concentration of $PM_{2.5}$ decreased by 62%, the local emission reduction reduced the concentration of $PM_{2.5}$ concentration by 30 micrograms per cubic meter, the meteorological conditions reduced the concentration of $PM_{2.5}$ by 11 micrograms per cubic meter, and the surrounding emission reduction reduced Beijing $PM_{2.5}$ by 15 micrograms per cubic meter.

The Ruhr industrial zone was once one of the most polluted areas in Germany. Due to industrial activities in the region, including heavy coal and steel production, significant emissions of exhaust and soot are emitted, leading to severe air pollution. In the early 1960s, the air pollution problem in the German Ruhr industrial zone became so severe that, in December 1962, the region experienced a severe haze disaster. The inversion weather lasted for five days, accumulating harmful substances in the air, containing more than 5 milligrams of sulfur dioxide per cubic meter, killing more than 150 people. In addition to sulfur dioxide, industrial pollutants also cause large areas of soil pollution, discharged seriously beyond the self-purification capacity of the soil. In addition, the Rhine River, due to industrial pollution has reduced oxygen levels, biological species and the river stinks. However, the Ruhr industrial zone in Germany has taken a variety of measures, and the air pollution control work has achieved significant results, and the air quality has been significantly improved.

Strict environmental regulations and measures: The German government has formulated a series of environmental regulations and measures for the air pollution in the Ruhr industrial zone, including the establishment of automatic chimney alarm system, each factory must establish devices to recover harmful gases and dust. These measures have effectively reduced the emission of air pollutants.

Energy structure adjustment: The Ruhr industrial zone actively promotes the adjustment of energy structure, phase out traditional energy sources such as coal, and uses clean energy sources, such as natural gas and solar energy, so as to reduce the emission of air pollutants.

Green transportation: The Ruhr Industrial Zone actively promotes green transportation, with a large number of bike lanes and public ev charging piles in the zone, encouraging employees to use low-carbon and environmentally friendly vehicles.

Environmental education: The Ruhr industrial zone also pays attention to environmental education and enhances people's awareness and participation in environmental protection. Through the publicity and promotion of environmental protection knowledge, the public's awareness of environmental protection and the enthusiasm of energy conservation and emission reduction will be enhanced.

Ecological restoration: While promoting economic transformation, the Ruhr industrial zone pays attention to ecological restoration. A large number of parks and forests have been built in the area, providing a beautiful and livable environment, and the quality of life of the local residents has been significantly improved.

According to the 2023 data, the air quality in the Ruhr industrial zone meets European standards. In addition, the concentration of fine particulate matter (PM) and sulfur dioxide (SO_2) in the Ruhr industrial zone has also dropped significantly.

(2) Water pollution prevention and control

In 2022, the Ganges River Rejuvenation of India and the Marine

Restoration of Abu Dhabi in the United Arab Emirates were rated as the first 10 "World Ecological Restoration Flagship Projects" of the United Nations, which attracted much attention.

The Ganges River is the holy river in the hearts of Hindus, but it has been heavily polluted in recent years. To control the pollution problem of the Ganges river, the Indian government has taken a series of measures. First, the Government of India launched the Ganges Action Plan in 1986, which aims to improve water quality by intercepting, diverting and treating domestic sewage, and to prevent toxic and industrial waste from flow into the river. The plan mainly includes measures to repair existing sewage systems, build sewage treatment plants and build sewage tributaries and diversion points. The scientifically treated Ganges sewage can be used not only for irrigation, but also for a variety of by-products, such as biogas and concentrated fertilizer. However, despite of these measures, the pollution problem in the Ganges remains. The reason is that the area where the Ganges River flows through is densely populated, and a large amount of domestic and industrial waste water is directly discharged into the river, resulting in serious water pollution. To address this problem, the Indian government launched an 18-year plan in 2014 to control the Ganges completely. The plan uses short, medium and long-term measures designed to reduce pollutants entering the Ganges and change Indian attitudes about the Ganges. The Indian government has soon installed more than a million household toilets and a number of garbage cans, and has forced plants to install sewage treatment equipment. In addition, the government has built more than 20 large sewage treatment plants and 10 electric crematoriums. These measures aim to reduce the number of contaminants entering the Ganges River. In the medium and long term, the Indian government plans to further repair existing sewage systems, build more sewage treatment plants, and build more sewage tributaries and diversion points. In addition, the government plans to change the Indian perception of the Ganges through publicity and education, putting them into the habit of not littering and dumping waste water. Governing the Ganges River is a long-term and arduous task, which requires the joint efforts of the government, society and individuals. Despite some progress made in the past decades, continued investment and efforts are needed to ensure continuous improvement in the Ganges water quality and protection of the river's environmental ecosystem.

The Abu Dhabi Ocean Recovery Program is part of Ocean World, Abu Dhabi, UAE, aiming to improve the health and sustainability of the coastal and marine ecosystems and promote the conservation and restoration of biodiversity. The specific implementation methods mainly include the following aspects: First, ecological restoration: including the restoration of seagrass beds, coral reefs, mangroves and other ecosystems. Second, the protection of marine life: through the establishment of marine life reserves, protect endangered species, strengthen the monitoring and investigation of marine life, understand the distribution, quantity and ecological habits of marine life, to provide scientific basis for the protection and restoration of marine ecosystems. Third, environmental monitoring and management: strengthen environmental monitoring and management, strict control of pollution sources, improve water quality and ecological environment. After the implementation of "ABU dhabi ocean recovery plan", has built a 25 million liters of water storage, accommodate more than 68,000 marine animals of marine creatures aquarium, and has a core landscape-Endless Vista, this is a 20 meters high vertical window, across multiple floors, can show amazing aquatic scene. In addition, the Yas SeaWorld Research and Rescue Center is established, the first dedicated marine research, rescue, rehabilitation and return center in the UAE. These measures will provide strong support for improving the health and sustainability of the coastal and marine ecosystems and promoting the conservation and restoration of biodiversity.

(3) Soil pollution prevention and control

Soil protection is crucial to the future agricultural food system, the restoration of ecosystems and all life on earth. Soil pollution is the major cause of land degradation and a central issue in the United Nations Decade on Ecosystem Restoration (2021-2030).

First, agricultural practice case: soil pollution prevention and control in the Berg Aukas mining area, Namibia, Africa. Soil pollution control in Berg Aukas, Namibia, Africa is an important environmental protection project. Long-term copper mining in the mining area has caused severe soil pollution in the surrounding area, including heavy metals and radioactive substances. These pollutants pose a serious threat to the local environment and the health of the residents. In order to solve this problem, the Namibian government and related enterprises have invested a lot of resources and manpower, and taken a series of measures to control soil pollution. Berg Aukas mine, located in Namibia, is a place where lead and zinc mining was used, and these metal elements enter the local farmland and produce through soil and water, posing health risks to the local people. To address this problem, the local government worked with international organizations to implement a program called "Youth Vocational Training". The program aims to reduce the risk of local population exposure to these heavy metals by relocating training facilities to safer locations and providing knowledge and skills on how to minimize lead and zinc uptake in soil and sediment. The plan also encourages local residents to adopt more environmentally friendly agricultural practices, such as growing lead-resistant plants, improving soil quality and optimizing water management, to minimize the risk of consuming trace elemental pollutants. These measures not only protect the health of the local people, but also improve their income and quality of life. Sustainable development can be achieved by combining the measures of environmental protection and agricultural development. Cooperation of governments, international organizations and local communities, as well as the delivery of knowledge and skills, are all crucial to reduce the risk of pollutants and improve the quality of life of local residents.

Second, the non-agricultural practice case: the United States Repower Program. The EPA has developed a "repowering" plan to encourage the use of contaminated sites such as landfills and mines for renewable energy generation. The EPA's "repowering" plan is a plan to boost renewable energy development and reduce greenhouse gas emissions. By using contaminated sites such as landfills and mining areas, the plan will not only reduce the negative environmental impact of these contaminated sites, but also promote the development of renewable energy and reduce carbon emissions. In addition, the plan supports investment in other renewable energy projects, such as wind and hydropower. These programs could help the United States achieve the Sustainable Development Goals, while also creating more jobs and economic activity. This case shows that environmental protection and economic development are not mutually exclusive. With the help of renewable energy technology, contaminated sites can be treated and inject new impetus into sustainable development.

IV. Experience and enlightenment of rural ecological governance

Land resources, water resources, forest resources, marine resources and other natural resources are the important ecological environment on which human beings survive and continue, and also the basic environment and important guarantee for the existence and development of rural areas, and an important link that needs urgent attention in the revitalization and protection of rural areas. From the guidance of ideas, to the constraints of laws and regulations, to the multi-directional support of science and technology and financing, all of them are making efforts and contributions to rural revitalization. Standing in the critical period of history, human beings have included ecological protection in the list of urgent problems to be solved. We should carry out comprehensive ecological protection from the concept, regulations, science and technology, and financing. Attach importance to the concept and regulations of ecological protection. In environmental protection and ecological governance, we must first be conscious. Science and technology is the key to realizing ecological governance. Science and technology are playing an increasingly important role in ecological governance. It can improve the efficiency of ecological protection and rural environmental governance. In the process of promoting ecological progress, the whole world needs to strengthen legislation, strengthen the legal system, and accelerate the establishment of a sound system of relevant laws and regulations. A perfect financing mechanism is one of the keys to ecological protection and rural revitalization, and also an important guarantee to effectively solve the funding problems for ecological protection and rural revitalization. At the same time, the government must also play a leading role in the process of promoting rural ecological governance and rural revitalization.

1. The concept guides all countries to jointly protect and restore ecosystems

As the guidance and supervision of ecological and environmental protection, the concept plays a vital role in the process of rural revitalization. In recent years, the international concept of ecological protection is evolving and gradually showing results. Since the 1950s, major ecological crises in the world have occurred more frequently and affected more widely. Against this background, the international community has started a campaign to protect the global ecosystem. In this movement, people have gradually formed a set of ideas based on the harmony between man and nature, and gradually formed a set of system to protect the natural ecosystem. It is roughly divided into several stages.

The first stage mainly focuses on the protection of natural resources. Since the 1950s, with the acceleration of industrialization and urbanization process, the natural resources in the world have suffered unprecedented destruction. The years 1950-1970 was the first "Anthropocene" period in human history. During this period, some important natural ecosystems began to degrade or destroy due to the intensified destruction of human activities to the ecological environment. After the 1960s, ecological protection became a global topic. UNESCO takes "ecological conservation" as one of the core concepts of sustainable development. In 1968, the United Nations Conference on Environment and Development issued the Declaration of "Our Common Future", which put forward the concept of "sustainable development" and became an important basis for developing countries to formulate policies on sustainable development.

In 1972, the United Nations Conference on Environment and Development adopted the Declaration on the Human Environment, which put forward four principles: respecting nature, making rational use of nature, protecting the environment and responding to environmental problems. The Declaration on the Human Environment marks ecological protection as a global issue.

The second stage is to pay attention to the ecosystem service function. After the 1970s, due to the increasing pressure on the ecological environment caused by climate change and population growth, countries began to pay attention to the function of ecosystem services and sustainable development. However, during this period, various countries have no consensus on the goal of ecological conservation. The Agenda 21 (the Millennium Agenda) of the United Nations Conference on Environment and Development sets out the goals of sustainable development, but countries have a different understanding of what a sustainable development is. In the 1990s, at the Conference of the Parties to the Convention on Biological Diversity in Brazil, consensus on biodiversity for the first time.

The third phase is greater emphasis on global ecosystems. Since the beginning of the 21st century, while understanding the ecological environment changes, we also pay more attention to the global ecosystem service function and sustainable development. With the promotion and implementation of the United Nations Sustainable Development Goals (SDGs), the global ecological protection cause has been moving forward. In 1992, the United Nations Conference on Environment and Development adopted Agenda 21, whose "Sustainable Development Goals" set a series of environment-related targets, indicators and policy recommendations. The concept of "sustainable development" began to take root among the people. Since the beginning of the 21st century, a series of ecological crises have occurred around the world. In this context, international organizations and governments represented by the United Nations began to pay attention to ecological issues. In 2004, the United Nations Environment Programme (UNEP) promulgated the United Nations Framework Convention on Climate Change (UNFCCC), which commenced implementation in 2007. In the same year, the Conference of the Parties to the UNFCCC introduced the "Framework Convention on Climate Change" and laid "Paris Agreement". Subsequently, in December 2010, the United Nations Conference on Sustainable Development, endorsed both the UNFCCC and the Paris Agreement. Concurrently, in October of the same year, the United Nations Conference on Environment and Development held in Madrid, Spain, adopted the 2030 Agenda for Sustainable Development, which embodies the concept of "Harmonious development across social, economic, and environmental dimensions."

The fourth stage focuses on proposing the concept of "biodiversity". Since 2012, the world has had extensive discussions about "biodiversity" issues. At the United Nations Summit on Sustainable Development, the Conference of the Parties at the Convention on Biological Diversity adopted the Paris Agreement. This agreement is an important outcome reached by the international community to promote global ecological protection. The Convention on Biological Diversity is by far the most comprehensive and complete global convention on biodiversity. In the Convention, its purpose is to promote global biodiversity conservation and sustainable utilization, aims to define "biodiversity" as "all organisms in their growth and life process formation and maintenance of a state", and "in the past and now has been present or in any way to contribute to the human welfare of various biological populations sum".

Through different understandings of the concept of "biodiversity", countries around the world have provided multiple ways and methods for "ecological conservation". At the United Nations Summit on Sustainable Development, national awareness of "biodiversity" has changed. At the United Nations Summit on Environment and Development in 2010, countries first included the concept of "biodiversity" into the Convention, which has two meanings: the emphasis on ecosystem service function and the combination of ecosystem service function and sustainable development.

One of the methods of ecological restoration, known as rewilding, which is to restore and improve the environment and make it more suitable for human needs. This method is also called ecological restoration. Rewilding refers to the reconstruction process of natural ecosystems after more human disturbance, that is, by restoring natural processes and all complete or nearly complete food webs at trophic levels to become self-sustained and resilient ecosystems. This approach can help to protect and restore the health of ecosystems, promote the prosperity of plants, animals and microorganisms, and thus achieve ecological balance.

Rewilding technology is a very complex restoration technique, including ecology, botany, soil science, ecology and agronomy. Rewilding technology is a very mature and effective ecological restoration technology in the world. It can repair the damaged ecosystem in a very short time and increase the species diversity and biological productivity of the ecosystem. Rewilding technology has the characteristics of replication, productivity and sustainability, and can fundamentally solve the problems of biodiversity loss and soil degradation.

The basic idea of rewilding comes from environmentalism, and its emergence and development also have a direct relationship with environmentalism. Environmentalists believe that one of the major problems in modern society is environmental pollution, and in this context, "dewilding" has become an important way for people to seek solutions to this problem. On this basis, the "rewilding" emerged at the historic moment. Rewilding theoretically originates from the criticism and reflection on the demolderalization, while it is an anti-modernity behavior in practice.

It has been achieved around the world, since the 1990s, most prominently in North America and Europe. Spanning the vast expanse of North America, the region specifically encompasses the northeastern United States, northern and western Canada, the mountainous forest and grassland areas of the American Midwest, and parts of Alaska, Indiana, and Virginia. Certain specific areas within these regions exhibit unique natural environmental characteristics, including diverse ecosystems such as mountains, forests, tundra, and deserts. Rewilding measures implemented in this area have shown significant results: the number of plant species in the region has doubled, and the density of natural vegetation has increased by the same magnitude, thereby effectively enhancing the level of biodiversity in the area. Another typical example in North America is the reintroduction of wolves in Yellowstone National Park: in 1995, Yellowstone National Park reintroduced wolves, which improved the structure and function of its ecosystem, gradually promoted its healthy development, and achieved great success. On a wider scale, Dave Foreman once again launched the North American Moors Project. The 1993 Yellowstone to Yukon Conservation Program, jointly initiated by Harvey Locke and others, aims to create an area of about 3,200 kilometers between Yellowstone in the United States and Canada, in order to achieve the purpose of harmony between man and nature.

Rewilding is also an important conservation issue due to the massive abandonment of agricultural land and the return of wildlife in Europe in recent years. In the high-intensity abandonment areas such as farmland and mines, a positive or negative behavior of abandonment will be triggered due to the high degree of abandonment. Practices related to European rewilding include pilot projects by European organizations in Iberia in the west, the Danube Delta and the Carpathian Mountains in the south; uninterference in wildlife recovery in the Swiss National Park and the Chernobyl barrier in Belarus. Rewilding is a promising method of ecological protection and restoration, which can help us protect and restore the natural environment and promote sustainable development and rural revitalization.

In the context of ecological civilization construction in China, rewilding plays a very important role in the protection and restoration of ecological environment, and it is urgent to carry out corresponding research and practice. First of all, China's land use has a long history, especially in the process of urbanization and rapid economic development, due to the intensification of human activities, the phenomenon of rewilding has undergone serious degradation in many areas, thus leading to the occurrence of rewilding phenomenon. On the other hand, in recent years, with the hollowing out of rural areas and the abandonment of agricultural land, and the restoration of the number of wild animals in some areas, the public's thirst for wild animals has provided a new opportunity for the rewilding. The concept of rewilding aligns closely with China's ecological protection and restoration strategies. It profoundly resonates with the core ecological civilization concept that "humans and nature are a community of life," jointly establishing a philosophical foundation that respects, conforms to, and protects nature, reflecting the beautiful vision of harmonious coexistence between humans and nature. Existing measures in China such as converting cultivated land back to forest, reverting grazing land to grassland, and reintroducing species have laid the groundwork for its rewilding efforts. Furthermore, initiatives like national spatial planning, establishing a natural conservation system primarily based on national parks, and implementing significant practices such as "mountains, waters, forests, farmlands, lakes, and grasslands" have provided new historical opportunities for its rewilding endeavors.

Rewilding is important in restoring biodiversity and ecosystem stability. However, at present, the research of rewilding at the community level mainly focuses on the recovery and reconstruction of native communities, and the research mainly focuses on the recovery of plant species diversity and its stability under specific conditions, and less attention is paid to the influence of soil habitat conditions, human activities and environmental changes on plant community structure.

2. Laws and regulations escort ecological protection and restoration

Laws and regulations are an important basis for ecological protection and restoration, and can provide a strong guarantee and support for ecological governance. Globally, governments have formulated a series of laws and regulations to ensure the healthy and sustainable development of the ecological environment. Since the 1970s, laws and conventions on global environmental protection represented by the United Nations Framework Convention on Climate Change and the Convention on Biological Diversity have been introduced successively. Their purpose is to promote global environmental protection and governance through laws, and encourage and limit the impact of human activities on the natural environment.

It can be seen from these global regulations that the protection and restoration of the natural environment is the prerequisite for the sustainable development of mankind. These laws and regulations have imposed mandatory constraints on the ecosystem through legal means, but there are also some limitations. For example, to solve the problem of environmental damage, laws and regulations usually conduct short-term control over the existing environment, while the laws and regulations are powerless for the fundamental solution of environmental damage problems. It is under this background that the concept of rewilding was born. It looks at environmental problems from a new perspective, combines ecological restoration with urban construction, and realizes the harmonious coexistence between man and nature.

In 1992, the United Nations Conference on Environment and Development adopted *Agenda 21*, listing "ecological protection and restoration" as an important goal of sustainable development. Since the 1990s, the United Nations Environment Programme, the World Bank and other international organizations have also started to conduct research on ecological protection and restoration. In 2015, the United Nations Environment Program me, pointed out that "sustainable development goals involves important areas include: economic growth, poverty reduction, education and health, environmental protection and climate change and sustainable use of natural resources". With the increasingly severe problem of global climate change, governments of all countries attach increasing importance to ecological protection and restoration. In June 2018, the United Nations Environment Programme issued the Framework Convention on Climate Change: Reduction and Adaptation, highlighting the responsibilities and obligations of governments in addressing climate change and putting forward specific recommendations on how to respond to climate change.

As the *United Nations Framework Convention on Climate Change*, the *Convention on Biological Diversity* and other international conventions have been widely observed and implemented around the world, governments have paid more attention to ecological protection and restoration, and their relevant laws and regulations have been improved. In 2010, the United Nations Environment Programme issued an assessment report on the implementation of the *Convention on Biological Diversity* by the parties, concluded that governments have taken measures to protect biodiversity and take actions to improve biodiversity. In 2015, the United Nations Environment Programme issued an assessment on the implementation of the 2030 Agenda for Sustainable Development, which evaluates and summarizes measures taken by countries between 2015 and 2030 and recommends that governments develop sustainable development strategies to address global environmental challenges.

In recent years, with the increasing attention of countries to ecological and environmental issues, the laws and regulations on ecological protection and restoration have been constantly improved, and have played a huge role in practice. In general, the main laws and regulations adopted by various countries in ecological protection and restoration include:

First, special legislation. Taking the United States as an example, it has issued a large number of laws and regulations on biodiversity protection, environmental protection and natural resources management, including climate change, water environment management, land use planning, mineral resources development and utilization, forest resources protection and sustainable utilization. For example, the *Clean Water Act*, the *Clean Air Act* , the *Environmental Policy Act* and *Freshwater wetlands protection Act* aureflect the great importance the United States attaches to ecological and environmental protection.

The European Union's Biodiversity Strategy 2020 adopts legislation to protect biodiversity and promote the restoration and management of ecosystems, serving as a guiding document for protecting and promoting biodiversity in Europe. The strategy highlights the importance of biodiversity in the sustainable development of the EU and "the key role of natural ecosystems in protecting and promoting biodiversity in the EU itself and in various regions of Europe". The strategy provides a specific path to achieve these goals, including formulating legislation to protect and promote biodiversity, exercising strict control of important ecosystems, promoting ecological restoration technologies, and strengthening cooperation with neighboring countries.

Japan has adopted a series of laws and regulatory measures in nature protection to improve its environmental protection system. Japan is one of the smallest countries in the world. It is very short of natural resources, but it has a wide variety of natural resources. In recent years, with the continuous development of Japan's economy and society, the problems such as population surge, accelerated urbanization process and shortage of resources have become increasingly prominent. To solve these problems, Japan has enacted a series of laws and regulations to promote ecological and environmental protection. In order to promote ecological environment protection and utilization of forest resources, Japan enacted the Law on the Protection and Management of Forest Resources (i. e., the Forest Law in the 1960s); In order to improve the utilization efficiency of water resources, Japan has enacted a series of laws and regulations on the protection of nature since the 1960s, such as the Environmental Basic Law and the Basic Law of Resource Management.

Second, it is to introduce special laws. In 1990, the United Nations Conference on Environment and Development adopted Agenda 21, pointing out that ecological and environmental issues have become a major issue facing the world, and taking environmental protection as an important part of global economic, social and cultural development. There are also many international conventions and agreements on ecological protection and restoration. In 1997, the United Nations General Assembly adopted the Convention on Biological Diversity, which defines the basic principles, objectives, mechanisms and specific action plans for the protection and promotion of biodiversity. In addition, the Framework Convention on Climate Change, the Statement of principles on Forests, and these agreements provide important guidelines and standards for global ecological conservation and restoration. In 2002, the United Nations General Assembly adopted the ecosystem management project section in Agenda 21. At present, more than 50 countries, including China, have formulated laws, regulations or treaties dedicated to the protection of nature and natural resources.

Since 2013, dense multiple files, actively promote rural environmental protection and governance. In 2021, the *Central Committee of the Communist Party of China under the State Council on Promoting Rural Revitalization to Accelerate the Modernization of Agriculture and Rural Areas* was put forward to promote agricultural green development, implement the five years action to improve the human settlements environment, In 2022, the *Central Committee of the Communist Party and the State Council about 2022 Comprehensively Promote Rural Revitalization of the Key Work Opinion* was put forward, in the implementation of rural living environment regulation improve action for five years. Positive progress has been made in the rural ecological protection work.

After Biden came to power, the United States has abandoned its previous passive stance on environmental protection, rejoining the Paris Agreement and actively participating in environmental governance and conservation. Russia is cold all the year and relies heavily on fossil fuels, but it strictly controls emissions and requires lower emissions than the EU. The EU undertook the heavy responsibility in the climate field, the European Climate Change Programme (ECCP) was initiated in the year 2000. and decided on a new emission reduction plan in 2007. In 2014, it adopted the Climate and Energy Policy Framework from 2020 to 2030, proposed "building a carbon neutral continent" in 2018, and a provisional agreement on the key elements of the "European Climate Law" was reached in 2021. However, from a global perspective, in some countries or regions, due to their own development restrictions, the implementation of the relevant environmental protection and governance agreements is insufficient, and the governance effect is poor. The formulation and implementation of laws and regulations plays a decisive role in ecological protection and restoration, and it still needs to be strengthened and improved in the future ecological governance work.

3. Scientific and technological innovation drives ecological governance, and needs further efforts

Scientific and technological innovation is playing an increasingly important role in the global rural ecological governance. Through scientific and technological innovation, the efficiency of energy utilization and sustainability in rural areas can be improved. The continuous scientific and technological and innovative achievements can provide strong support for ecological restoration, resource utilization, environmental monitoring and other aspects, and at the same time can improve the efficiency and precision of ecological governance to achieve the goal of sustainable development. Scientific and technological innovation is an important driving force to promote rural sustainable development. Compared with other forms of technology, technological innovation is more sustainable and more efficient, and it is more adaptable to environmental changes. At the same time, scientific and technological innovation is also conducive to promoting industrial structure adjustment and industrial upgrading, so as to improve labor productivity and income level. According to the UN-Habitat's report on Rural Ecological Governance: Sustainable Development Goals and Innovation, global rural ecological governance is facing many challenges, including water shortage, frequent agricultural disasters, biodiversity loss and land degradation.

In the context of climate change, since the 1950s, the United Kingdom, Germany, the United States, Japan and other countries have begun to conduct research on clean energy, and have invested a lot of manpower and financial resources. In the mid-1960s and early 1970s, the United States used nuclear fusion technology for power generation in the Manhattan Project to reduce its dependence on oil. In the late 1970s, Britain and other countries began the research of nuclear power generation. Germany has carried out a more comprehensive research on geothermal energy, solar energy and wind energy. Among them, in the face of carbon dioxide pollution, "carbon capture and storage" (CCS) technology can effectively reduce carbon dioxide emissions, is an important way to achieve the global carbon neutrality goal. At the same time, CCS technology can protect the earth's ecosystem and improve the function of ecosystem services by storing the carbon dioxide in the atmosphere. The use of CCS technology can reduce carbon dioxide emissions in rural areas and provide new development opportunities for rural areas.

In the background of water resources pollution, water shortage areas bear the brunt and should be adapted to local conditions. In recent years, a number of water ecological environment restoration technologies have appeared at home and abroad. These technologies adopt different processing methods for different regions, different industries and different objects, according to local conditions and emerge as The Times require. Compared with the major developed countries, Japan has a relatively late urbanization level, and its rural sewage treatment level and treatment technology are significantly higher than that of the major developed countries, mainly thanks to the sewage treatment and purification tank. Japan's purification tank is mainly divided into three kinds: one is contact oxidation method, the second is biofilm technology, the third is purification tank. Biofilm technology is mainly through the form of biofilm organic matter, nitrogen and phosphorus and other nutrients in sewage through the transformation of the action of microorganisms, so as to achieve the purpose of purifying sewage. This technology does not need follow-up treatment, simple and easy to run, easy to operate and maintain, produce less sludge, can reduce secondary pollution. The purification tank technology can convert the nitrogen and phosphorus and other nutrients in the sewage into simple inorganic substances, and then the inorganic substances are absorbed and degraded through the plants in the constructed wetland, so that they can meet the discharge standard. Compared with other technologies, the purification tank technology has the advantages of small footprint and low construction and operation cost. This technology is an ideal rural sewage treatment mode with low cost, high efficiency, convenient management and good effluent quality. Japanese domestic sewage treatment purification tank is composed of two parts, respectively is the main body and the blower. First, the sewage is collected into the purification tank, and at the same time, the air is collected and sent into the transmission fan, and the oxidation reaction is conducted. Then the treated water can flow directly into the natural water, which can effectively alleviate the problem of water shortage.

In the context of a biodiversity threat, Kunming, China's Yunnan province, has built a home for biological species: the Southwest China Wildlife Germplasm Resource Bank, a wildlife germplasm collection facility established according to international standards, with only two in the world[70]. In recent years, Chinese researchers have continuously collected and preserved the required seeds, and 85,046 seeds of 10,601 species have been preserved. In the process of preservation, the time, place, temperature, humidity, longitude, altitude and other information have been recorded in detail.

Countries also need to fully promote the combination of science and technology and rural ecological governance, follow the laws of nature, and adapt measures to local conditions. Rural ecological governance also needs to make full use of scientific and technological innovation achievements. On the one hand, we should strengthen the supporting role of scientific and technological innovation in ecological governance. Technologies such as artificial intelligence and big data can realize real-time monitoring and evaluation of environmental changes; equipment such as robots and drones can realize efficient management and utilization of ecological resources in rural areas; and big data analysis and other technologies can provide more accurate and scientific decision-making basis for rural ecological governance. The combination of digital technology and infrastructure construction such as rural Internet can provide more convenient, efficient and accurate social services for rural areas; Big data analysis technology can identify and address key factors affecting environmental change.

In the face of new challenges in global rural ecological governance, more attention should be paid to the combination of scientific and technological innovation and practical application. Firstly, we should strengthen basic

70 Fan Zhang, Maoying Li, Chuanzeng Ye. The Wildlife Germplasm Resource Bank in Southwest China gives biological species a "safe home" [N]. People's Daily, 2021-October 14 (013). DOI:10.28655/n.cnki.nrmrb.2021.010794.

research to break through the technical bottlenecks restricting industrial development and environmental governance; secondly, pay attention to the practical application of scientific and technological innovation achievements in ecological governance, and constantly improve relevant supporting policies and regulations. The application of scientific and technological innovation achievements in rural ecological governance can provide more accurate technical services for agricultural production. While solving problems such as rural labor shortage and low agricultural production efficiency, it can also promote the transformation and upgrading of rural industries and create new opportunities for farmers to increase their income and become rich.

Scientific and technological innovation to drive ecological governance should follow scientific laws. The history of the development of human society shows that every scientific and technological progress will lead to changes in the way of production and life. Especially at the critical stage of social development, scientific and technological innovation has provided strong support for ecological and environmental protection. With the continuous development and progress of science and technology, human society has entered the information age. Digital technology and the Internet have provided more convenient, efficient and accurate scientific and technological support for ecological and environmental protection. Therefore, we must respect the natural law of ecological and environmental protection, and give full play to the supporting role of scientific and technological innovation in rural ecological governance.

Scientific and technological innovation should take full account of different regions, different levels of development and different historical and cultural traditions. In some areas, clean energy is often available for large scale due to poor natural geographical conditions, backward economy and weak infrastructure; in some areas, it is often difficult to implement clean energy replacement due to excessive population density and inconvenient transportation; in some areas, it is often difficult to build perfect infrastructure due to their low level of economic development.

Technology Empowering Rural Development 2022: Digital Technology

Empowering Rural Industry Development points out that digital agriculture with data and knowledge as the core elements can reduce food loss , control environmental non-point source pollution, promote energy conservation and emission reduction, and thereby promote sustainable agricultural development. The water shortage is the main cause of the shortage of agricultural irrigation water, and it is also one of the biggest environmental problems in the world. Agricultural drought is the most common climate change phenomenon in the world, and it is also one of the main causes of problems such as crop production reduction, food security and ecosystem degradation. Many countries face severe agricultural drought problems, and these problems need to be solved through measures such as technological innovation and policy innovation.

Technological innovation should become the core engine driving ecological governance, actively leading the trend of green development, with the aim of realizing the beautiful vision of harmonious coexistence between humans and nature. With the development of economy and society, human production and life has had a huge impact on the ecological environment, and even brought great pressure. Therefore, promoting green development is the fundamental way to solve the global ecological and environmental problems. Scientific and technological innovation plays an increasingly important role in rural ecological governance. On the one hand, energy efficiency and sustainability can be improved; on the other hand, scientific and technological innovation can improve ecosystem service function and carbon absorption capacity. Therefore, to promote green development, we must adhere to the principles of harmonious coexistence between man and nature, protection of the ecological environment and sustainable utilization of resources.

4. Financing is an important means of rural ecological environment governance

Ecological governance not only needs the guidance of ideas and regulations and the support of technology, but also the greater demand behind this is the demand for capital. At present, the financing channels for ecological environment protection and restoration are relatively single, and the scale is relatively small, which mainly depends on the government's fiscal expenditure. At the same time, the ecological protection and restoration project has a long period and a large scale. Large investment and slow income make it difficult to attract social capital. In order to solve these difficulties, the government, enterprises and all sectors of society need to work together to promote the smooth development of the international rural ecological environment governance work by increasing capital investment, optimizing the investment structure, establishing a clear investment return mechanism and strengthening the investment in the monitoring system.

So far, 138 countries have set carbon neutrality targets, the rest have set carbon reduction targets, and some countries have not set targets of carbon peaks in several major economies (Table 4.5). The World Bank Group provided a record $31.7 billion to help countries address climate change in fiscal year 2022, and $31.7 billion accounted for 36% of the World Bank's total loans in fiscal year 2022, exceeding the target set in the *2021-2025 Climate Change Action Plan* for an average of 35% of the total.

Table 4.5　Timing of carbon peak and carbon neutrality for major economies

Countries/Regions	Carbon peak time	Carbon neutrality time
the United States	2007	2050
European Union	1990	2050
Canada	2007	2050
the Republic of Korea	2013	2050
Japan	2013	2050
Australia	2006	2040
South Africa	2025	2050
Brazil	2012	2060

Data source: collated according to individual countries' carbon peak and carbon neutrality policies.

Private companies and public entities join the environmental financing ranks. In addition to the funding provided by international organizations and countries to address climate change, "perpetual" and "green" bonds are also one of the sources of funding provided by private businesses and government agencies to support investment in climate and the environment. In 2022, green bond issuance experienced the first year-on-year decline in a decade, reaching $487.1 billion, down 16 percent from 2021. Current market conditions lead to a decline in bond issuance across all categories. Green bonds accounted for 3% of the total issuance, and green labels continued to lead the issuance of global theme bonds, accounting for 56% of the issuance of green, social responsibility and sustainable development bonds, sustainable development linked bonds and transformation bonds (GSS + bonds), with a total of $2.2 trillion. So far, demand for green bonds has far exceeded supply, and this continues with green bond issuance in 2022.

As an important supplement and extension to the green financial market, the development of transformation finance-related products has become a topic of more attention in the sustainable finance field. Currently, industries such as real estate, transportation and utilities have a relatively sound low-carbon transition path, and entities from them can easily use green bonds to finance their projects, assets and specific expenditures. For many high-carbon emission industries, such as cement, steel and basic chemicals, the transformation related path in the market has just begun to be developed, and there is still a lack of guidance to clarify the use of the raised funds for specific industries. For these high-carbon corporate entities, sustainable linked bonds (SLB), which are not limited to raising funds, have become a popular financing vehicle in the market. Sustainable development linked bond is a debt financing instrument that links the bond terms to the issuer's sustainable development Goal. Compared with green bonds, carbon neutral bonds and other products that limit the purpose of raising funds, it is more flexible in terms of issuer, fundraising purposes and bond structure. The SLB market has grown Strongly over the past two years as SLB allows issuers to finance for general purposes and institutional entities to set their own key performance indicators (KPIs) and Sustainable Performance Targets (SPT). In terms of size, the Climate Bond Initiative (CBI) had issued $76.4 billion by 2022, down 32% from $112.1 billion in 2021.

According to China's Transformational Bond Market Is Ready to Develop, China is the world's largest green bond issuance market in 2022 in terms of the scale of green bond issuance that meets the CBI definition (Figure 4.20). In 2022, China's green bonds included in the CBI green bond database reached $85.4 billion (575.2 billion yuan), leading the world in scale. By the end of 2022, the issuance of domestic and foreign labeled bonds reached $489 billion (RMB 3.3 trillion), with the CBI definition reaching $286.9 billion (RMB 1.9 trillion). The green labeled bonds issued in China accounted for 1.5% of China's total onshore bond issuance, up from 1% in 2021, and there is still huge room for growth.

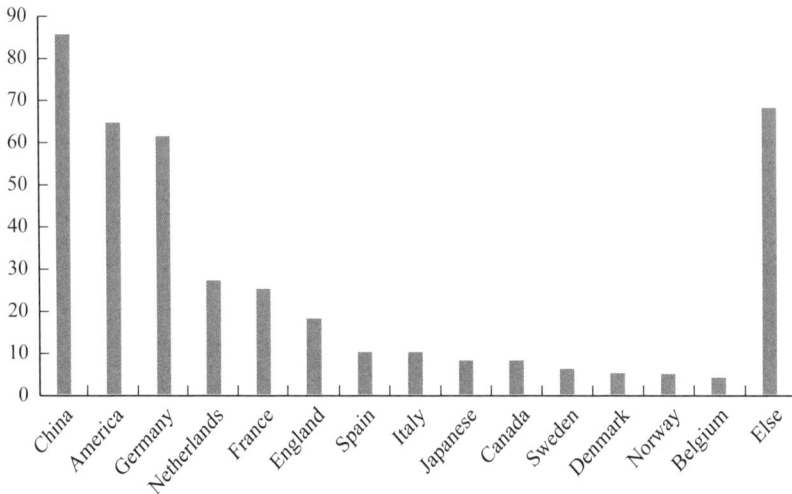

Figure 4.20   Green bond issuance in major countries in the world in 2022 (unit: $1 billion)

Data source: drawn based on the Global Sustainable Bond Market Report 2022.

According to UNEP's *state of Finance for Nature*, the total investment demand will reach $8.4 trillion by 2050, exceeding $536 billion per year, four times the current investment scale (Figure 4.21, Figure 4.22).

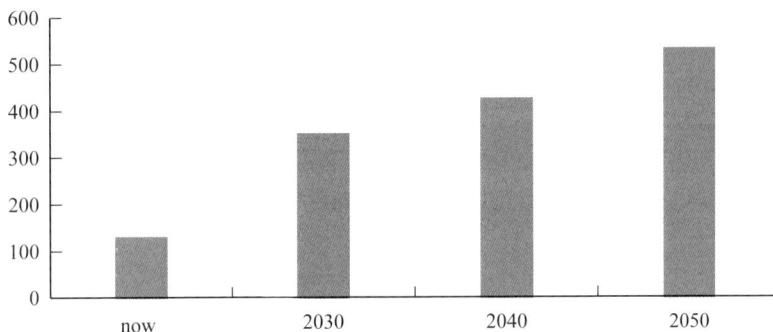

Figure 4.21   Annual investment demand for future natural financing (unit: $1 billion/ year)

Data source: drawn based on the 2022 UNEP's *State of Finance for Nature.*

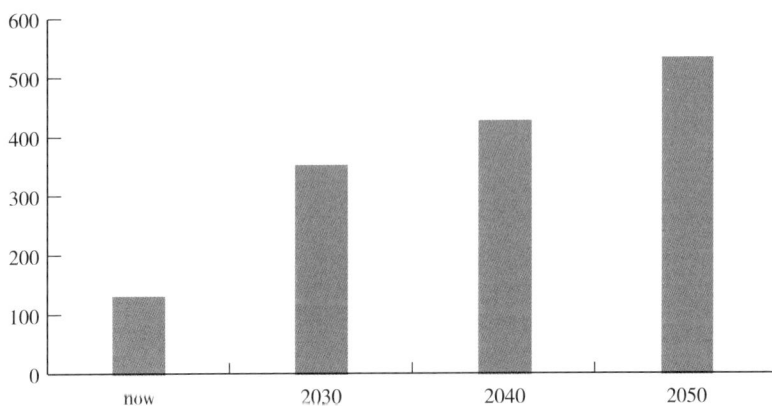

Figure 4.22   Future demand for natural financing in 2021-2050 (unit: $1 billion/year)

Data source: drawn based on the 2022 UNEP's *State of Finance for Nature.*

From the national level, the United States through different bills and projects to provide financial support for rural environmental protection, the implementation of a number of plans, such as land fallow, soil and water conservation, wetland protection, grassland conservation, wildlife habitat protection, Which are the rural environmental protection special funds support focus, in addition to rural non-point source water pollution treatment of clean water state rolling fund, etc. For example, the Agricultural Law 2002 provides subsidies for agricultural ecological environment protection, which provides up to $22 billion over the six-year period, mainly to support rural clean energy projects, ecological environmental protection programs, water quality improvement, soil protection and so on. The US Department of Agriculture has spent $600 million on rural clean energy projects to reduce national emissions and improve energy security. In the financing and use of environmental protection funds, the US government pays attention to the cooperation with non-governmental organizations and the private sector, and jointly promotes the development of rural environmental protection through public-private partnerships and government subsidies. Switzerland has adopted a variety of strategies and methods in the financing of rural construction, including government subsidies and incentive policies, emphasis on environmental beautification and infrastructure, diversified financing channels and ecological environment financing mode. These strategies and methods jointly promote the sustainable development of rural construction in Switzerland. For example, xFarm Technologies, a Swiss smart agriculture company, raised 17 million euros, one of the largest Series B-rounds of financing in the field of agricultural science and technology in Europe. This shows that Switzerland is also carrying out active investment and financing activities in promoting agricultural modernization and intelligence.

In summary, there is the problem of insufficient financing in international rural ecological governance, but the world organization and various countries are actively designing relevant financing products for financing, and private companies and public capital have a strong willingness to join. By providing stable sources of funds, guiding the participation of social capital and promoting the development of rural economy, financing can provide strong support and guarantee for rural ecological environment governance. It is imperative to actively explore diversified financing mechanisms, foster enhanced cooperation and coordination among governments, enterprises, and various sectors of society, and jointly promote the smooth progression of rural ecological and environmental governance.

◎ Chapter V Development of International Rural Organizations

Abstract

Rural organizations are an important force in achieving rural revitalization, referring to groups that exist in rural areas of various countries or regions to perform certain social functions, achieve specific social goals, and establish common activities in a certain form. The development of rural organizations cannot be separated from government policy guidance. The government jointly assists the development of rural organizations by providing financial support, improving laws and regulations, or integrating various social resources. Rural organizations have made significant progress under the support and guidance of the government. However, due to significant differences in the development stages, political systems, historical experience, traditional customs in each country or region, the specific modes of rural organizations also have their own characteristics. Ten cases were selected from developed countries, emerging economies, and developing countries for analysis. Through case studies in Japan, the United States, France, Germany, China, India, Brazil, Pakistan, Ethiopia, and Mauritius, experience and inspiration on the construction of international rural organizations are drawn.

I. The development status and policy measures of international rural organizations

1. The development status of international rural organizations

(1) Agricultural cooperatives are the most traditional form of rural organization

Throughout the history of global agricultural development, the traditional form of rural organization, agricultural cooperatives, had already emerged in Britain in the mid-19th century. Currently, there is a cooperative model in both developed and developing countries, and agricultural cooperatives are also an important organizational form in the agricultural field in various countries around the world. In developed countries such as Sweden, the agricultural cooperative model plays an important role in business management. Farmers joined cooperatives and became one of the owners of cooperative enterprises. The Swedish government improved the regulations and behaviors of cooperatives through the intervention and coordination function of central institutions, thereby promoting the transformation of the agricultural industry.

In the United States, agricultural cooperatives are composed of farmers, suppliers, and traders. According to the *"Summary of Agricultural Cooperation Statistics (2021)"* released by the US Department of Agriculture, there are 1,699 farmers, ranchers, and fishery cooperatives in the United States. The US government supports the development of agricultural cooperatives through a formal agricultural policy assistance system, such as the US Department of Agriculture funding new value-added cooperation projects, and the Department of Agriculture's Rural Utilities Service providing revolving loan special funds to utility cooperatives. In the latter half of the 1990s, traditional cooperatives were no longer able to meet the needs of economic development and social progress. Cooperatives had emerged with new development trends such as corporatization, shareholding, and openness.

In China, after the founding of the People's Republic of China in 1949, the CPC gradually organized and guided farmers through the development of mutual aid groups, primary cooperatives and other forms, rapidly liberating and developing agricultural productivity. After entering the 21st century, the development of agricultural cooperatives has entered a new stage of development. The *Law of the People's Republic of China on Farmers' Professional Cooperatives* was promulgated in 2006, which legally limits the conditions that should be met for the establishment of agricultural cooperatives, as well as the rights and obligations of members of farmers' professional cooperatives. In recent years, the Chinese government has actively explored ways to enhance the self-development ability and service level of farmers' cooperatives in order to guide them to adapt to market competition, and promoted the transformation of farmers' cooperatives growth both in quantity and quality.

(2) Diversification of governance entities in the process of rural development

At present, rural governance has shifted from a single government entity to multiple government entities. In grassroots rural areas in China, the main bodies of governance include grassroots party committees, grassroots governments, village supervision agencies, and autonomous institutions. In village level administrative units, the grassroots party committee is the village branch committee, the grassroots government is the township government, the village supervision institution is the village affairs supervision committee, and the village autonomous institution is the village committee. In specific operations, an organizational system is implemented with the grassroots organizations of the Party as the core, villagers' autonomy and village affairs supervision organizations as the foundation, collective economic organizations and farmers' cooperative organizations as the link, and various economic and social service organizations as supplements.

In the process of rural revitalization in the United States, market mechanisms were actively introduced, and the United States utilized its own advantages to establish many large-scale family farms. Some of these large-scale family farms implemented partnerships or shareholding systems, and they themselves became market entities. In terms of rural regional planning in the United States, the federal government and local governments have a clear division of labor, often with the former responsible for investment and construction of rural roads, and the latter responsible for infrastructure construction in areas such as garbage and sewage treatment and water supply. In the evolution of support for rural development in the United States, the federal government has also actively relied on market forces to gradually strengthen the partnership between the government and the private sector. For example, the funding sources for rural development in the United States are not only government subsidies, but also important loans and subsidies provided by various partners to rural areas. These partners include the White House Rural Committee, the Rural Foundation, local development employees from the Department of Agriculture, non-profit organizations, and more.

In short, actively coordinating the relationship between the government, market, and society, forms a joint force to promote rural development, and provides financial support and public services for rural revitalization.

(3) The status of farmers varies among different rural organizational models

Farmers have different positions in different rural organizational models. In East Asian rural organizations, villagers hold a dominant position. For example, the Japan Farmers' Association focuses on solving production and living problems that individual farmers cannot solve or cannot solve well, establishing close connections between dispersed small farmers and large markets, overcoming the limitations of small-scale household management, and improving agricultural management efficiency. In addition, farmers' cooperatives enhance their market position through cooperation, benefiting farmers in market transactions, integrating collective resources to extend the industrial chain, and achieving economies of scale. The construction planning, agricultural production, and other important affairs of rural areas in the Republic of Korea are all decided by the local villagers' assembly, and farmers have full voice and decision-making power in rural governance.

In Europe and America, villagers and governments are on an equal footing. The government hands over the power of rural governance to farmers, and farmers decide on public affairs related to village governance through parliamentary meetings. For example, developed countries in Europe and America, represented by France and the United States, focus on streamlining rural administrative structures and fully leveraging the autonomous role of farmers in rural governance. The rural areas of both countries have established dual administrative organizations with deliberative and executive organizations as the core. Civil agricultural cooperation organizations maintain consultation and communication with government management agencies, discussing rural public affairs closely related to farmers' interests, such as rural planning and construction, bill and regulation setting, and effectively reducing barriers to communication between farmers and the government.

In some countries in Africa and Latin America, rural governance systems are not perfect, and the position of farmers is relatively passive. In Africa, after countries became independent and implemented land reforms, agricultural production was mainly based on scattered small-scale farmers and family farms. However, this small-scale, scattered, and low-level production model is difficult to adapt to the needs of modern agricultural development. In recent years, African countries have increasingly attached importance to independent development of agriculture and rural areas. By seizing their own autonomy in agricultural and rural development, they have promoted rapid development of agriculture and rural areas, worked hard to solve food security and nutrition problems, and explored improving the commercial and technical capabilities of farmers' organizations and trade associations. In Latin America, the rapid urbanization process has caused many problems such as urban diseases, large income gaps between rich and poor, and backward rural construction and development. In order to stabilize rural order and protect the legitimate rights and interests of farmers, governments around the world are focusing on adjusting rural production relations, increasing infrastructure construction in rural areas, and improving rural governance systems.

2. Policy measures of international rural organizations

The development of international rural organizations cannot be separated from government policy guidance. The government jointly assists the development of rural organizations by providing financial support, improving laws and regulations, or integrating various social resources.

(1) Government guidance for the development of international rural organizations

The role played by governments varies in different types of countries and regions. In developed countries in Europe and America, the active agricultural policies of the United States began with the Roosevelt administration during the Great Depression. After World War II, the European Community established the *Treaty of Rome* to increase agricultural productivity, improve the living standards of agricultural populations, stabilize markets, and ensure the supply of products to consumers at reasonable prices. By the 1980s, the original agricultural policies mainly focused on government intervention had led to problems such as agricultural overproduction, declining farmers' income, and excessive government financial expenditure. Agricultural policies in various countries gradually shifted to emphasizing the fundamental role of market mechanisms in regulation and guidance. From the perspective of the development of farmers' agricultural cooperatives in various countries, effective government support is an essential external condition for the development of cooperatives. In the growth and growth of farmers' agricultural organizations, government support and guidance are crucial.

In emerging economies in East Asia, governments play an important role in the development of agriculture and rural areas. In 1994, the government of the Republic of Korea issued the *Basic Law on Agricultural Land* to support agricultural development. With the "New Village Movement", the government of the Republic of Korea actively guided the organization and specialized functions of agricultural cooperatives, making them gradually grow into independent, autonomous, and multifunctional agricultural cooperative organizations. In African and Latin American countries, the failure of government agricultural and rural development policies often stems from government systems and their governance capabilities outside of agricultural policies. In China, governments at all levels attach great importance to the modernization of grassroots governance systems and governance capabilities, promoting the growth and development of social organizations through government procurement of services, and guiding and regulating the level of service provided by social organizations. Overall, the government's guidance on the development of rural organizations is mainly reflected in four aspects: firstly, establishing corresponding affairs departments responsible for guiding agricultural development in government departments; secondly, provide policy guidance and financial support for agricultural development; thirdly, the government often guides the development of rural organizations through legislation to ensure the sustainability of policies; fourthly, the government also coordinates and integrates social resources with social organizations to form a joint force and jointly support the development of rural organizations.

For example, in North America, the governments of the United States and Canada have taken various measures to support the development of agricultural cooperatives. Firstly, both countries have established specialized agencies responsible for the development of farmers' cooperatives. The United States Department of Agriculture has the Agricultural Cooperative Development Bureau, and the Canadian government department has a Cooperative Secretariat responsible for cooperative affairs. Secondly, both governments provide financial and tax support for the development of cooperatives. The US government provides various forms of direct or indirect assistance to the Agricultural Cooperation Organization, such as research, management, and education assistance. Farmers' Cooperative Organizations can enjoy loans provided by cooperative banks at lower market rates. The Canadian government not only allocates funding subsidies to cooperative alliances every year, but also allocates special funds for funding at any time based on the approval of business projects proposed by cooperatives. Once again, both countries attach great importance to using laws to guide the development of cooperatives. For example, the United States passed early legislation on cooperatives in six states between 1865 and 1870. Canada also has a relatively complete cooperative legal system. The Canadian Federal Cooperative Law was promulgated in 1970 and revised in 1999. In addition, the two governments also coordinate various rural public service organizations and other community organizations to form strong support for the development of farmers' cooperatives. The North Dakota Coordination Committee is formed by the United Organization of Rural Power Cooperatives and Farmers' Credit Services in North Dakota, the North Dakota Farmers' Union, and other cooperatives.

In Europe, some governments of EU member countries actively guide the development of rural organizations. In 1867, Germany enacted the first *Cooperative Law*, and in 1895, Sweden enacted the *Cooperative Association Law*. Spain enacted the *Cooperative Law* in 1885, and after multiple revisions, a new *Cooperative Law* was passed again on July 16, 1999. The French government also announced the relevant laws and regulations on cooperatives on September 10, 1947, and revised them in 1992. The support of EU countries for the development of rural organizations is also reflected in the financial aspect. The governments of France, Germany, Italy and other countries pay special attention to financial and tax support for farmers' professional cooperatives. For example, newly established agricultural cooperatives in Germany can enjoy entrepreneurial assistance within 5 years and investment assistance within 7 years. Any cooperative established in France to serve agriculture is subsidized by the government with an investment subsidy of approximately 25%, and is exempt from industrial and commercial profit taxes, business taxes, and property taxes that are usually payable. The Italian government invests in agricultural, animal husbandry, and agricultural product processing cooperatives in poverty-stricken areas according to a certain proportion of shares, usually ranging from 30% to 40%, with some reaching as high as 70%.

In Asia, governments of emerging economies in East Asia and some developing countries also focus on guiding rural development through legislation, taxation, and policy formulation. For example, Japan was the first country in Asia to enact a cooperative law. It successively promulgated three laws on agricultural cooperatives in 1900, 1943, and 1947, forming Japan's unique cooperative legal system. The Japanese government clearly defines the agricultural sector as the administrative management agency of the Agricultural Cooperation Organization. There is a Management Bureau in the Ministry of Agriculture, Forestry, and Fisheries, under which there are agricultural association courses. Each prefecture and county also has agricultural association courses, responsible for guiding, managing, supervising, and supervising the agricultural association. In 1994, the government of the Republic of Korea issued the *Basic Law on Agricultural Land* to support agricultural development. With the "New Village Movement", the government of the Republic of Korea actively guided the organization and specialized functions of agricultural cooperatives, gradually transforming them into independent, autonomous, and multifunctional agricultural cooperative organizations. The government of the Republic of Korea also provides low interest loans to farmers through the Farmers' Association, with the interest difference subsidized by the government and a certain handling fee paid to the Farmers' Association to provide financial support. Other Asian countries such as India proposed in the first five-year plan to support and support the establishment of cooperatives, and each subsequent five-year plan will have content on the development and support of cooperatives. The sixth five-year plan for the national economy formulated by Thailand in 1987 pointed out that the government should support the business activities of cooperatives as much as possible, provide timely economic information, and the financial department should provide loans and interest incentives to help cooperatives improve business efficiency.

In China, the central government and local governments at all levels attach great importance to guiding rural organizations. The *Law of the People's Republic of China on Farmers' Professional Cooperatives* has been implemented since July 1, 2007. In August 2022, the General Office of the

Central Committee of the CPC and the General Office of the State Council issued the *Opinions on Regulating the Work of Village level Organizations, Mechanism Brands and Certification Matters*. In October of the same year, the report of the 20th Congress of the CPC clearly proposed that we should accelerate the construction of a powerful agricultural country and solidly promote the revitalization of rural industries, talents, culture, ecology and organizations. These five aspects of revitalization are interrelated and complementary, among which organizational revitalization is not only one of the goals of rural revitalization, but also the fundamental guarantee for the other four revitalization. In China, both the CPC and the government attach great importance to the modernization of grass-roots governance system and governance capacity, promote the growth and development of social organizations by means of government purchase of services, and guide and standardize the service level provided by social organizations.

(2) Legal protection for the development of international rural organizations

The laws and regulations on agricultural development issued globally and in major regions are important guarantees for promoting rural revitalization. In the history of agricultural development, Germany enacted the first *Cooperative Law* in 1867, the United States enacted the *Capper-Volstead Act* in 1922, and Japan enacted the *Agricultural Cooperative Act* in 1947. These laws and regulations provide legal basis and protection for the traditional mode of agricultural economic development - the activities of cooperatives. With the passage of time and the changes in domestic and international situations, these laws are also constantly being revised and improved. For example, in 1947, Japan promulgated the *Agricultural Cooperative Act*, which was revised 85 times. The revision and improvement of laws are aimed at better protecting the interests of farmers or farmers in the new situation.

In Japan, the *Agricultural Cooperative Act* promulgated in 1947 stipulates that the Agricultural Cooperative is a legalized farmers' autonomous cooperative organization with the goal of "improving agricultural production capacity, enhancing farmers' socio-economic status, and achieving national economic development". The various businesses engaged in by the Agricultural Cooperative are to contribute to its members to the maximum extent possible, and are not for the purpose of profit. In the following decades, Japan's *Agricultural Cooperative Act* underwent dozens of revisions, but its purpose remained unchanged despite any modifications. The *Agricultural Cooperative Act* of Japan made principle provisions on the purpose, legal status, business content, management, organizational structure, and other aspects of agricultural associations from a national perspective, which played an important role in ensuring the development of agricultural associations and protecting farmers' rights and interests. In 1961, the Japanese government formulated the *Basic Law on Agriculture* to improve the efficiency of agricultural land resource utilization and change the fragmentation pattern of arable land. It established the goal of expanding the scale of land management and encouraged and guided the transfer of agricultural land ownership among farmers. Afterwards, in order to further promote land transfer and achieve large-scale operation, the Japanese government has repeatedly revised the *Agricultural Land Law* and *Agricultural Cooperative Act*, and introduced legal documents such as the *Agricultural Land Use Promotion Law*, *Special Area Law for Structural Reform*, *Basic Plan for Food, Agriculture and Rural Affairs*, and *Promotion of Agricultural Land Intermediary Management Business Law* to provide legal protection for agriculture, rural areas, and farmers.

In the United States, although the federal government does not have a separate bill targeting cooperatives, each state has introduced its own agricultural cooperative bill based on its actual situation. Since the promulgation of the *Capper-Volstead Act* in 1922, the *American Agricultural Cooperative Act* has been keeping up with the times for over a century, constantly improving and revising specific legal provisions to adapt to changes in the external environment. The revision of the *Agricultural Cooperative Act* in the United States mainly reflects the improvement of financing, decision-making, and benefit distribution mechanisms, and maximizes the preservation of the basic principles of cooperatives, thus providing legal protection for the sustainable and healthy development of cooperatives. The US federal and state governments have adjusted existing laws and successively enacted and implemented the Limited Partnership Act. The earliest state to introduce such laws was Wyoming, which was the first to enact and implement the Wyoming Processing Cooperatives Act in 2001. By 2006, similar laws were enacted and implemented in Minnesota, Tennessee, Iowa, and Wisconsin. In 2007, the United States National Uniform State Law Commission drafted the *Uniform Limited Cooperative Association Act (ULCAA)*. Afterwards, Nebraska, Utah, Oklahoma, Colorado, and other states adopted the law.

In Europe, as the birthplace of agricultural cooperatives, the UK passed the world's first cooperative law, the Industrial and Credit Union Act, in 1852. Over the past 100 years, European and American countries have continuously promoted legislative work and model constitutions, standardized legal relationships within cooperatives, between cooperatives, and between cooperatives and other economic organizations, ensured the legitimate rights of members and the legal status of organizations, and promoted agricultural cooperatives to receive policy support in tax reduction, loan financing, and other aspects. Germany is also one of the important birthplaces of agricultural cooperatives, and in 1867, the first cooperative law, the *Law on the Private Legal Status of Business and Economic Cooperatives*, was promulgated. The current German cooperative law *Industrial and Commercial Cooperatives and Economic Cooperatives Law* was formulated in 1889, and has been revised several times in response to changes in the economic situation. The legal provisions have surpassed those of the European Union in terms of strictness and specificity. After more than 150 years of development, the types of German agricultural cooperatives have become increasingly diverse and their systems have become increasingly perfect. Agricultural cooperatives throughout the country provide comprehensive services to their members, helping German farmers participate in modern agricultural development. In addition, other European countries such as Sweden enacted the Cooperative Association Act in 1895, while Spain enacted the Cooperative Act in 1885. After multiple revisions, a new Cooperative Act was passed again on July 16, 1999. The French government also announced the relevant laws and regulations on cooperatives on September 10, 1947, and revised them in 1992.

In China, the *Law of the People's Republic of China on Farmers' Professional Cooperatives* came into effect on July 1, 2007, which was the first cooperative law since the establishment of the People's Republic of China. It grants farmers' professional cooperatives legal status and independent legal personality, allowing them to enter the market as legal market entities and develop business relationships with other economic entities, giving small farmers the power to organize their entry into the market. Among them, Article 8 clearly stipulates the basic policies of the government to support the development of professional cooperatives, that is, the state promotes the development of farmers' professional cooperatives through measures such as financial support, tax incentives, financial, technological, talent support, and industrial policy guidance. Since the implementation of the *Farmers' Professional Cooperatives Law* in 2007, it has effectively promoted the development of professional cooperatives, and the number of farmers' professional cooperatives has been increasing rapidly.

(3) Social assistance for the development of international rural organizations

Rural organizations do not exist in isolation, they are closely related to the government, the market, and other social organizations. Rural organizations, supported or guided by government policies, connect with the market and also interact with other social organizations.

In China, the Chinese government also encourages social organizations to assist in rural revitalization. The Chinese Ministry of Civil Affairs and the National Rural Revitalization Bureau have issued three important policies on the participation of social organizations in rural revitalization. Propose to improve the mechanism for participating in assistance cooperation and promote various types of assistance cooperation among national and provincial social organizations, as well as social organizations in the eastern region and poverty-stricken areas; require the organization to mobilize some key social organizations to provide coordination and assistance to 160 national key counties for rural revitalization, consolidate and expand the achievements of poverty alleviation and effectively connect with rural revitalization, and implement specific measures for the policies of social organizations to assist rural revitalization.

In Pakistan, the development model of the Aga Khan Rural Support Program (AKRSP) is relatively successful and has been recognized by the World Bank. This project was initiated by the Aga Khan Foundation and supported by multiple international institutions. The support plan began in 1982 with the basic goal of enhancing the self-development ability of people in remote mountainous areas through human resource development and the management and development of natural resources, enabling them to steadily and fairly improve their income and welfare, and promoting the sustainable development of impoverished communities.

In Africa, such as the F.A.L.C.O.N Association of Mauritius, which was officially registered in 2004 as a social organization in the field of agriculture in Mauritius, aims to explore the path of sustainable agricultural development and is committed to developing local agriculture. The F.A.L.C.O.N Citizens' Union of Mauritius has long supported farmers and farmers' organizations in conducting production, marketing, and promotional activities on the agricultural industry both internationally and domestically, creating employment opportunities for vulnerable groups, and providing education and training in ecological agriculture and commercial cooperatives; actively participate in ecological and environmental governance, carry out campaigns to address climate change, and strive for environmental protection and sustainable development.

II. Practical cases of the development of international rural organizations

Rural organizations have made significant progress with the support and guidance of the government. Due to significant differences in development stages, political systems, historical experiences, and traditional customs among different countries or regions, the specific manifestations of rural organizations also have their own characteristics. Here, ten cases were selected from developed countries, emerging economies, and developing countries for analysis.

1. Farmers' cooperative economic organizations in Japan: dual role of half officials and half civilians

The Japan Agricultural Cooperative Association (JACA) was officially established as a non-governmental cooperative economic organization after the *Agricultural Cooperative Association Act* was passed by the Japanese parliament in 1947. After the end of World War II, in order to consolidate the achievements of post-war agricultural land reform and solve the problem of poor and weak small farmers connecting with the big market, the Japanese authorities decided to establish a farmers' self-organizing group, namely the Farmers' Association. Supported and encouraged by a series of policies, finance, and taxation from the Japanese government, the Japan Farmers' Association has developed rapidly and quickly. By 1950, the Japanese Farmers' Association had attracted over 99% of farmers from across the country, basically achieving coverage of rural areas throughout the country. At the same time, a three-level agricultural association organization was established, including grassroots farmers' associations in cities and villages, agricultural federations in prefectures and counties, and national central federations, improving the organizational structure. Grassroots farmers' associations refer to the agricultural collaborative combination of administrative regions in cities, towns, and villages; County Farmers' Association refers to the agricultural collaborative combination at the county level of prefectures, the National Agricultural Association refers to the central level agricultural collaborative combination.

The Japanese Farmers' Association is the most important rural social organization, playing a role in organizing farmers to strive for political and economic interests, and participating in various aspects of rural construction. As mentioned earlier, the Japan Farmers' Association focuses on solving production and living problems that individual farmers cannot solve or cannot solve well, establishing close connections between dispersed small farmers and large markets, overcoming the limitations of small-scale household operations, and improving agricultural management efficiency. Secondly, the Japan Farmers' Association plays a role as a link between the government and farmers in Japanese society. The Association has close ties with the government, and the Japanese government will provide assistance in agricultural development, such as financial subsidies and tax preference, etc. The Japan Farmers' Association also cooperates with the government to provide faster and more comprehensive agricultural data. Once again, the Japan Farmers' Association can sometimes influence party member elections. For example, during the Japanese House of Representatives election, the Japan Farmers' Association gathers farmers together and conducts vote analysis for them, encouraging voters to vote for candidates that are conducive to agriculture. On the contrary, the call and organization of the Japan Farmers' Association will lead candidates to attach great importance to the development of agriculture and the interests of farmers. Many local candidates also come from rural areas, representing the interests of the Japanese Farmers' Association and taking into account the needs of farmers.

The Japan Comprehensive Farmers' Association has a wide range of business scope and has played an important role in the production and daily life of farmers and rural public utilities. Since its establishment, the Farmers' Association has had a semi-official nature. As an intermediary between the government and farmers, it implements various government policies and measures, and is also seen as a spokesperson for farmers' interests, expressing opinions on behalf of farmers and influencing political decision-making. Firstly, the Farmers' Association relies on its connections with political parties to gain political negotiation status and has a certain influence in the national strategic decision-making agenda, improving farmers' negotiation ability and status. Secondly, with the help of agricultural product control and market monopoly measures, the Farmers' Association resolved the contradiction between small farmers and large markets, promoted farmers' income growth, and protected regional agricultural interests. Thirdly, the Farmers' Association provides its members with socialized services in the fields of farmers' lives and agricultural production. It is a protective and service organization that promotes agricultural production and farmers' lives from the primary stage to the high development stage.

It can be said that the Japanese Farmers' Association takes administrative villages as the basic unit, and through the multi-layer network of county-level federations and national central councils, it unites farmers across the country into a whole. The Farmers' Association not only provides guidance to farmers in production and daily life, but also serves as the executor of national policies. At the same time, it represents the farmers' group to strive for various government support, serving as a link between the government and farmers. The Japan Farmers' Association and the administrative system have formed a model of mutual cooperation, playing a huge role in rural governance in Japan.

2. Farmers' cooperative economic organizations in the United States: scaled enterprise operation

The farmers' cooperative economic organizations in the United States are mainly farmers' professional cooperatives, which serve farmers and lead them to benefit, providing them with the necessary fertilizers, technology, and agricultural loans. Due to the fact that family farms are the basic agricultural production units in the United States, farmer cooperatives, also known as farmer cooperatives, are characterized by their well-organized, large-scale, widely distributed, and fully functional nature. They are the main forms of modern agricultural production, processing, and sales in the United States. The US Department of Agriculture once defined farmer cooperatives as organizations voluntarily formed by people with joint ownership on a non-profit basis to provide the services they need. The Capper-Volstead Act, passed by the United States Congress in 1922, established the legal status and government preferential policies enjoyed by farmers' professional cooperatives.

The development scale of farmers' professional cooperatives in the United States is relatively large. The productivity of grain in the United States accounts for about 1/5 of the world's total grain production, but 80% of its grain production is produced and processed by professional farmers' cooperatives. There are over 4,000 professional farmers' cooperatives with over 3 million members, an annual turnover of over 100 billion US dollars, and a net profit of over 2 billion US dollars. They have become an important economic entity in American agriculture. Almost all farmers in the United States participate in farmer cooperatives, and some even join several different types of farmer cooperatives at the same time. Farmers' professional cooperatives have an effective connection function between the upper market and the lower farmers, playing a leading role in agricultural development. The following is a detailed introduction to the specific operation process of American farmer cooperatives, taking Oregon as an example.

In Oregon, there are currently 55 farmer professional cooperatives, including 36 farmer professional cooperatives that produce specific agricultural products (such as milk, vegetables, meat and sheep farmer cooperatives, etc.), and 10 farmers' professional cooperatives with specific functions (such as agricultural education, agricultural law, water resource protection, etc.), 5 comprehensive farmers' professional cooperatives (such as farm alliances) and 4 farmers' professional cooperatives targeting specific populations (such as female farmer cooperatives and future farmer cooperatives). These farmers' professional cooperatives have clear responsibilities and a sound internal organizational structure. All members of the farmers' professional cooperative elect a board of directors, which hires a full-time manager to be responsible for daily affairs. Major matters are decided by the general meeting of all members. For example, the Farm Alliance, a farmers' professional cooperative in Oregon, elected 22 directors and established a board of directors. The board hired one executive manager, who recruited 12 full-time employees to assist in handling daily affairs.

Although there is no leadership relationship between different levels of cooperatives and cooperative members in the entrepreneurial operation model of American farmers' professional cooperatives, and the status is relatively loose, the role played by farmers' professional cooperatives has not weakened. Firstly, farmers' professional cooperatives in the United States provide members with various education and training programs. For example, customized education programs for local cooperative members, training courses and information programs for cooperative leaders and employees, inviting cooperative leaders and their members to participate in the annual meeting of the cooperative, providing a "think tank" role for cooperative leaders. Secondly, cooperatives actively participate in relevant legislative activities of the state legislature, reflect the interests and demands of members, and safeguard the interests of cooperatives. The association not only establishes a wide network of legal contacts, but also arranges two dedicated lobbyists to supervise relevant legislation and adjustment activities. Thirdly, cooperatives provide members with assistance in council innovation, long-term planning, mergers, acquisitions, or corporate restructuring, as well as assistance in creating new companies, project feasibility analysis, project coordination and outcome analysis, financial consulting, and services. Fourthly, cooperatives provide members with opportunities to connect with other cooperative leaders, enabling cooperatives facing special challenges to find answers and help.

3. Farmers' cooperative economic organizations in France: public service oriented

The development of French farmers' professional cooperatives has gone through a considerable period of time. As early as 1880, the organization of French peasant associations had a considerable foundation, and these peasant associations gradually became cooperatives. In 1945, the French government promoted the establishment of the National Union of Farmers' Professional Cooperatives. Later, France enacted many agricultural regulations, such as the 1960 *Agricultural Guidance Law*, the 1962 *Agricultural Production Economic Organization Law*, the 1972 *Agricultural Cooperation Charter Law*, and the EU Common Agricultural Policy, which had a significant impact on the development of French farmers' professional cooperatives. Therefore, since the 1960s, with the active support of the government, the French Farmers' Cooperative Economic Organization has achieved unprecedented development and gradually formed various service-oriented organizations, industry associations, and service enterprises, serving various stages of agricultural production before, during, and after production through various forms.

Farmers' professional cooperatives are the main body of the agricultural service system provided by society for French farmers. According to statistics from the French Ministry of Agriculture, 75% of French farmers have joined more than one cooperative, which purchases 91% of the country's pigs, 70% of grains, 55% of milk, and 51% of wine. From the perspective of development history, French farmers' cooperatives have gone through a process of first development, then standardization, and gradually becoming larger and stronger, generally showing a trend of decreasing in quantity and expanding in scale. Until 2018, the number of French agricultural cooperatives has decreased from around 7,500 in 1965 to 2,400. On the other hand, a group of large cooperatives have been formed through mergers and acquisitions, becoming not only giants in the domestic market, but also multinational groups with significant influence in the European Union and even global markets.

French farmers' professional cooperatives, as mutual aid organizations spontaneously formed by farmers, have less government intervention in cooperatives. However, the industry organizations formed from the bottom up and a large number of professional service organizations provide strong guidance and services for cooperatives. In France, there are three national level cooperative industry organizations, including the Higher Council of

French Agricultural Cooperatives (HCCA), the French Association for the Regulation of Agricultural Cooperatives, and the French Union of Agricultural Cooperatives. The branches of the three major industry organizations are located in 13 major regions, provinces, and municipalities in France, forming a complete organizational system. The Higher Committee, Regulatory Association, and Alliance are respectively responsible for the registration, financial audit, and business guidance services of cooperatives.

The French Union and Federation of Agricultural Cooperatives were developed on the basis of the organization of French agricultural cooperatives. The cooperative alliance belongs to a higher-level cooperative organization, which is a large-scale organization established strictly in accordance with the articles of association and relevant national laws and regulations. Its members are also various cooperatives. The scope of activities of cooperative alliances can be either regional or national, and according to different situations, cooperative alliances can be classified as professional or comprehensive. At present, 22 economic zones in France have established regional cooperative alliances, and each region has established professional alliances for milk, fruit, meat, and other sectors within each region. The large enterprises established by various cooperative alliances have greater power than dispersed cooperatives. The cooperative enterprise invested and established by farmers is the first level of the cooperative, and each member farm becomes the agricultural product production workshop of the regional cooperative alliance. Enterprises established by regional or professional alliances belong to the second level, and they help to supply and sell agricultural products, further uniting the pre- production and post production departments of agricultural production.

The complete cooperative system in France runs through various aspects of agriculture, including production, supply, sales, credit, insurance, and social services. It plays a huge role in reducing agricultural production costs, increasing farmers' income, improving farmers' quality, achieving agricultural modernization, and promoting rural economic development.

4. Farmers' cooperative economic organizations in Germany: led by government credit support

Agricultural cooperatives are a relatively common agricultural service organization in Germany, covering various parts of Germany, providing farmers with various agricultural services for production and operation. As an important pillar of the German cooperative organization system, agricultural cooperatives solve the contradiction between small-scale agricultural production and market economy through efficient and modern agricultural cooperative organizations. German agricultural cooperatives developed in the mid to late 19th century. After more than 150 years of development, the scale of German agricultural cooperatives continued to grow, their coverage became wider, and their system became increasingly perfect. From the organizational level, German agricultural cooperatives mainly include four gradients: central level cooperatives, local level cooperatives, township cooperatives, and rural cooperatives. From the perspective of business operations, German agricultural cooperatives mainly involve different fields such as production, credit, consumption, purchase and sales, and labor services.

Among them, agricultural credit cooperatives are an important component of the German financial industry and an organizational carrier for implementing agricultural financial policies. Their purpose is to provide financial credit support for the healthy development of agricultural cooperatives, with agricultural production cooperatives as the main lending entity, taking into account other agricultural cooperatives, and focusing on solving problems such as insufficient funds and large transactions in agricultural activities. Agricultural credit cooperatives establish direct credit connections with farmers through branches. It is to solve the financial difficulties faced by farmers, and the German government vigorously develops farmers' cooperative economic organizations, establishes a unique credit cooperation system, coordinates the German Cooperative Financial Organization, the German Central Cooperative Bank, and three regional cooperative banks, among which grassroots local cooperative banks composed of rural banks play a leading role. German cooperative finance has greatly alleviated the funding shortage of German farmers in agricultural product production and sales by providing preferential credit loans to farmers.

The efficient operation of German agricultural cooperatives is inseparable from Germany's sound financial policy support system. Germany has a developed credit cooperative system, and rural cooperative finance received attention from the German government at the beginning of its establishment, and relevant regulations and legislation were implemented for rural cooperative finance. This type of credit cooperative aims to absorb public deposits, issue credit loans to members of agricultural cooperatives and large cooperatives, and provide other commercial financial activities for them. A sound social credit system is the foundation of a sound agricultural financial policy support system. Germany strengthens the interest connection and credit protection between members, members and cooperatives, and cooperatives and cooperatives through a standardized public credit information system and private credit service system. The good social integrity environment promotes the German agricultural finance credit policy to serve agricultural cooperatives and their members to the maximum extent possible.

The proportion of agriculture in Germany accounts for 1% of GDP, but agricultural loans account for 2.5% of the total loans of financial institutions, and almost all banking and financial institutions are involved in rural credit market activities. In Germany, due to the fact that land belongs to individual farmers, farmers generally use land as collateral when applying for loans. In addition, the European Union, the federal government, and state governments encourage the development of small enterprises and farms, providing direct assistance to projects that comply with the European Common Agricultural Policy. Especially impoverished farmers can use fallow subsidies and government aid funds as repayment guarantees. Therefore, there are few financial institutions in Germany that refuse farmers' loan applications. To encourage financial institutions to participate in rural credit activities, the government implements interest subsidies for rural credit, covering all farming and breeding industries, agricultural production materials, agricultural product processing, water conservancy facilities, land improvement and consolidation, housing construction, agricultural structural adjustment, ecological agriculture, environmental protection, tourism, and the establishment of new enterprises.

For example, the German Agricultural Real Estate Mortgage Bank is mainly responsible for balancing and adjusting the supply and demand of rural credit funds between regions under the supervision of the Federal Bank, ensuring the long-term credit fund demand in various fields of the rural economy at preferential interest rates (generally no less than 4 years, up to 25 years), and managing and distributing the interest subsidy funds used by the Federal Bank and the federal government for rural credit. The German Agricultural Real Estate Mortgage Bank has implemented four special projects in rural credit activities, namely the special credit project for the planting and breeding industry, the special credit project for young farmers, the special project for village and town renovation, and the special credit project for regional structural adjustment, which are 0.1 to 1 percentage point lower than the credit market interest rate. The special credit project for young farmers has been a measure taken by the government since the 1980s to encourage and support young farmers to engage in agricultural production. Young farmers under the age of 40 can receive special preferential loans or subsidies, with interest rates about 0.25 percentage points lower than the special credit project for the breeding industry. The maximum credit limit was about 50,000 marks higher at that time. The purpose of implementing this policy is to encourage more young people to participate in rural economic activities and cultivate a new generation of rural business operators.

5. Rural revitalization organizations in China: party-led governance and social participation

Organizational revitalization is the political guarantee for rural revitalization in China, and the concrete embodiment of the Communist

Party of China (for short CPC) leading rural revitalization. In China, the main body of rural organization revitalization mainly includes four parts, namely, rural grassroots party organizations, rural professional cooperative economic organizations, social organizations, and village self governance organizations. The revitalization of rural organizations should establish and improve an organizational system with the CPC's grass-roots organizations as the core, villagers' autonomy and village affairs supervision organizations as the foundation, collective economic organizations and farmers' cooperative organizations as the link, and various economic and social service organizations as the supplement.

In China, the Communist Party is the leading core of various undertakings, and the rural grass-roots party organizations are the basis of all the work and combat effectiveness of the CPC in rural areas; rural grassroots party organizations comprehensively lead various organizations and work in townships and villages; rural grassroots party organizations are also the leading force for rural revitalization in China. It can be said that the construction of grassroots party organizations in rural areas is a prerequisite for establishing and improving the modern rural social governance system in China. Therefore, the CPC attaches great importance to the construction of rural grass-roots party organizations and the selection of the person in charge of rural grass-roots party organizations. For example, rural governance in China's Zhejiang Province has become a demonstration benchmark for national learning. These benchmark well-off demonstration villages have fully played the leading role of village party branch secretaries, guided grassroots party members and cadres to set an example, united and led the farmers to promote rural revitalization, and have achieved remarkable results.

China's rural revitalization has also consolidated the foundation of villagers' autonomy and village affairs supervision organizations. The village committee fulfills the functions of grassroots mass autonomous organizations and enhances the villagers' abilities in self-management, self-education, and self-service. The village affairs supervision committee plays a supervisory role in decision-making and disclosure of village affairs, property management, construction of engineering projects, and implementation of policies and measures that benefit farmers. For example, the rural grassroots units in contemporary China are townships, towns, and villages. The secretary of the township party committee and members of the party committee shall promptly identify and study solutions to problems such as rural grassroots party organization construction, rural governance, and mass production and life, and establish a stable system for ensuring the operation of village level organizations with financial investment as the main focus. The director of the village affairs supervision committee is generally held by a party member, and can be concurrently held by members of the village party organization team who are not members of the village committee, implementing the leadership of party members and cadres in village affairs construction.

China's rural revitalization organizations also need to play the role of a link between collective economic organizations and farmers' cooperative organizations. Collective economic organizations refer to the role they play in managing collective assets, reasonably developing collective resources, and serving collective members. Farmers' cooperative organizations and other economic and social organizations refer to fully exercising their powers in accordance with national laws and their respective articles of association. The secretary of the village party organization serves as the director of the village committee and the head of village level collective economic organizations and cooperative economic organizations through legal procedures. Members of the village committee and village affairs supervision committee cross serve to jointly guide the development of the collective economy.

In addition, China also encourages social organizations to assist in rural revitalization. The Chinese Ministry of Civil Affairs and the National Rural Revitalization Bureau have issued three important policies on the participation of social organizations in rural revitalization in 2022 and 2023. In the first notice, *Notice on Mobilizing and Guiding Social Organizations to Participate in Rural Revitalization Work*, it was proposed to improve the mechanism for participating in assistance cooperation, and promote various types of assistance cooperation among national and provincial social organizations, as well as social organizations in the eastern region and poverty-stricken areas. The second notice "Special Action Plan for Social Organizations to Assist Rural Revitalization" requires the organization and mobilization of some key social organizations to provide docking and assistance to 160 national key counties for rural revitalization, and to do a good job in consolidating and expanding the achievements of poverty alleviation and effectively connecting with rural revitalization. The third notice, *List of Paired Assistance between National Social Organizations, Social Organizations of Eastern Provinces (Municipalities), and 160 National Key Counties for Rural Revitalization,* is a specific implementation measure for the above two policies.

In short, China's rural revitalization organizations, under the leadership of the CPC, give full play to the role of grass-roots party organizations as a fighting fortress, work together with the villagers' committee and the village affairs supervision committee, and take rural collective economic organizations and farmers' cooperative organizations as the starting point to jointly promote China's rural revitalization. Meanwhile, social organizations also contribute to China's rural revitalization.

6. Farmers' cooperative economic organizations in India: a complete private official assistance system

India established its first cooperative in 1904 and also passed the *Credit Cooperative Act*, with the aim of promoting farmers to provide production funds in the form of cooperation and self-help, and freeing them from the cruel exploitation of high-interest loan merchants. The independence of India in 1947 entered a new historical stage in the development of the cooperative movement. In the more than 30 years since independence, not only has the number of cooperatives, members, and funds steadily increased, but the types, business scope, and scale of cooperatives have also undergone significant changes. So far, after more than 110 years of development, India has formed the world's largest agricultural cooperation organization system.

Indian Agricultural Cooperative is a voluntary organization that is open to all individuals without discrimination based on gender, social status, race, politics, or religion. Anyone can participate as long as they are able to fulfill their rights and obligations as members. At the same time, Indian cooperatives are also democratic organizations managed by cooperative members themselves, with members participating in decision-making and having the right to elect representatives and management bodies for the cooperatives. The agricultural cooperatives in India adopt a democratic management approach in their operation, making daily decisions through the election of members, as well as determining the representatives and management institutions of the cooperatives. The council is the highest management body of a cooperative, elected by the general assembly of members, with a term of up to 5 years. The general assembly of members is usually held once a year to review the work of the cooperative. At the national level, cooperative alliances have both management and coordination functions, and the council is appointed by the government.

The rapid development of India's agricultural cooperation movement is mainly due to the strong advocacy and support of the government. After India's independence, the Indian government attached great importance to the cooperative movement. By formulating corresponding laws, the Indian government stipulated the rights, obligations, and types of business operated by agricultural cooperatives, effectively promoting their orderly development. The Indian government believes that this is the best way to achieve grassroots democracy and economic planning, and regards cooperatives as one of the most important institutions for rural development and construction. The government has incorporated the development of cooperative economy into the national five-year plan in response to the development status of agriculture in various regions of the country. Develop corresponding development policies, increase investment in education, infrastructure construction, and technology, establish good financing channels, raise more funds, establish supporting services such as processing factories, and encourage more farmers to participate in the daily management of cooperatives. With strong government support, agricultural cooperatives have achieved unprecedented development.

However, India also faces some problems in developing cooperatives, as following aspects, the scale of grassroots cooperatives is small, their strength is weak, their service functions are limited, their infrastructure is poor, there is more administrative intervention from the government, the management personnel lack professional quality, and there is a large gap between regions. In order to further promote the healthy development of agricultural cooperative organizations, the Indian government introduced the National Policy on Agricultural Cooperatives in 2001. The policy stipulates that the state should provide necessary support, encouragement, and assistance to agricultural cooperative organizations, ensuring the independent, autonomous, and democratic management of cooperatives, in order to make important contributions to the development of the national economy. The main objective of national policy is to ensure that cooperative organizations operate in accordance with the basic values and principles of cooperatives proposed at the 1995 International Cooperative Union Conference; revitalize the cooperative organization system, especially the agricultural credit cooperation organization system; strengthen the construction of agricultural cooperatives in underdeveloped areas and states through the support of the central government and state governments, and narrow regional differences; strengthen education, training, and human resource development to improve the professional management level of cooperatives; strengthen the participation of members in cooperative management; revise the Cooperative Law and remove provisions that restrict the development of cooperatives; ensure that the profits of cooperatives can benefit impoverished groups, and encourage the participation of impoverished groups and women in the management of cooperatives.

In short, Indian farmers' cooperative economic organizations have a typical private official assistance nature, and the Indian government has always attached great importance to the development of cooperatives. In 1958, India established the Cooperative Department, which was a deputy ministerial level institution under the Indian Ministry of Community Development at that time. In 1979, India established the Ministry of Agriculture and Cooperatives, which was a sub-ministerial level institution under the Ministry of Agriculture and Irrigation at that time. Currently, the Ministry of Agriculture and Cooperatives is still a deputy ministerial level institution under the Ministry of Agriculture of India, responsible for policy formulation for national agricultural cooperatives; coordinate and manage relevant national agricultural cooperation organizations; carry out cooperative education and training. At the same time, the Indian government provides significant financial and technical support for cooperatives in terms of economic support. The Indian Ministry of Agriculture and Cooperatives also provides financial support to various agricultural cooperative organizations through institutions such as the National Cooperative Union, the National Agricultural Cooperative Sales Federation, the National Cooperative Development Group Corporation, and the National Consumer Cooperative Union.

7. Rural organizations in Brazil: spontaneous organization participation and promotion

The Brazilian cooperative organization has a wide coverage and comprehensive service provision. The cooperative based agricultural industrialization operation model has made the cooperative organization a link and bridge for effective communication between agricultural producers and operators and the market. It is also an important force in the agricultural socialization service system and has played a positive role in promoting the development of agriculture in Brazil. The social development of rural areas in Brazil mainly relies on spontaneous agricultural production cooperatives and agricultural industrial joint ventures, without the most grassroots rural government institutions. According to the 1988 Constitution, only areas with over 20000 residents can establish "city" governments with political decision-making and executive functions. In rural areas without a "city", due to the lack of government agencies, general enterprises and institutions are unwilling and unable to effectively carry out work such as organizing the settlement system, improving village living facilities, and rural development environment. Many rural areas have inconvenience in living and lack necessary development planning.

Brazilian cooperative organizations have four levels, from high to low, namely national cooperative organizations, state cooperative organization centers, cooperatives, and grassroots cooperatives. From the perspective of cooperative categories, there are mainly supply and marketing cooperatives, fishery cooperatives, and rural electrification cooperatives. The supply and marketing cooperative is responsible for providing production materials to farmers, providing individual producers and farms with services such as agricultural product packaging, processing, storage, transportation, sales, and market information technology training; fishery cooperatives guide fishermen in purchasing fishing equipment, conducting deep processing of fishery products, and providing technical training in freezing, processing, and transportation of fishery products; rural electrification cooperatives raise funds for the construction of rural power supply facilities, manage the charging and taxation of agricultural electricity, promote regional economic development, and improve the production and living conditions of farmers. These professional cooperatives mainly provide farmers with a series of services such as technical information, relevant training, agricultural product storage, processing, transportation and sales, infrastructure construction, etc. Some well managed cooperatives have developed into large-scale agricultural and industrial comprehensive enterprises, engaged in the processing of agricultural products such as sugar, wine, and coffee.

Cooperative organizations implement the basic principle of "voluntary membership and freedom of withdrawal". Joining the organization is the self choice of members, and the normal operation of cooperative organizations relies on the collective action of members in unity. In the implementation of agricultural socialized services by cooperative organizations, the main position of members ensures that they are active selectors of technical service technology promotion, rather than simply passive recipients. This ensures that the content of agricultural socialized services meets the requirements of the majority of farmers, thereby improving the effectiveness of agricultural technology promotion and services. The organizational system of Brazilian cooperatives is a combination of sections. From horizontal level, it refers to cooperatives in 12 industries across the country, each with its own headquarters. From vertical aspect, it refers to the establishment of cooperative headquarters at both the state and national levels, which are joint organizations of 12 industry cooperatives and do not engage in business activities. The main tasks are to maintain the interests of cooperatives, reflect their wishes, coordinate relationships, promote joint provision of training and information services, and are actually industry associations.

In short, Brazilian agricultural cooperatives organize dispersed small and medium-sized farmers and establish economic consortia through collective and individual forms, which not only promotes the development of agricultural production but also contributes to rural industrialization. Agricultural cooperatives have also improved the market competitiveness of small producers, laying a solid foundation for the development of agriculture in Brazil.

8. Rural organizations in Pakistan: foundation participation in governance

The Aga Khan Rural Support Program (AKRSP) in northern Pakistan was initiated by the Aga Khan Foundation and supported by multiple international institutions. The support plan began in 1982 with the basic goal of enhancing the self-development ability of people in remote mountainous areas through human resource development and the management and development of natural resources, enabling them to steadily and fairly improve their income and welfare, and promoting the sustainable development of impoverished communities. AKRSP has a history of 40 years since its establishment, and its development model is successful.

The Aga Khan Rural Support Project in Pakistan mainly includes projects such as rural infrastructure, rural basic education, health, large-scale agriculture, human resource development, training and services. Initially organized and implemented in the Gilgit region of northern Pakistan, it gradually expanded to the Chitral region from 1985 onwards. The implementation of the project not only improved the basic conditions of agricultural production, increased crop yield, and increased farmers' income, but also improved the education, nutrition, and health care status of farmers, enhancing their quality. More importantly, through project implementation, it has influenced and changed the mindset of local people, making them believe that they can rely on their own strength to achieve development goals.

In recent years, its achievements have included a doubling of income, the construction and restoration of over 4,000 small-scale infrastructure projects, the planting of tens of millions of trees and the development of hundreds of acres of marginal land, the development of over 50,000 community activist backbone, the mobilization of nearly $50,000 in village savings, and the establishment of over 4,990 community organizations. The community organizations supported by AKRSP have established participatory, democratic, transparent, and accountable local governance models for their members, and are now jointly establishing local support organizations at the level of the trade union council.

The Aga Khan Support Project in Pakistan has the following characteristics: firstly, strengthen and enrich the management institutions at all levels of the project, and adjust and layout the grassroots project management institutions. In project management, the power of project implementation management is gradually delegated to the regional level project office, and "Field Management Units" are successively established below the region, and corresponding full-time officials with professional technical background and practical project management experience are equipped to enrich and strengthen each specific management level of project operation and improve the level of project management. The main responsibilities of these project implementation management units are to liaise with village organizations and women's organizations. Each full-time project officer equipped is composed of carefully selected representatives of local indigenous peoples and hired external professionals, and the project management personnel are constantly supplemented and improved at any time.

Secondly, in the specific operation process, the Aga Khan Rural Support Project focuses on integrating resources and multiple interests. The Aga Khan Rural Support Project establishes and supports the development of rural organizations. With the joint promotion of rural organizations, at least 75% of villagers have participated. Through rural organization alliances, promote the development of farmers' autonomous organizations and fully mobilize the enthusiasm and initiative of participating farmers. In terms of project selection, farmers first make requests, and then rural social organizations and women's organizations provide support through project applications submitted to the foundation. This approach closely combines the economic interests of various organizational members participating in project operation with the interests of the foundation, as well as the interests of multi-level project officials, forming a cohesive force, thereby ensuring the success of project implementation and project benefits.

Thirdly, the Aga Khan Rural Support Project has improved the status and cultural level of local women. Throughout the Aga Khan rural support project activities, the widespread involvement and benefits of women have become a theme in project design and implementation. This project approach that introduces gender and highlights the status of women is highly likely to receive assistance from relevant international organizations. The project strengthens the training and monitoring of women through the implementation of human resource development activities. At the same time, through years of effort, the proportion of women in the management of the entire Aga Khan rural pillar project has also been continuously increasing.

9. Rural organizations in Ethiopia: highly autonomous villagers

Ethiopia is located in northeastern Africa, with a weak domestic industrial foundation and mainly relies on agriculture and animal husbandry. Its farmers and herdsmen account for over 85% of the total population, mainly engaged in planting and animal husbandry, as well as a small amount of fishing and forestry. Ethiopia's agriculture is mainly based on small-scale farming, with a wide range of crops and a thin harvest. It relies on the weather for food and is often short of food. Cereal crops such as bran and wheat account for 84.15% of grain crop yield. In recent years, due to the government's cancellation of agricultural product sales monopolies, relaxation of price controls, encouragement of small-scale agricultural loans, strengthening of agricultural technology promotion and fertilizer use, grain production has increased.

Ethiopia is a traditional agricultural country, and its grassroots rural governance has its own characteristics, namely, government support and guidance, high autonomy of villagers, and potential support for religious culture. The role of the Ethiopian government in maintaining rural stability is mainly reflected in, firstly, the government provides transactions and distribution of important agricultural investment products, such as fertilizers and seeds. The second is that the government has established an agricultural technology promotion system, responsible for promoting new agricultural technologies. The third is to provide necessary public services, such as the maintenance of transportation, public security, and market order, as well as financial and educational services. The national administrative system in Ethiopia is divided into four levels: states (municipalities directly under the central government), districts, Warida, and Kobele. Taking the agricultural technology promotion system of the Ethiopian government as an example, the Federal Agricultural Office is the highest level agricultural institution, followed by the Regional Agricultural Bureau, District Agricultural Office, and Warida Agricultural Office. There is a promotion group under the Warida Agricultural Office, which is composed of agricultural technology promotion personnel responsible for the implementation of agricultural technology promotion. Agricultural technology extension personnel will also provide necessary technical training to farmers.

Agricultural production in Ethiopia is based on farmers, but due to the backward level of agricultural technology production, it is difficult for a single family to independently complete the entire process of agricultural production. All farmers spontaneously established agricultural cooperatives. Agricultural cooperatives are established in the most grassroots administrative unit, Kobele. Agricultural cooperatives implement a membership system, with the majority of farmers being members. Agricultural cooperatives, as representatives of the local collective economy, play an important role in the agricultural production of farmers. For example, due to strict government control over fertilizers and seeds, farmers cannot purchase them separately and can only purchase them collectively through agricultural cooperatives. Secondly, agricultural cooperatives play a role in the storage and sale of food. Agricultural cooperatives have large iron sheet warehouses, and when the rainy season comes, farmers can choose to store their grain in the agricultural cooperatives and sell it at a higher price before the next year's grain harvest. After 2006, the Ethiopian government gradually relaxed its control over rural markets, allowing almost all agricultural inputs and products to be freely traded by farmers in the market.

The villagers' autonomy in Ethiopia is also reflected in two aspects: agricultural production activities and self management of rural affairs. Firstly, in terms of self-management of agricultural production activities. Ethiopia's agricultural production faces many unfavorable conditions, such as climate drought, inconvenient transportation, outdated production technology, poor terrain and soil quality. Local farmers have developed mechanisms such as agricultural cooperatives, labor rental markets, and market markets to overcome these difficulties, effectively ensuring the smooth progress of agricultural production activities. Secondly, in terms of self-management of rural affairs. Agricultural cooperatives not only have the task of managing agricultural production activities, but also have the function of managing rural affairs. The discussion and decision-making of daily affairs in rural areas shall be resolved through consultation among all members of the agricultural cooperative. All members will also elect permanent members, usually appointed by highly respected individuals, to represent the entire village and negotiate disputes with other villages and their subjects. Rural affairs are resolved through consultation and negotiation, and there is basically no recourse to the government or the law.

The relatively closed rural areas in Ethiopia, the hardships faced by farmers, the extreme scarcity of cultural life, and the abundance of free time are all powerful elements in the development of religious activities. Most Ethiopians believe in Eastern Orthodoxy and regularly participate in religious activities. Religion has established norms in the handling of personal affairs and interpersonal relationships, forming binding social customs. Religious activities are the most important cultural activities for local residents, playing an important role in calming people's emotions, regulating neighborhood relationships, and regulating moral behavior. Therefore, religious culture has become a component of the informal system in rural Ethiopia, and can also be said to be an invisible organizational force, which is an important supplement to explicit organizations, particularly prominent in economically backward impoverished rural areas.

10. Rural organizations in Mauritius: participation of civil society organizations

Mauritius is an island country in eastern Africa, with an arable land area of 110,800 hectares, accounting for 46% of the total national area, including 76,186 hectares of sugarcane fields and 5,262 hectares of grain fields. Approximately 200,000 tons of grain need to be imported annually. Other crops include tea, tobacco, onions, fruits, etc. Animal husbandry mainly focuses on raising cattle, sheep, pigs, deer, chickens, etc. 80% of dairy products and 90% of beef rely on imports, while pork, chicken, and vegetables are basically self-sufficient.

The F.A.L.C.O.N Association of Mauritius is a non-governmental organization officially registered in the field of agriculture in Mauritius in 2004. It aims to explore the path of sustainable agricultural development and is committed to the development of local agriculture. The F.A.L.C.O.N Citizens' Union of Mauritius has long supported farmers and farmers' organizations in conducting production, marketing, and promotional activities on the agricultural industry both internationally and domestically, creating employment opportunities for vulnerable groups, and providing education and training in ecological agriculture and commercial cooperatives; actively participate in ecological and environmental governance, carry out campaigns to address climate change, and strive for environmental protection and sustainable development.

The F.A.L.C.O.N Citizens' Union of Mauritius, as a farmers' cooperative organization in Mauritius, mainly serves local farmers in agriculture, animal husbandry, organic agricultural product networks, and cooperation projects. It is implementing its purpose of "working hard for a cleaner, greener, and safer world". The F.A.L.C.O.N Citizens' Union of Mauritius also actively participates in international cooperation. In 2018, it signed a memorandum of cooperation with Beijing Vocational College of Agriculture, agreeing to engage in in-depth exchanges and cooperation in agricultural training and talent assistance. For example, teachers at Beijing Vocational College of Agriculture once taught the cultivation techniques of tomatoes and edible mushrooms to members of the F.A.L.C.O.N Citizen Union in Mauritius. The members of the F.A.L.C.O.N Citizens' Union in Mauritius have applied these technologies to agricultural production in Mauritius, greatly improving production efficiency and profitability.

III. Experience and inspiration from the construction of international rural organizations

Rural organizations are an important force in achieving rural revitalization.

In the process of rural organization development, government guidance, legal protection, and social organization assistance jointly promote the development of global rural organizations. Ten countries, including Japan, the United States, France, Germany, China, India, Brazil, Pakistan, Ethiopia, and Mauritius, were selected from three types of developed countries, emerging economies, and developing countries for case analysis to draw experience and inspiration on the construction of international rural organizations.

1. Improving organizational policy guarantee to assist rural development

Although the government plays a different role in different types of rural revitalization models, the policies that support rural development can be determined through financial and tax policies, laws and regulations, or institutional means to ensure the sustainability of rural development. Government support and legislation are indispensable and important conditions for protecting rural development. The financial and tax support, laws and regulations of governments in Europe and America are relatively complete, while the government support and protection efforts of Latin American and African countries are insufficient. The governments of Japan, China, and India in Asia are providing certain policy support for the development of rural organizations and formulating corresponding laws and regulations to assist rural development.

2. Strengthening organizational coordination, guiding and integrating social resources

The government plays an organizational and coordinating role in the process of rural revitalization, especially grassroots government organizations are the core force in coordinating various actors at the grassroots level. Therefore, not only should the government play a good role in planning guidance and policy support, such as the transmission of higher-level government policies, national financial support, cross departmental and cross industry cooperation, but also enable grassroots governments to organize and mobilize various forces, integrate various resources, and cooperate to promote rural revitalization. For example, grassroots farmers' associations in Japan, grassroots party organizations in China, and Kobele in Ethiopia are all ties that connect grassroots governments, villagers, and collective economic cooperation organizations.

3. Mobilizing market forces and collaborating to serve rural development

The government is an indispensable leader in rural construction. By making decisions, implementing policies, and integrating resources, the government can also integrate various social forces to effectively achieve various goals of rural construction and revitalization. In the process of rural construction, rural organizations often assist small farmers to unite and face the coordinators between large markets, which can overcome the limitations of small-scale household operations and improve agricultural efficiency. On the contrary, the market economy environment has also given rise to the development of rural enterprises or collective cooperative economies. Therefore, in the process of rural revitalization, market forces can be mobilized to jointly serve rural development.

4. Fully leveraging the joint efforts of various social organizations

Social organizations include various types of civil organizations, social groups, etc. Social organizations have public service functions and undertake different social division of labor from governments and enterprises. Social organizations are one of the main bodies of grassroots governance, serving as an important bridge and link between the market, enterprises, and farmers. They play a positive role in promoting the development of rural industrial entities and stimulating their endogenous motivation. In the process of rural revitalization, rural organizations, under the policy support or guidance of the government or political parties, will also connect with the market and interact with other social organizations in the current market economy. Therefore, it is necessary to actively mobilize the collaborative participation of different types of social organizations to form a synergy.

5. Strengthening international cooperation in agriculture to assist the development of rural organizations

Currently, there are significant differences in the development level of rural organizations among developed countries, emerging economies, and developing countries. The *Transforming Our World: 2030 Agenda for Sustainable Development* adopted by the United Nations General Assembly in 2015 stated that "eradicating all forms of poverty, hunger, achieving food security, improving nutritional status, and promoting sustainable agriculture worldwide". Therefore, developing countries can strengthen cooperation in the field of agriculture with developed countries and emerging economies through bilateral or multilateral platforms, learn from the experience of rural organization development, and jointly promote the development of global agricultural modernization.

◎ Chapter VI Rural Revitalization and Practice in China

Abstract

This chapter first analyzes the effect of China's promotion of rural revitalization, explains the value of China's countryside to global rural development, reviews China's rural revitalization policies, and explains how consolidating and expanding the achievements of poverty eradication can be effectively connected with rural revitalization; secondly, the annual experience of China in promoting rural revitalization is summarized. High-quality development of rural industries, expanding employment opportunities, developing and enlarging new types of rural collective economies, and enhancing poverty alleviation capabilities through skill training, are all important measures to strengthen the intrinsic motivation of impoverished areas and their residents. To continue advancing rural revitalization, it is necessary to learn from and implement typical practices, which include but are not limited to promoting high-quality development of rural industries, vigorously advancing the construction of livable and business-friendly beautiful villages, and improving the rural governance system led by organizations.

I. Analysis of the effect of China's promotion of rural revitalization

1. The value of China's rural revitalization to global rural development

The revitalization of China's countryside is a development that takes up the cause of poverty eradication in China. At the stage of poverty eradication, the value of China's achievements in the field of poverty governance and rural development has been recognized by the world. UN Secretary-General Guterres has spoken highly of China's approach to poverty reduction, saying, "A precise poverty reduction strategy is the only way to help the poorest people and achieve the ambitious goals of the *2030 Agenda for Sustainable Development*. China has lifted hundreds of millions of people out of poverty, and its experience can provide useful lessons for other developing countries". In the resolution *Eradicating Rural Poverty and Implementing the 2030 Agenda for Sustainable Development* adopted by the 73rd session of the UN General Assembly, the UN dovetailed China's experience in poverty governance with the *UN 2030 Agenda for Sustainable Development*, proposing new ideas for achieving the 2030 Sustainable Development Goals and a basic policy framework for eliminating world poverty based on China's practice in poverty eradication. In this new stage, China's rural revitalization will also continue to highlight China's global value in the governance of the "three rural issues".

China's large rural population base determines that rural revitalization has global representation. During the stage of poverty eradication, China, which accounts for nearly 20% of the world's population, has completed its poverty eradication and achieved the poverty reduction target of the *United Nations 2030 Agenda for Sustainable Development* 10 years ahead of schedule. According to the World Bank's international poverty standard, China has reduced poverty by more than 70% of the global poverty reduction population in the same period. China's fight against poverty has lifted hundreds of millions of Chinese people out of poverty while significantly lowering the global poverty rate. Today, China's rural population still accounts for about 15% of the world's rural population[71], and rural China remains a huge and critical part of the world's rural development map. Against the background that the global rural development situation is still severe, China's rural revitalization project not only carries the development hope of more than 500 million rural people in China, but also has the important responsibility of guiding the way for the world's rural development.

China's rural revitalization contributes Chinese solutions and experience to global rural development. General Secretary Xi Jinping has repeatedly proposed that China should "propose Chinese solutions" and "contribute Chinese wisdom" to world development, and build "a community with a shared future of mankind with no poverty and common development" together. "The Chinese government has been promoting the development of the countryside since the implementation of the rural revitalization strategy. Since the implementation of the rural revitalization strategy, China has gradually worked out "counterpart support", "cultural tourism to help farmers", "e-commerce to help farmers", "two mountain banks "three-tier logistics system in rural areas" and other experiences and practices with Chinese characteristics. They also contain general laws and methodological principles of rural development, are distinctly universal and international, and have important reference values for global rural development work. In addition, China's rural revitalization has also demonstrated to the world the governance ability of the Communist Party of China and the political advantages of the socialist system. To ensure the effective promotion of poverty eradication and rural revitalization, the CPC has taken a series of original and unique initiatives based on China's national conditions, and explored a path with Chinese characteristics, such as the "Trinity" poverty alleviation pattern, the developmental approach to poverty alleviation, the precise poverty alleviation strategy, and the social mobilization

---

71   Data source: World Bank database (rural population) https://data.worldbank.org/indicator/SP.RUR. TOTL?end=2021&most_recent_value_desc=true&start=1960& view=chart.

mechanism with the participation of the whole nation. These are important experiences of the Marxist anti-poverty movement. These important experiences are the theoretical crystallization of the combination of Marxist anti-poverty theory and China's anti-poverty practice, and are the latest theoretical achievements of the Chinese Communist Party in leading the Chinese people in exploring and practicing the road to poverty eradication and rural revitalization, contributing Chinese wisdom and Chinese experience to global poverty governance.

China has deeply practiced the concept of community of human destiny to promote international cooperation in rural revitalization. China has been actively participating in global rural revitalization and poverty governance for many years, and has provided assistance to developing countries in various ways. **First, it has provided financial support for the cause of rural revitalization and poverty reduction in the world.** China has repeatedly made donations to the World Bank and other international development organizations to address the problem of insufficient funding for global poverty governance. China has initiated the establishment of the Asian Infrastructure Investment Bank to support infrastructure development in Asia and promote development and poverty reduction in Asia and other regions. In addition, China has proposed the "One Belt, One Road" cooperation initiative and funded the Silk Road Fund to provide investment and financing support for infrastructure, resource development, industrial cooperation and financial cooperation projects in countries along the "One Belt, One Road" route, providing substantial financial assistance for poverty reduction and development in countries along the route. China has provided substantial financial assistance to poverty reduction and development in countries along the route. **Second, China has actively engaged in South-South cooperation to help other developing countries escape poverty.** Over the past 60 years, China has provided assistance to 166 countries and international organizations, dispatched more than 600,000 aid workers, forgiven the debt of least developed countries to China seven times, and provided assistance to more than 120 developing countries to implement the UN Millennium Development Goals. In addition, China established the International Development Knowledge Center (IDKC) in 2017 to "work with other countries to study and exchange development theories and practices that are appropriate to their own conditions"[72] and help developing countries explore the path to poverty reduction and revitalization that is appropriate to their own conditions. In the future, China will still uphold its role as a great power and persistently promote international cooperation on rural revitalization.

2. Retrospective of China's rural revitalization policies

Strong institutional guarantee and policy support. China's rural revitalization strategy was first proposed in the report of the 19th National Congress made by General Secretary Xi Jinping in 2017, reflecting the great importance the country attaches to solving Issues of agriculture, farmer and rural area. Subsequently, during the period of poverty eradication, the state has issued a series of documents represented by *Opinions of the State Council of the Central Committee of the Communist Party of China on Implementing the Strategy of Rural Revitalization, National Strategic Plan for Rural Revitalization (2018-2022), Guidance Opinions of the State Council on Promoting the Revitalization of Rural Industries, Opinions on Adjusting and Improving the Use of Land Transfer Revenue to Support Rural Revitalization in Priority*, etc.; after the task of poverty eradication has been completed, the state has issued a series of documents to support the revitalization of rural areas. After the completion of the task of poverty eradication, in the stage of consolidating and expanding the achievements of poverty eradication and rural revitalization, a series of documents have been issued, such as *Opinions on Accelerating Agricultural Modernization by Comprehensively Promoting Rural Revitalization, Opinions on Accelerating the Revitalization of Rural Talents, Opinions on Realizing the Effective Interface between Consolidating and Expanding the Achievements of*

72　Xi Jinping. (2015). UN Development Summit.

Poverty Eradication and Rural Revitalization, Law of the People's Republic of China on Promoting Rural Revitalization, Opinions on Making Good Efforts to Promote Rural Revitalization in 2022, etc. *Opinions on Promoting the Key Work of Rural Revitalization in 2022, Implementation Plan of Rural Construction Action,* etc. are a series of laws and documents (Table 6.1). As China's "three rural issues" change and work progresses one after another, the state attaches more and more importance to the rural revitalization strategy in its policies and regulations, and this is reflected in the increase in the number of relevant policies and regulations, the expansion of dimensions, the elevation of the status and the extension of depth.

Table 6.1   Retrospective of China's rural revitalization policies, 2017-2022

Period	Policies / Regulations	Release time	Main content
The period of poverty alleviation	*The Great Victory of Socialism with Chinese Characteristics in the New Era by Winning the Comprehensive Completion of a Well-off Society*	October 18, 2017	For the first time, he proposed the strategy of revitalizing the countryside, pointing out that the issue of agriculture, rural areas and farmers is a fundamental issue related to the people's livelihood, and that the solution of the "three rural" issues must always be the top priority of the work of the whole Party.
	Opinions of the State Council of the Central Committee of the Communist Party of China on the Implementation of Rural Revitalization Strategy	February 4, 2018	By 2020, important progress will be made in rural revitalization, and the institutional framework and policy system will be basically formed; by 2035, decisive progress will be made in rural revitalization, and agricultural and rural modernization will be basically realized; by 2050, the countryside will be fully revitalized, and strong agriculture, beautiful countryside and rich farmers will be fully realized.

(Continued)

Period	Policies / Regulations	Release time	Main content
The period of poverty alleviation	*National Strategic Plan for Rural Revitalization (2018-2022)*	September 26, 2018	The key tasks for the next five years are clearly defined, 22 specific indicators such as the contribution rate of agricultural science and technology progress are proposed, and a countryside revitalization index system is established for the first time. According to the four types of clustering and upgrading, suburban integration, characteristic protection and relocation and evacuation, the methods and steps to promote rural revitalization by category are clarified. The work of rural revitalization was refined and actualized, and 82 major projects, plans and actions of digital agriculture and rural areas and smart agriculture were deployed.
	The Guidance of the State Council on Promoting the Revitalization of Rural Industries	June 28, 2019	Adhere to the general policy of giving priority to the development of agriculture and rural areas, take the implementation of the rural revitalization strategy as the general grasp, take the structural reform on the supply side of agriculture as the main line, focus on the integrated development of one, two, three industries in rural areas, effectively connect with poverty eradication and urbanization, fully explore the multiple functions and values of the countryside, focus on key industries, gather resource elements, strengthen innovation leadership, highlight clusters into chains, extend industrial chains, improve value chains, cultivate new momentum for development, accelerate the formation of a modern agricultural industrial system, production system and operation system, and lay a solid foundation for the modernization of agriculture and rural areas. Cultivate new momentum for development, accelerate the construction of modern agricultural industry system, production system and operation system, promote the formation of urban-rural integration development pattern, and lay a solid foundation for agricultural and rural modernization.
	Opinions on Adjusting and Improving the Use of Land Transfer Revenue to Support Rural Revitalization on a Priority Basis	September 23, 2020	According to the requirement of "taking from agriculture and mainly using it for agriculture", it will adjust the urban-rural distribution pattern of land transfer proceeds, steadily increase the proportion of land transfer proceeds for agriculture and rural areas, focus on supporting the key tasks of rural revitalization, accelerate the short board of development of "three rural" areas, and provide strong support for the implementation of the rural revitalization strategy. This will provide strong support for the implementation of the rural revitalization strategy.

(Continued)

Period	Policies / Regulations	Release time	Main content
Rural revitalization period	*Opinions on Accelerating Agricultural Modernization by Comprehensively Promoting Rural Revitalization*	February 21, 2021	We will place rural construction in an important position of socialist modernization, comprehensively promote the revitalization of rural industries, talents, culture, ecology and organizations, give full play to the functions of agricultural product supply, ecological barrier and cultural heritage, take the road of socialist rural revitalization with Chinese characteristics, accelerate the modernization of agriculture and rural areas, accelerate the formation of a new type of industrial-agricultural-urban-rural relationship with mutual promotion, urban-rural complementarity, coordinated development and common prosperity, and promote agriculture of high quality and high efficiency, livable and livable countryside, and rich and affluent farmers.
	Opinions on Accelerating the Revitalization of Rural Talents	February 23, 2021	The key to the revitalization of the countryside lies in people. Strengthen the overall leadership of the Party on the work of rural talents, adhere to the priority development of agriculture and rural areas, adhere to the priority of human capital development in rural areas, vigorously cultivate local talents, guide urban talents to the countryside, promote professional talents to serve the countryside, attract all kinds of talents to build up their work in rural revitalization, improve the institutional mechanism of rural talents, strengthen the guarantee measures for the revitalization of talents, cultivate a "three rural" work team that understands agriculture, loves the countryside and loves farmers, and provide strong talent support to comprehensively promote rural revitalization and accelerate agricultural and rural modernization. In order to cultivate a "three rural" work team that understands agriculture, loves the countryside and loves farmers, and provide strong talent support to comprehensively promote rural revitalization and accelerate the modernization of agriculture and rural areas.

(Continued)

Period	Policies / Regulations	Release time	Main content
Rural revitalization period	*Opinions on Realizing the Effective Interface between Consolidating and Expanding the Results of Poverty Alleviation and Rural Revitalization*	March 22, 2021	It is proposed to set up a 5-year transition period after the completion of the target task of poverty eradication. By 2025, the results of poverty eradication will be consolidated and expanded, rural revitalization will be comprehensively promoted, the economic vitality and development momentum of the areas out of poverty will be significantly enhanced, the quality, efficiency and competitiveness of rural industries will be further improved, the level of rural infrastructure and basic public services will be further enhanced, the ecological environment will be continuously improved, the construction of beautiful and livable villages will be solidly promoted, the construction of rural style civilization will make significant progress, the construction of rural grassroots organizations will be The long-term mechanism to help the rural low-income population is gradually improved, and the growth rate of farmers' income in areas out of poverty is higher than the national average level of farmers. By 2035, the economic strength of the areas out of poverty will be significantly strengthened, significant progress will be made in the revitalization of the countryside, the living standard of the rural low-income population will be significantly improved, the urban-rural gap will be further narrowed, and more obvious and substantial progress will be made in promoting the common prosperity of all people.
	Law of the People's Republic of China on the Promotion of Rural Revitalization	April 29, 2021	For the first time, special legislation is enacted for rural revitalization to provide important legal guarantee for the implementation of rural revitalization strategy.
	Opinions on the Key Efforts to Comprehensively Promote Rural Revitalization in 2022	February 22, 2022	It is proposed to make every effort to grasp food production and the supply of important agricultural products, strengthen the basic support of modern agriculture, adhere to the bottom line of not returning to poverty on a large scale, focus on industry to promote rural development, solid and steady promotion of rural construction, highlighting the effectiveness of improving rural governance, increase policy protection and institutional innovation, adhere to and strengthen the Party's overall guidance of the work of the "three rural" areas and other eight aspects.

(Continued)

Period	Policies / Regulations	Release time	Main content
Rural revitalization period	*Implementation Plan for the Countryside Construction Action*	May 23, 2022	Focusing on the construction of universal, basic and bottom-up livelihoods, strengthening planning and leading, coordinating resources and elements, mobilizing efforts from all sides, strengthening the construction of rural infrastructure and public service systems, establishing a bottom-up, villagers' self-governance and farmers' participation implementation mechanism, doing the best we can and doing what we can, seeking good rather than fast, doing one thing to make one thing, trying to make rural areas have better living conditions, and building beautiful villages that are livable and workable.

We should take into account the current situation and promote rural revitalization. The evolution of the policy on rural revitalization reflects the continuous deepening of China's rural revitalization work, which is manifested in "two shifts" and "four changes"[73] . The "two shifts" are adjustments in the general direction, i.e., in terms of work objectives, the work objectives have been upgraded from solving the "two worries and three guarantees" for the poor people with fixed records to realizing the prosperity of rural industries, ecological livability, civilized countryside, effective governance and affluent living; in terms of work tasks, it has shifted from concentrating resources on supporting poverty eradication to consolidating and expanding the results of poverty eradication and promoting rural revitalization, i.e. the task has shifted from absolute poverty governance to solving relative poverty governance problems through effective linkage and rural revitalization, but the main content still revolves around industry, ecology, culture, organization, education, consumption and other aspects. This is an adjustment in the general direction and in line with the current development of the "three rural areas" in China. The

---

73 Yongxiu Bai, Haixin Huang, Liting Song. The policy evolution and logic of consolidating and expanding the achievements of poverty eradication and rural revitalization [J]. Journal of Northwestern University (Philosophy and Social Science Edition), 2022, 52 (5): 73-86.

"four changes" are reflected in the specific contents, namely, the change from poverty alleviation industries to sustainable rural revitalization industries; the change from "moving out and stabilizing" to "having employment and getting rich"; and the change from cultural poverty alleviation to "having employment and getting rich". The change is from poverty alleviation industry to sustainable development of rural revitalization industry; from "moving and stabilizing" to "having employment and getting rich"; from cultural poverty alleviation to cultural tourism integration; and from ecological poverty alleviation to beautiful and livable.

3. Consolidate and expand the effective connection between the results of poverty alleviation and rural revitalization

When presiding over a meeting of the Standing Committee of the Political Bureau of the CPC Central Committee at the end of 2021 to study the "three rural" areas, General Secretary Xi Jinping emphasized that consolidating the achievements of poverty eradication is a prerequisite for rural revitalization, and that it is essential to maintain a firm commitment to ensure that the quality of life for those who have emerged from poverty is significantly improved and elevated to the next level. We should continue to promote the organic connection with the rural revitalization strategy to ensure that no large-scale return to poverty will occur, so as to effectively maintain and consolidate the great achievements in the war against poverty. Subsequently, the CPC Central Committee and the State Council made deployments, requiring firmly guarding the two bottom lines of ensuring national food security and no return to poverty on a large scale, and doing a solid and orderly job of rural development, rural construction and rural governance key work to promote new progress in rural revitalization and new steps in agricultural and rural modernization. In February 2022, the State Council issued the *14th Five-Year Plan for Promoting Agricultural and Rural Modernization*, which clearly sets "consolidating and expanding the achievements of poverty eradication and rural revitalization, enhancing the endogenous development capacity of areas out of poverty, allowing people out of poverty to live a better life and gradually embarking on the road to common prosperity" as the "14th Five-Year Plan". One of the seven key tasks to promote the modernization of agriculture and rural areas in the 14th Five-Year Plan period. At present, significant progress has been made in consolidating and expanding the effective connection between poverty eradication and rural revitalization, and the results of poverty eradication have been consolidated and expanded, while the connection of working mechanisms, policies and measures, institutions and teams has been promoted in an orderly manner.

First, the policy convergence has been fully implemented. All 33 articulated policies identified by the Central Leading Group for Rural Work have been introduced, and financial, financial, land and talent support guarantees have been strengthened, gradually realizing a smooth transition from concentrating resources to support poverty eradication to comprehensively promoting rural revitalization. The Ministry of Agriculture and Rural Affairs, the National Rural Revitalization Bureau and other 10 departments jointly issued the *Implementation Opinions on Supporting National Rural Revitalization Key Support Counties*, which put forward tilted support policies in 14 aspects, including finance, land, talents, projects, ecology and infrastructure. The study and introduction of the implementation plan for consolidating and expanding the achievements of poverty eradication and rural revitalization in the key counties of national rural revitalization support, and promoting the implementation of projects to make up for shortcomings and promote development. The *Opinions of the Central Committee of the Communist Party of China (CPC) and the State Council on the Effective Connection between Consolidating and Expanding the Achievements of Poverty Eradication and Rural Revitalization* state that a sound long-term mechanism should be established to consolidate and expand the achievements of poverty eradication, and to maintain the overall stability of the main support policies. During the transition period, the strict implementation of the "four do not take off" requirements, take off the responsibility not to take off, to prevent slackening; take off the policy not to take off, to prevent the emergency brake; take off the help not to take off, to prevent a withdrawal; take off the supervision not to take off, to prevent the rebound of poverty. The continuation of the existing help policy, the optimization of the optimization, the adjustment of the adjustment, to ensure policy continuity. The underwriting assistance class policy should continue to remain stable. The implementation of education, medical care, housing, drinking water and other livelihood protection policies for the general public, and according to the actual difficulties of the population out of poverty to give moderate inclination. Optimize industrial employment and other development policies. The opinion emphasizes the need to do a good job of financial investment, financial services, land support, talent and intellectual support policy convergence. **Second, the help articulation is solid and effective.** Adjustment, improve the East-West collaboration twinning relationship, eight eastern provinces (cities) twinning to help the western 10 provinces (autonomous regions and municipalities), invested 22.87 billion yuan in financial assistance funds, mutual cadres and 23,000 talents. Maintain the overall stability of the work of 305 central units to help 592 counties out of poverty, and invest and introduce 66.9 billion yuan of help funds to the counties targeted. All 563,000 cadres stationed in villages, including 186,000 first secretaries, have been rotated and the baton has been handed over smoothly[74] . Implementing the action of "Ten Thousand Enterprises for Ten Thousand Villages" and mobilizing private enterprises and other social forces to participate in rural revitalization. **The third is the orderly and powerful assessment connection.** The post-assessment of consolidating the results of poverty eradication, the assessment and evaluation of east-west collaboration and the assessment and evaluation of the effectiveness of the work of the central units in helping the central units are combined into the assessment and evaluation of consolidating and expanding the results of poverty eradication and rural revitalization, so as to reduce the burden of the grassroots. **Fourth,**

74　Saiqun Zhang. Orderly bridging precise poverty alleviation and rural revitalization strategy [EB/OL]. https://baijiahao.baidu.com/s?id=1678599109461362930&wfr=spider&for=pc.

the team convergence is basically in place. The rural work leading groups of party committees at all levels have assumed the responsibility of consolidating and expanding the results of poverty eradication and attacking and comprehensively promoting rural revitalization, and all provincial and rural revitalization agencies in cities and counties involved in agriculture have been listed.

II. Typical practices for continuing to promote rural revitalization

1. Promote high-quality development of rural industries

The first is to focus on developing characteristic industries. Accelerate the development of modern rural service industries and cultivate new rural industries and new business formats. **The second is to strengthen support for agricultural science and technology.** Accelerate the improvement of the national agricultural science and technology innovation system; continue to strengthen basic agricultural research; significantly enhance the status of enterprises in agricultural science and technology innovation; stimulate the innovation vitality of agricultural science and technology innovation talents. **The third is to make the agricultural products processing and distribution industry bigger and stronger.** Implement actions to improve the agricultural product processing industry, support family farms, farmer cooperatives, the SMEs in developing primary processing of agricultural products in origin, and guide large agricultural enterprises to develop intensive processing of agricultural products. **The fourth is to cultivate and expand industries that enrich the people in the county.** Improve the spatial layout of rural industries in the county, enhance the industry carrying and supporting service functions of the county, and enhance the agglomeration function of key towns. Implement the "one county, one industry" project to strengthen the county and enrich its people. Support national high-tech zones, economic development zones, and agricultural high-tech zones to jointly host county industrial parks.

2. Solidly promote the construction of livable, industrial and beautiful countryside

The first is to strengthen village planning. Adhere to county-wide coordination, support villages with conditions and needs to prepare village plans by division, and reasonably determine village layout and construction boundaries. Incorporate village planning into the list of village-level discussions and consultations. Standardize and optimize the administrative divisions in rural areas, and strictly prohibit the annexation of villages and the establishment of large communities against the wishes of farmers. **The second is to solidly promote the improvement of rural living environment.** We will increase efforts to renovate public spaces in villages and continue to carry out village cleaning operations. Consolidate the results of the investigation and rectification of rural household toilet problems, solidly promote the renovation of household toilets, and effectively improve the quality and effectiveness of rural toilet renovations. Strengthen the construction and maintenance of sanitary public toilets in rural areas. Promote rural domestic sewage treatment by zoning and classification, and strengthen the treatment of black and odorous water bodies in rural areas. Improve the rural domestic waste collection, transportation and disposal system, and promote source classification and reduction where conditions permit. **The third is to continue to strengthen rural infrastructure construction.** We will deepen the demonstration and creation of "Four Good Rural Roads", strengthen the construction of hardened roads for natural villages (groups) with large populations and qualified rural households, and promote rural road construction projects to be more oriented towards villages and households. Promote the construction of large-scale rural water supply projects and the standardized transformation of small-scale water supply projects, accelerate the resolution of seasonal water shortages in rural areas and temporary drinking water difficulties due to drought, and continue to consolidate the results of drinking water safety. We will continue to consolidate and improve the level of rural electricity security, carry out the construction of rural energy revolution pilot counties, accelerate the clean and low-carbon energy transformation in rural areas, promote the in-depth integration of digital technology with rural production and life, and continue to carry out digital rural pilots. **The fourth is to improve basic public service capabilities.** Promote the sinking of basic public service resources and focus on strengthening weak links. Promote the high-quality and balanced development of compulsory education within the county and improve the level of rural schools. Implement the living subsidy policy for rural teachers. Promote county-level coordination of medical and health resources, and strengthen the construction of rural-level medical and health and medical security service capabilities. We will coordinate and resolve the issues of salary distribution and benefits security for rural doctors, and promote the professionalization and standardization of the rural doctor team.

3. Improve the rural governance system led by party organizations

The first is to focus on the construction of grassroots democracy and strengthen the political and organizational functions of rural grassroots party organizations. In the process of rural governance, it is necessary to give full play to the role of villagers' committees, strengthen villagers' autonomy, allow villagers to participate in decision-making and management, and improve villagers' participation and satisfaction. At the same time, it is necessary to strengthen the construction of villagers' congresses and villagers' councils, so that villagers have more voice and decision-making power, and promote the democratization and legalization of rural governance. **The second is to focus on cultural inheritance and innovation and strengthen the construction of rural spiritual civilization.** In the process of rural governance, we must pay attention to inheriting and promoting local culture, exploring and exploring rural cultural resources, promoting the development of cultural and creative industries, and increasing the influence and attraction of rural culture. At the same time, we must focus on innovation, promote the modernization and technologicalization of rural governance, introduce new technologies and new models, and improve the efficiency and quality of rural governance. **The third is to focus on ecological protection and green development to improve the quality and sustainability of the rural ecological environment.** Promote the exploration and implementation of modern agricultural and rural ecological environment governance models. Strengthen the construction of modern ecological environment management capabilities in agriculture and rural areas. Promote the implementation of ecological environment system governance in agriculture and rural areas. Strengthen scientific and technological innovation and application in agricultural and rural ecological environment management.

◎ Chapter VII   Looking to the Future of Rural Development

Abstract

This chapter looks at the future of rural development from a global perspective. Currently, the global countryside is facing many difficulties, population loss is a serious challenge to rural revitalization, improving infrastructure construction is an urgent task for rural revitalization, lack of education and medical resources is a problem for rural revitalization, a single industrial structure restricts rural revitalization, and environmental protection and ecological issues are the key to the sustainable development of rural revitalization. Facing the future of the global countryside, we put forward five development goals in the areas of rural industry, talents, culture, ecology and organization, and give countermeasures and suggestions.

I. Current difficulties and challenges

From a global perspective, rural population loss, lack of infrastructure, lack of education and medical resources, single industrial structure, and environmental pollution have become universal problems facing global rural revitalization.

Population loss is a serious challenge to rural revitalization. With the acceleration of urbanization, more and more people are moving to the cities, especially young people. This has led to a decline in population in rural areas and an increasingly prominent shortage of rural labor. First, there is a shortage of young laborers in the countryside. A large number of young people have left the countryside to seek better employment opportunities and living conditions in the cities, leading to the gradual aging of the labor force in rural areas. Older people's low participation in agricultural production makes it difficult for them to perform heavy physical labor and heavy rural work, thus limiting the development of agricultural production. Second, population loss has exacerbated the lack of provision of rural schools, hospitals and other public service facilities in rural areas. Schools are facing a decline in students, and there is a serious shortage of educational resources to meet the educational needs of children who remain in the countryside. The lack of medical resources makes it difficult for rural residents to receive timely and effective treatment and services when they face illnesses and health problems. In addition, population loss has brought about difficulties in rural economic development. Agricultural production requires significant labor inputs, but the shortage of rural labor due to population loss has led to the abandonment of farmland and a decline in agricultural productivity. There are also fewer opportunities for economic activities and entrepreneurship in rural areas, hindering the diversification and further development of the rural economy.

Improving infrastructure construction is currently an urgent task for rural revitalization. Compared with cities, infrastructure construction in rural areas is relatively lagging behind, with obvious gaps in transportation, electricity and communications. This gap is not just a superficial phenomenon, but a direct limitation on the economic development of the countryside, the quality of life of residents and employment opportunities. First of all, the imperfect transportation infrastructure limits the development of villages. Narrow roads and inconvenient transportation in rural areas have brought great trouble to the distribution of agricultural products. This not only increases logistics costs, but also makes it more difficult to keep agricultural products fresh, affecting the development of the rural economy. In addition, underdeveloped transportation also restricts the employment opportunities of rural residents, and many young people have to choose to go out to work in order to seek better development opportunities. Secondly, the imperfections in electricity infrastructure also contribute to the difficulty of rural revitalization. In rural areas, unstable electricity and insufficient power supply capacity are common problems. Frequent power outages in many places have caused great inconvenience to the lives of residents and the production of enterprises. This has not only caused problems for the daily use of electricity by rural families, but also constrained the development of some rural enterprises. The lack of a stable power supply prevents the industrial chain in rural areas from being perfected, thus limiting the income of farmers and the growth of the rural economy. In addition, the lagging communication infrastructure has also brought many troubles to rural areas. Due to unstable network signals and imperfect coverage, rural residents have encountered many problems in the process of information acquisition, communication and business. Especially in modern agriculture, e- commerce and telecommuting, rural areas are lagging behind in the pace of economic development because of the digital divide created by poor communications.

The lack of educational and medical resources is a challenge to rural revitalization. Compared with urban areas, education resources in rural areas are generally lacking. Rural schools are small, with insufficient teachers, poor educational facilities and limited educational quality. Many children in the countryside are unable to acquire good knowledge skills and learning experiences due to the lack of access to good educational resources, resulting in the highlighting of the problem of educational inequality. The lack of educational resources in rural areas has led to unequal educational opportunities. The fact that children in the countryside do not receive a good education limits their possibilities for personal growth and development, and also leads to a further widening of the education gap between urban and rural areas. It is difficult to upgrade the knowledge and skill levels of rural residents, limiting their competitiveness in the job market. Difficulty in obtaining high-quality labor in the rural economy restricts the development of the rural economy. The generally low quality of rural education has led some rural high school and even college graduates to go out to work or take up jobs in cities. The large-scale loss of rural talents has further affected the development potential of villages. In addition, medical resources in rural areas are relatively scarce. There are few medical facilities and few medical personnel in rural areas, and the quality and level of medical services are low. Due to the distance from medical institutions and inconvenient transportation, it is difficult for rural residents to seek medical treatment, resulting in the lack of timely treatment for common illnesses, which seriously affects the health of the residents. The lack of medical resources in the countryside makes it difficult for residents to prevent and treat common diseases, which makes the health of rural residents overall poorer, with a higher incidence of chronic and infectious diseases, seriously affecting the quality of life and longevity of farmers. In addition, the lack of specialized medical services has increased the cost of medical care for rural residents, creating a financial burden for rural residents, and families are often plunged into poverty in the event of serious illness. The heavy burden of medical costs also discourages many rural residents from seeking medical care, leading to delays in illness and further exacerbating the problem of poverty.

A single industrial structure constrains the development of rural revitalization. Many rural areas still rely mainly on the traditional agricultural industry and lack a diversified industrial structure, leading to the vulnerability of their economies to natural disasters and market fluctuations, which increases the risks of rural development. First, the heavy reliance on the agricultural industry in rural areas means that the economies of rural areas are more vulnerable to natural disasters. Natural disasters such as natural calamities and epidemics often have a great impact on the growth of crops, farming and other agricultural industries, which leads to a sharp decline in the economic income of the rural areas, or even face difficulties in survival. Secondly, because of their single industrial structure, rural areas are relatively weak in their ability to cope with market fluctuations. Changes in domestic and foreign markets and fluctuations in consumer demand will have a direct impact on the main agricultural industries in rural areas. When market demand drops or overcapacity occurs, the agricultural industry in rural areas is unable to adjust quickly, resulting in increased economic and employment pressures. In addition, rural areas often lack diversified employment opportunities due to a single industrial structure. A large number of farmers can only engage in agricultural labor, resulting in limited employment space in the countryside and a lack of development platforms for young people, causing a large number of talented people to lose to the city, further exacerbating the economic homogenization and instability of rural areas.

Environmental protection and ecological issues are key to the sustainable development of rural revitalization. With the rapid advance of industrialization and urbanization, many rural areas are facing serious environmental pollution and ecological degradation. Traditional agricultural production methods and habits, such as large-scale use of chemical fertilizers and pesticides and indiscriminate logging, have led to ecological deterioration such as declining soil quality, pollution of water sources, and destruction of vegetation, which seriously affects the sustainable development of rural areas. In the process of rural revitalization, how to strike a balance between economic development and ecological environmental protection has become an important challenge. On the one hand, villages need to actively develop economic industries, raise the income level of residents and promote agricultural modernization. However, the traditional high-energy-consuming and high-polluting industrial model can no longer meet today's requirements for environmental protection. Therefore, the revitalization of the countryside needs to optimize the industrial structure, promote green development, and introduce environmentally friendly technologies and clean energy in order to reduce the adverse impact on the environment. On the other hand, rural areas need to focus on ecological protection and the sustainable development of the ecosystem. Organic and refined agriculture should be promoted, the use of pesticides and chemical fertilizers should be reduced, the ecological environment of the soil should be restored and protected, and the quality and nutritional value of agricultural products should be improved. In addition, rural areas should strengthen water environment management, protect water sources and wetlands, and prevent water pollution and over-exploitation of water resources.

II. Towards a global future for rural development

At the International Conference "Urban and Rural Development: The Future of Historic Villages and Towns", focusing on the theme of "rural revitalization, poverty alleviation and cultural inheritance", UNESCO put forward the following experiences on how to promote the future development of historic villages and towns: "Maintain the quality of the human environment; Place culture at the heart of rural development policies; improve traditional production creativity and cultural innovation; establish township networks and develop new forms of cooperation; strengthen cultural protection and achieve environmental sustainability."

Based on the above experience, this report proposes the following rural development goals.

1. Rural industry development goals

The Global Rural Industry Development Goals cover industrial diversification, rural economic upgrading, and agricultural product quality and branding, and are designed to promote the sustainable development of rural economies and improve farmers' incomes and quality of life.

Diversification of rural industries can reduce the economic risks associated with reliance on a single industry and provide more employment opportunities. For example, through the development of the agricultural products processing industry, agricultural products can be processed into high-value-added agricultural and sideline products, increasing farmers' incomes. Rural tourism can capitalize on the unique natural and cultural resources of the countryside to attract tourists while also promoting employment for rural residents. Rural e-commerce, on the other hand, breaks down geographical constraints through e-commerce platforms, enabling agricultural products to be sold more conveniently to national and even global markets.

Improving the rural economy is an important goal of rural industrial development. Through the development of modern agricultural technology and innovation in agricultural science and technology, the output and quality of agricultural products can be improved, and farmers' incomes will rise. In addition, rural industrial development can also lead to the development of related service industries, such as logistics, catering and tourism services, further increasing employment opportunities and economic income.

Strengthening the quality and branding of agricultural products is the key to improving the competitiveness of rural industries. Villages can improve consumer trust and satisfaction with rural agricultural products by promoting organic and green agriculture, reducing the use of pesticides and chemical fertilizers, ensuring the safety and environmental friendliness of agricultural products, and providing relevant quality certification, traceability systems and other measures. At the same time, villages can also create agricultural products with regional characteristics and branding effects by means of marketing and publicity to enhance the added value and market competitiveness of their products.

2. Rural talent development goals

The goal of talent development in the global countryside is to attract talent to the countryside and to improve the education and vocational skills of farmers. Through the establishment of a quality education system, rural talents will be trained and urban talents will be attracted to the countryside to work in agricultural production and rural development, thus promoting the modernization of rural industries and societies.

Attracting talents to the countryside is an important measure to promote the modernization of rural industries and society. Villages can attract urban talents to innovate and start businesses in villages by providing good working and living conditions, and also need to provide opportunities and platforms suitable for their development. Villages can establish innovation and entrepreneurship incubation bases and provide financial support and policy concessions to attract more talents to the development of rural industries.

Improving the education level of farmers is key to the talent development goals. Villages can provide good educational resources, build modern schools and educational institutions and improve rural educational conditions. At the same time, villages can also strengthen training and vocational education, improve farmers' vocational skills and innovation ability, and cultivate talents that meet the needs of rural industrial development. The Government and society should increase their investment in and support for rural education to provide a better environment and opportunities for the cultivation of rural talents.

Upgrading vocational skills is an important direction for talent development. Villages can provide opportunities for farmers to participate in vocational skills training by organizing training courses, skills competitions and other activities. At the same time, villages can also cooperate with colleges and universities and research institutions to introduce advanced agricultural technology and management experience to improve farmers' production skills and management level. Governments and enterprises can provide appropriate training subsidies and incentives to motivate farmers to continuously improve their vocational skills.

3. Rural cultural development goals

The goal of cultural development in the global countryside is aimed at preserving local cultural traditions, promoting cultural diversity and fostering the integration of culture and tourism. Only by protecting and passing on the cultural heritage of the countryside and promoting cultural diversity can we enhance the attractiveness of the countryside, realize the creative and innovative development of rural culture and further promote the revitalization and development of the countryside.

The preservation of local cultural traditions is one of the important directions of the cultural development objectives of villages. Villages can protect their unique cultural traditions by collecting, recording and passing on village history, folklore, traditional customs and handicrafts. The Government and society should increase their efforts to protect and support rural culture, set up relevant cultural institutions and programs, and provide professional guidance on protection and transmission to ensure that rural cultural traditions are effectively protected.

The promotion of cultural diversity is also an important element of the goal of cultural development in villages. Villages can promote exchanges and cooperation between different regions and cultures through the organization of cultural and artistic activities, cultural exchanges and exhibitions, and so on, in order to enrich the cultural content of villages. The Government and society can also encourage the pluralistic development of rural culture and protect and pass on diverse cultural resources by providing financial and policy support.

Promoting the integration of culture and tourism is one of the key strategies for promoting rural development. Rural villages can utilize their own historical and cultural resources to develop cultural-themed tourism activities and provide tourists with rich cultural experiences. At the same time, villages can also create cultural brands with cultural characteristics and attractiveness through the development of cultural and creative industries, attracting more tourists and foreign talents and promoting rural economic and social development.

4. Rural ecological development goals

The goal of ecological development in the global countryside is aimed at protecting the ecological environment, promoting sustainable agricultural development and improving the efficiency of resource utilization. Only by realizing the protection of the ecological environment and the development of sustainable agriculture will it be possible to establish a harmonious relationship between human beings and nature and achieve ecological prosperity and sustainable development in the countryside. The protection of the ecological environment is one of the core objectives of ecological development in villages. Villages should take active measures to reduce pollutant emissions and environmental damage, establish environmental monitoring and management systems, and strengthen the protection and management of natural resources, especially natural ecosystems such as water sources, forests and wetlands. The Government and society should increase investment in environmental protection and encourage rural residents and farmers to adopt sustainable production methods to promote green development in the countryside.

The promotion of sustainable agricultural development is also an important element of the goal of ecological development in villages. Rural villages should encourage farmers to adopt organic and ecological agricultural methods for agricultural production, reduce the use of pesticides and chemical fertilizers, and improve the quality and safety of agricultural products. At the same time, villages should also strengthen agricultural technology innovation and promotion, improve the ability of crops to resist pests and diseases, and increase the efficiency of agricultural production. Governments can introduce appropriate agricultural support policies, provide technical training and financial support, and guide farmers to transition to sustainable agriculture.

Improving the efficiency of resource utilization is another important aspect of the goal of ecological development in villages. Villages can reduce the consumption and waste of resources and improve the efficiency of resource utilization by promoting energy-saving and environmentally friendly technologies and recycling modes. The Government can strengthen the planning and management of energy, water and land resources in villages, establish a scientific mechanism for resource utilization, and encourage the adoption of low-carbon lifestyles and green modes of travel to promote the sustainable use of resources.

5. Rural organization development goals

The goal of organizational development in the global countryside is aimed at establishing a rural governance system, promoting the development of social organizations and strengthening farmers' participation. Only by achieving the benign development of rural organizations and establishing a sound rural governance system can we achieve harmony and stability in rural society and promote rural development and progress.

The establishment of a rural governance system is one of the important directions of development objectives of rural organizations. Villages should strengthen capacity-building for rural governance and establish a multi-level, multi-party rural governance mechanism, including village committees, farmers' cooperatives and agricultural associations. The Government can increase its support for rural governance by providing policy, legal and financial support, promoting community self-governance, rural cooperation and collective economy, and facilitating consultation, participation and governance in rural society.

Promoting the development of social organizations is also an important element of the objective of organizational development in villages. Villages can encourage and support the development of various social organizations, including agricultural cooperatives, farmers' professional cooperatives, family farms and rural mutual aid organizations. Social organizations can play the main role of farmers, helping them to solve production, management and living problems, and promoting industrial development and rural economic prosperity. The Government can provide relevant policies, funding and services to guide social organizations to play an active role in promoting rural development.

Strengthening farmers' participation is key to the goal of organizational development in villages. Villages should encourage farmers to participate in decision- making and management and improve their capacity and level of self-governance. Farmers should participate in the construction of rural governance and social organizations through appropriate means, express their opinions and demands, and participate in decision-making and planning for agricultural production, so as to promote rural economic development and social progress. The Government can provide relevant training and support to strengthen the organizational capacity of farmers and provide a strong guarantee for their participation.

III. Suggestions and recommendations

Upgrading agricultural and rural industrial development. Agricultural and rural industrial development is one of the core tasks of rural revitalization, which can promote rural revitalization and achieve sustainable development of the rural economy. First, the scientific and technological development and application of agricultural science and technology can be strengthened through increased investment in scientific and technological innovation, so as to improve the science and efficiency of agricultural production. For example, advanced planting techniques and equipment can be introduced to improve the precision of farmland irrigation and fertilization, reduce the use of pesticides and chemical fertilizers, and improve the quality and safety of agricultural products. In addition, it can promote the industrialization of agriculture, encourage farmers to organize themselves, build brands for agricultural products, and increase the added value and competitiveness of their products. By integrating rural resources and building a processing and marketing system for agricultural products, the added value of agricultural products can be increased and farmers' incomes expanded. In addition, in rural revitalization, attention should be paid to the adjustment and optimization of the rural industrial structure. Encourage farmers to adapt to market demand and develop competitive specialty agricultural and rural industries, such as agro-tourism, agro-paradise, and rural tourism. By fostering new industries such as leisure agriculture and rural tourism, we can increase employment opportunities for farmers and enhance the level of rural economic development.

Strengthening rural infrastructure. Infrastructure is the support and guarantee for rural development, directly affecting the socio-economic development of rural areas and the quality of life of residents. First, strengthening rural transportation is one of the important infrastructure tasks. Constructing and improving rural roads can open up transportation bottlenecks in rural areas, improve the convenience of exporting and selling agricultural products, and promote rural economic development. In addition, strengthening the construction of rural transportation networks, including railroads, highways and bridges, can facilitate farmers' travel and improve the efficiency of agricultural production and rural logistics. Secondly, improving water and power supply facilities in villages is also a very important infrastructure development task. Providing reliable water and power supply services not only meets the daily needs of rural residents, but also promotes the development of agricultural production. A modern water supply system should be built for rural areas to solve the problem of farmers' drinking water difficulties; the construction of rural power networks should be strengthened to ensure the needs of farmland irrigation and agricultural mechanization, and to improve the efficiency and quality of agricultural production. In addition, the construction of rural communication facilities should be strengthened to promote the process of rural informatization. Provide high-speed broadband network coverage to promote the development of new business forms such as rural online sales and e- commerce. Through the provision of high-quality communication services, it will expand farmers' access to information, help them understand market demand and new technologies, and promote agricultural modernization. In the process of strengthening infrastructure development, the government should increase investment and strengthen planning and management. It should guide social capital and enterprises to participate in rural infrastructure construction by formulating appropriate policies and planning.

Promoting rural education development and skills training. Education is the foundation of talent development and one of the key drivers of rural development. First, strengthening the allocation of rural education resources is key. It is necessary to improve the conditions of rural schools and provide quality educational resources and facilities to ensure that rural children receive a good education. In addition, it is necessary to increase the training of rural teachers to improve their teaching standards and professionalism, so that they can better impart knowledge and guide students. Secondly, emphasis should be placed on vocational education and skills training for rural youth. Through the opening of vocational skills training courses and specialized technical schools, rural youth should be helped to learn and master various types of employment skills, and their overall quality and employability should be improved. At the same time, it is necessary to encourage and support rural youth to participate in the development of the agricultural industry chain and rural specialty industries, carry out practical training and entrepreneurial counseling, and cultivate innovative and entrepreneurial talents. In addition, it is necessary to emphasize lifelong education and skills upgrading for farmers. Through the development of farmers' evening schools and rural community colleges, farmers are provided with opportunities for continuing education and skills training, and agricultural technology training and the popularization of modern agricultural management knowledge are widely carried out. By upgrading the cultural quality and vocational skills of farmers, their ability to adapt to modern social and industrial development will be improved, promoting the upgrading of rural industries and the sustainability of rural development.

Accelerating the promotion of digital village construction. In the process of global rural revitalization, promoting the construction of digital villages is a key task, through promoting the application of information technology in rural development, building digital agriculture and digital villages, and upgrading the level of informationization and service capacity in rural areas. First, it is necessary to strengthen the construction of rural information infrastructure. This includes the construction of rural broadband networks to provide stable, high-speed network connections covering all corners of the countryside; and the construction of a rural intelligent Internet of Things (IoT) to realize the sharing and management of information on agricultural equipment, farmland, farmers and other aspects of the countryside. Second, the development of digital agriculture should be promoted. Digital agriculture is a modern agricultural method that utilizes information technology, cloud computing, big data, artificial intelligence and other technical means to improve the efficiency and quality of agricultural production. Farmland monitoring, precise fertilization, early warning of pests and diseases, and other functions can be realized through intelligent farm machinery, drones, sensors and other technologies to improve the scientific and sustainable nature of agricultural production. At the same time, it is necessary to build digital villages to improve the level of informationization and service capacity in rural areas. Through the construction of rural e-commerce platforms and traceability systems for agricultural products, online sales and traceability management of agricultural products will be realized; through the promotion of the application of technologies such as e-payment and intelligent logistics, the efficiency and convenience of rural financial and logistics services will be enhanced; and through the development of rural e- commerce and Internet+Agriculture projects, farmers' participation in the Internet economy and entrepreneurship and innovation will be encouraged and supported. In addition, it is necessary to strengthen IT training and awareness spreading among farmers. Through the conduct of farmers' training courses and rural e-commerce mentor programs, farmers' IT application capabilities will be improved; through publicity and promotion, farmers' awareness of and participation in digital village construction will be increased, and they will be encouraged to use IT to participate in agricultural production and rural development.

Strengthening ecological environmental protection. In order to realize a win-win situation between economic development and ecological environmental protection, it is necessary to formulate and implement strict environmental protection policies and measures, strengthen ecological protection in rural areas and promote sustainable development models such as eco-agriculture and eco-tourism. First of all, it is necessary to strengthen the construction of agricultural ecology. Agriculture is one of the most important industries in rural areas, and the sustainable development of agricultural production can be realized through the implementation of eco-agriculture. This includes adopting techniques and methods of organic and green agriculture, reducing the use of pesticides and chemical fertilizers, improving soil quality and crop quality, and protecting the stability and health of farmland ecosystems. Secondly, it is necessary to strengthen rural ecological environment protection.

The ecological environment of rural areas is the basis of agricultural production and rural residents' life, and also an important resource for attracting tourists and promoting the development of rural tourism. Therefore, it is necessary to strictly control the sources of pollution in the rural ecological environment, strengthen the construction of infrastructure such as sewage treatment and garbage disposal, and ensure that the air in the countryside is fresh, the water quality is clean and the ecological balance. At the same time, it is necessary to promote the development of ecotourism. Eco-tourism is a sustainable development model that combines natural resources and cultural heritage, and can provide employment opportunities and economic growth points in rural areas. Through the development of rural tourism, it can promote farmers' income and prosperity, protect the sustainable use of natural and cultural resources, and realize a win-win situation for the upgrading of the agricultural industry and the development of the rural economy.

Strengthening rural governance and social management. Improving the rural governance system and raising the level of rural social management can provide a solid foundation and guarantee for rural revitalization. First, improving the rural governance system is the key to strengthening rural governance. The improvement of the rural governance system involves the construction of rural grass-roots organizations, the building of a rural rule of law environment, and the strengthening of democratic decision-making in rural areas. By establishing and improving the villagers' self-governance mechanism and rural social organizations, the ability of rural residents to participate in decision-making can be improved, the interests of villagers can be better realized, and rural revitalization can be promoted. Secondly, improving the level of rural social management will help maintain the harmony and stability of rural society. Strengthening rural social management requires strengthening the prevention and solution of rural social problems, including labor force employment, social security, education and medical care. In addition, strengthening the guidance of rural social structure, values and cultural inheritance is also an important element of rural social management.

By creating a good social environment and moral culture, it can promote the harmonious development of rural society and the process of rural revitalization. Again, strengthening the leading role of party organizations is an important way to enhance rural governance and social management. Party organizations play an important leadership and organizational role in rural development, and can better promote the various tasks of rural revitalization through their organizational construction, cadre training and policy propaganda. In the process of rural revitalization, party organizations should strengthen their contact and coordination with various types of rural organizations, so as to form a unified working force and promote the vigorous development of rural revitalization.

Strengthening international cooperation and exchanges. By drawing on and learning from successful experiences in international rural development, we can better promote rural revitalization and achieve sustainable development. First, international cooperation can introduce high-quality agricultural technology and advanced management experience to rural areas. Different countries and regions have unique experience and technical advantages in agricultural development. Through cooperation with other countries and regions, we can learn from their advanced practices in agricultural production, agricultural product processing and agricultural supply chain, and apply them in the process of rural revitalization. This will help improve the productivity and quality of agriculture and promote the development of the rural economy. Second, international exchanges can promote openness and innovation in the rural revitalization process. Through exchanges with other countries and regions, we can learn about the rural development models and policy measures of different places, thus providing reference and inspiration for our own rural revitalization. At the same time, international exchanges can also promote cultural integration and innovation in rural areas, providing more possibilities for the diversification of the rural economy and the development of specialty industries. In addition, international cooperation and exchange can also promote the development of rural tourism. Rural tourism is a multifaceted industry, including tourist attraction development, tourism product design, tourism promotion and marketing and so on. Through cooperation with other countries and regions, we can attract more international tourists to rural tourism, promote the development of tourism and provide more economic growth points for rural revitalization. At the same time, the Government should also strengthen its co-operation with relevant rural revitalization agencies and international organizations to share experience and resources and jointly promote the process of rural revitalization. In addition, enterprises and non-governmental organizations can also participate in international cooperation and actively engage in technical cooperation and project cooperation to promote the process of rural revitalization.